Business Brilliant

ALSO BY LEWIS SCHIFF

The Armchair Millionaire
The Middle-Class Millionaire

Lewis Schiff

Business
Brilliant

SURPRISING LESSONS

FROM THE GREATEST SELF-MADE

BUSINESS ICONS

HARPER
BUSINESS

An Imprint of HarperCollins*Publishers*
www.harpercollins.com

FIRST EDITION

Designed by Fritz Metsch

Library of Congress Cataloging-in-Publication Data has been applied for.

ISBN: 978-0-06-225350-7

13 14 15 16 17   OV/RRD   10 9 8 7 6 5 4 3 2 1

Author's Note and Acknowledgments

I began work on this book in early 2009, just as the world was coming to understand the full extent of the financial meltdown that took place only a few months earlier. As it turns out, 2009 may well come to be regarded as a historic milestone, marking the end of the longest period of economic expansion this nation has ever enjoyed. For more than half a century, stretching back to World War II, Americans could confidently follow a clear roadmap to prosperity: get a degree from a good school, find a job at a good company, and work hard long enough to fund a secure and happy retirement. That familiar scenario is no longer viable. Today, there are far too many forces—longer life spans, rising health-care costs, vanishing natural resources, and globalization, to name a few—arrayed against such a quaint notion.

Instead, just as the world continues to become more complex, so must our strategies for success. The time has come to reset our goals and the ways we go about achieving them. *Business Brilliant* is the story of how wealth is created now. It showcases the greatest success stories of our time because that's the way good stories are told. Nobody wants to read about the guy who screwed up his courage to ask his boss for a 5 percent raise. We'd rather read about Richard Branson's exotic adventures to build a global empire. But make no mistake: you, reader, and Sir Richard or any of the other great wealth creators featured in this book, are in the same boat. Each of us must figure out how to use our behavior, attitudes, temperament, and skills to create financial security for our families and ourselves. While this will lead to different results for each of us (because we are all differently abled), the process is fundamentally the same.

The seven principles for wealth creation identified in this book are not just about getting rich, although for some readers that's exactly what will happen. They are about realigning our career-development practices with the world we live in today. The opening chapter shares a few stories of people who were willing to look upon old beliefs with fresh eyes. This is the first threshold you must pass in order to achieve financial security in the new economy and your first indication of how you will fare on this journey.

There are many people to thank for the information you will find in this book. The past half-dozen years have been among the most exciting of my life in terms of my own education as an entrepreneur and as a wealth creator. My teachers include the collaborator on my previous book, Russ Alan Prince, as well as the whole team at *Inc.* magazine, most notably Bo Burlingham and Bob LaPointe. Also, the great entrepreneurs who are part of the *Inc.* community, including Norm Brodsky, Jack Stack, Paul Spiegelman, and the rest of the "Small Giants." Many thanks to Arthur Klebanoff for providing me with great advice and Hollis Heimbouch for spotting the merits of this story instantly and decisively. And Noel Weyrich for his unflinching commitment to excellence.

Finally, I'd like to offer my deepest thanks to the community of incredible entrepreneurs who make up *Inc.*'s Business Owners Council. They have taught me what it means to be brilliant in everything I do.

Contents

Business Brilliant

1

"Business Brilliant"

➤ The Coach Who Cracked the Football Code

Football is a warrior's game. Fans love to watch because every game has one winner and one loser: there's no in-between. Few have embodied that singularity more thoroughly than Joe Gibbs, the legendary coach of the Washington Redskins. Gibbs was so passionate about winning that he famously slept in his office during football season, such was his dedication to game preparedness. His multiple Super Bowl wins and lifetime game-winning average of .683 (behind only Vince Lombardi and John Madden) earned him a slot in pro football's hall of fame and the allegiance of Redskins fans everywhere. Charley Casserly, noted NFL analyst for CBS and former general manager of the Redskins under Gibbs, calls him "arguably the greatest coach in the history of the league."

Among the many facets to building a successful team is identifying up-and-coming talent and Gibbs's scouts, like those of other NFL teams, scoured the country's football fields in search of the next big thing. But Gibbs was frustrated with the limitations of the traditional aptitude tests that were widely used, including the SATs, to measure the abilities of prospective players.

"We were looking for a test that wasn't educationally biased," says Casserly. In other words, one that did not rely upon reading and writing, two skills that are of little use on the field in a game that is won or lost based on split-second decisions.

Beginning in 1984, Gibbs worked with vision specialists Harry Wachs and Ron Berger, optometrists from George Washington University, to develop a new test that would be customized to the unique aptitudes required for success in football. Gibbs met Dr. Wachs when he had successfully treated Gibbs's son, improving both his school performance and his football performance. To design the test, Gibbs offered Wachs and Berger four of his best players, those he believed instinctively knew how to make the most of every football play, as baseline examples of the capabilities the test should identify.

"We specialized in vision, not just sight." This is how Dr. Wachs, now retired, described his field of study. "For example, you know the expression, 'I see what you mean'? That's about vision." The Wachs-Berger test they created assessed sight, coordination, motivation, and a player's ability to keep cool under stress.

The Redskins recruiting benefited from the Wachs-Berger test because it measured a player's ability to think during a battle whereas the traditional tests just measured the player's ability to think, period. "Say you're on defense," says Casserly. "There's a call and a player's in motion. Now responsibilities have to change and the players have to visualize all of that change." Redskins scouts traveled the country carrying a Wachs-Berger toolkit made up of goggles that distorted lines of vision and small blocks and other plastic shapes the size of tiddlywinks, among other peculiar items. After the scouts started using the Wachs-Berger test to analyze players, the Redskins on to win two Super Bowls (in 1988 and 1992) under Coach Gibbs.

Wachs told the *Los Angeles Times* that the test "taps into the human potential anywhere in the world." Gibbs agreed but he was only focused on one thing: winning football games. Gibbs didn't need to know if a player was smart in a general way. He embraced the Wachs-Berger test because he believed it could assess whether or not a prospect was truly "football brilliant."

Just as Coach Gibbs sought to identify what made certain players brilliant on the football field, this book seeks to identify what makes certain people brilliant in the business field, what it takes to be "Business Brilliant."

In the coming pages, you will see how Business Brilliance, just like football brilliance, has little to do with IQ or education. You will learn how Richard Branson became a billionaire *because* he can't read a financial spreadsheet. You will discover how a high school–educated circus clown used his Business Brilliance to become the billionaire founder of Cirque du Soleil. You will find why a Brooklyn entrepreneur needed to listen to his lowest-paid employees, and how a $100 million line of business was the result. You will see how the famously impulsive founder of JetBlue uses his Business Brilliance to build soaring successes atop his many crushing failures.

In the process you will witness the debunking of some very popular myths about success. You'll see how Warren Buffett started getting rich as soon as he *stopped* investing the "Warren Buffett Way." How Suze Orman built her personal wealth by ignoring her own gospel of frugality. How Bill Gates made the business deal of the century not because he's a computer genius or an "outlier" but because he executed doggedly on a simple three-step business strategy that anyone can learn. You will see how Steve Jobs stumbled into his greatest fortune by sheer accident—and then rewrote history so it looked like it had been his plan all along.

But most important, the seven Business Brilliant principles in the coming chapters will help you learn about yourself. You'll see why it's just as important to follow the money as it is to follow your passion. Why a "big idea" won't help you succeed, but the person in the cubicle next to you probably can. Why your network needs fewer people, not more. And why you're better off doing only the very few things that you do exceptionally well. You'll also learn about some behaviors that might be holding you back. Why you fail to ask for what you want at the very moments you're most likely to get it. Why you feel bad when you *win* a negotiation. And why failure itself is a bad thing *only* if, like most people, you try to push it out of your mind by taking on something new.

I didn't figure out these principles on my own. They are the products of years of original research, careful study, persistence through setbacks, and lots of help from other people. In fact, the book you are holding is the product of all seven of the Business Brilliant principles it explores. It is a project that had its beginnings a dozen years ago, when I first teamed up with a good friend of mine named Russ Alan Prince.

➤ The Wealth Whisperer

We all know people who have a knack for making money. They appear to be naturals at it. Opportunities seem to find them. They always know the right people. Their risks pay off more often than not, or at least it looks that way.

For the past 25 years, Russ Prince has worked with some of the world's richest individuals to uncover the secrets behind these behaviors, much the same way that Joe Gibbs reverse-engineered his best players' performances to discover the fundamental elements of football brilliance. Behind thick glasses and an athlete's tall and lean frame, Prince, a former mixed martial arts competitor in Hong Kong in the 1980s, operates today out of a well-guarded eighteen-acre compound in rural Connecticut.

After a chance meeting and subsequent friendship with one of Asia's richest people during his competitive martial-arts days (he has never revealed who this individual is), Prince was ushered into a realm of wealth most of us will never know. Since then, he has probed and surveyed the best practices and personal beliefs of very successful people, including probably more in-depth conversations with billionaires than any other social scientist on earth.

"I'm a failed academic," says Prince, whose thick Brooklyn accent can't hide a childhood far away from great wealth in the Canarsie section of Brooklyn. "But I know what makes people rich."

His lifetime of study has made Prince a "wealth whisperer" of sorts, a coach to some of the world's richest families who will pay or do almost anything in the pursuit of more treasure. Prince shows his already successful clients how to attain financial goals that most of us can't imagine, such as making the Forbes 400 list—the annual ranking of the country's richest individuals.

Impressed by his years of coaching success, I asked Prince to share his methods for this book. I wanted to identify the kind of brilliance that allows the self-made wealthy to make the most of every business opportunity in much the same way that Gibbs sought to discover what makes some of his players football brilliant.

Prince and I go back a ways. Besides having spent countless hours over chocolate milkshakes arguing about whether or not the techniques that lead to wealth can be learned, we first worked together in 2000 when we collaborated on a curriculum to teach financial advisers how to support their wealthiest clients. In 2006, Prince and I teamed up again for a research project that resulted in the book now known in its paperback edition as *The Influence of Affluence*. That project focused more on my own area of interest, related to what the financial services industry calls the "mass affluent" and what we called the "middle-class millionaire."

We wanted to look at the thoughts, behaviors, and purchasing decisions of people who had attained millionaire status but hailed from middle-class upbringings.

We restricted our research only to people who received little or nothing in the way of gifts or inheritance from their families and now have net worths ranging between $1 million and $10 million. For comparison's sake, our researchers asked the same questions of a sampling of middle-class households with above-average incomes in the $50,000 to $80,000 range—the upper third quartile of U.S. household income.

From the start, we discovered that the middle-class people whose accumulated wealth puts them in the top 10 percent among U.S. households are, on average, no smarter than the rest of the middle class. In fact, despite the great disparity in household wealth, these two groups have a lot in common in terms of educational attainment and personal values.

About 90 percent of both groups were college graduates and at least 40 percent of each held graduate degrees. Three-quarters of both groups were married, and just about two-thirds of them were on their second marriages. The middle-class families were slightly bigger on average, but more than 95 percent of both groups had at least one child.

Even their financial aspirations were similar. In this 2006 survey, a large majority of respondents from both our middle-class and our self-made millionaire groups reported what might be called a typically healthy middle-class respect for money. They agreed with near unanimity that love and health are more important than money, but they also agreed that "money is essential to living a full life." More than 85 percent of both groups concurred with the statement, "Money can buy happiness."

It seemed to us that almost all our survey respondents felt that having money was important to their personal happiness and satisfaction with life. Where they differed was in their beliefs about how best to acquire it.

For instance, most middle-class respondents believed that if you "do what you love, the money will follow," but only 2 percent of self-made millionaires felt the same. Likewise, the importance of "cutting back on little expenditures" was embraced by the middle class, but totally rejected by self-made millionaires. The vast majority of the middle class agreed that "putting your own capital at risk," "diversifying the ways you make money," having a "success attitude," and "thinking like a millionaire" are all important ways to attain financial success. And to each of these statements, the middle-class millionaires said: Wrong. Wrong. Wrong. Wrong.

Instead, we discovered that the self-made millionaires subscribed to a completely different set of priorities. Most overwhelmingly agreed that, among other things, if you want to succeed you should obtain an ownership stake in your work, persuade others to invest with you, get to know a lot of people, and learn from your bad business decisions. And yet, *the importance of each of these ideas was rejected by the vast majority of the middle class!*

The starkness of the gap between the two groups was stunning. It was also just a little heartbreaking. After all, the vast majority of the middle-class survey respondents said they wanted to be financially successful. For the sake of their families' well-being and their own personal happiness, they wanted to make more money. But their ideas about how to achieve financial success conflicted with the practices of those *who had actually achieved it*. Picture a person who claims a desperate need to get to some far-off city, but refuses to drive on the interstate. That became our image of the middle class.

➤ The Magic of the Mundane

In reviewing the survey results from that 2006 project, it became clearer to me why so many members of the middle class might consider the wealthy as somehow a breed apart, as people with unique and even mysterious gifts or talents for making money. Just as the Wachs-Berger test identified football-brilliant skills that traditional aptitude tests couldn't measure, our survey revealed a gap between middle-class assumptions about money and the actual practices and attitudes of their middle-class peers who had become millionaires. Our middle-class respondents seemed to be blind to the mechanisms of how wealth is produced in ways that our wealthy survey respondents weren't.

If financial success remains a mystery to the middle class, it might be because the wealth-creation process practiced by Prince and his clients does not in any way resemble middle-class notions of stable, steady progress. The Business Brilliant system described in this book is characterized by a "synergy" of its various parts. *Synergy* is a word frequently abused in the business press to describe mergers or acquisitions that purport to make the resulting companies stronger than the sum of their parts. In truth, synergy describes the way complex systems and processes—such as a football play or the way a poison gas combines with an explosive metal to produce ordinary table salt—can produce outcomes that are unexpected and unrecognizable from their component parts. In a synergistic system, a set of simple and mundane individual factors can interact and affect each other in improbable ways, creating results that can seem breathtaking and—to the uninformed—mysterious in origin.

Later, I commissioned Prince to run another survey—which we called the "Business Brilliant survey." The new survey, run in the spring of 2009, was similar to our previous work together, but it posed more questions that were based on Prince's successful coaching methods. We wanted to dive deeply into the details of what it takes to be successful and find out if the earlier pattern of misguided assumptions by the middle class would hold up. We asked questions about goal setting, personal autonomy, work habits, business relationships, retirement, and more. We went back to the same two population groups as in the previous survey, but we added two more groups: self-made millionaires in the $10 million to $30 million range of net worth, and self-made millionaires in the above–$30 million range. Fundamentally, we wanted to find out what beliefs and behaviors separate the mass middle class from the affluent, but we were also curious about what factors might spell the difference between the merely affluent in the $1 million to $10 million range and *the truly rich.*

This book is the result. It represents my attempt to lay bare the mysteries of wealth creation in the twenty-first century. By using the Coach Gibbs method, by reverse-engineering the results Prince was achieving with his wealthy clients and testing them against a statistically significant sample of Americans, we were able to identify seven distinct principles that have allowed people who are born into the middle class to become wealthy exemplars of what I call Business Brilliance.

Through these survey results and the accompanying stories and discussions, you will be able to appreciate for the first time the crucial factors essential for financial success in these turbulent times. This book shows that while fortune often smiles on people in ways that seem arbitrary, fortuitous, and unpredictable, it is synergy, not serendipity, that is usually at work behind the scenes. There are elemental factors to account for, and simple replicable steps you can take, in order to steer yourself toward what may only appear at a distance to be a confluence of lucky connections and happy coincidences. Beginning with the way you pursue your livelihood, which of your talents you develop, and how you negotiate the terms of your work, each of these factors and others collude to determine how far you might go.

Do I think that anyone who reads this book can become a million-aire? Of course not. Even Prince has serious doubts about the ability of ordinary people to learn and adopt his wealth-building techniques. But this book is not written for just anyone. It's written for a very special segment of the population: the millions of educated and intellectually curious people who have made a good living playing by rules that might not be working very well for them anymore.

If you are one such person, I believe that if you master one-half or just one-third of the Business Brilliant techniques described in this book, your income will rise. If you get really good at most or all of them, you just might grow wealthy enough to become one of Prince's clients.

But first you have to be willing to accept that changing your behavior and following through on a few everyday practices can bring you financial successes you may have only dreamed of. Does that seem too simple? Too obvious? Before you go any farther, I want to tell a story that demonstrates exactly how this mastery of simple, mundane techniques can produce near-miraculous results with far greater certainty than all our more traditional notions of talent, education, and training. The story tells how a Pittsburgh hospital saved lives at an unprecedented rate by modeling its intensive-care-unit procedures on a zero-defect process borrowed from the auto industry. You will see the magic of the mundane in this story, but you will also see why there is resistance to its magic, and why so many secrets of success are doomed to remain just that—secrets.

➤ The Toyota Way of Medical Care

In May 2003, Dr. Richard Shannon took on a project that many deemed utterly impossible. As head of medicine at Allegheny General Hospital in Pittsburgh, Shannon put his intensive-care-unit staff on a mission to completely eradicate life-threatening infections.

Tens of thousands of hospital patients die from infections every year. One estimate puts the number at 250 per day, which is greater than the death toll from breast cancer, air crashes, car crashes, and AIDS combined. Countless medical conferences have been held to address this terrible waste in money and human lives and most hospital administrators insist they do everything humanly possible to limit, treat, and contain infection. But no hospital had ever even tried to attain zero infections.

The previous year, Shannon had taken a five-day training course with a local health consortium that had developed a health-care-delivery process adapted from the Toyota car-making system. He started the week highly skeptical that simple factory methods using standardized parts could translate into providing treatment for patients with an endless array of illnesses. By the end of the week, though, Shannon was a believer. To his mind, Toyota's quality regime with its zero-defect focus was not only applicable to medicine but absolutely essential in a field dedicated to the preservation of human life.

Intensive-care patients in hospitals are most susceptible to infections at the point where catheters are inserted into their arteries. These infections are called CLABs—central line–associated bloodstream infections. In 2003, there had been 47 documented CLABs at Allegheny General's two intensive-care units, and 19 of the infected patients had died. Shannon wanted to reconfigure operations of both units using the Toyota factory model. The goal was zero infections and zero deaths within 90 days.

The Toyota Way is a legendary management philosophy built around 14 principles that emphasize quality, efficiency, and continuous improvement. Most of the principles are aspirational in nature ("Become a learning organization" is the thrust of Principle 14) but others emphasize the importance of standardizing every conceivable task, organizing tools and processes so that no problems are hidden, analyzing every error, and, most critically, allowing every member of the team to stop to fix any defect or deviation from standard procedure.

Allegheny General had never studied just how patients acquire infections while under its care. Treatment standards existed, but each doctor and nurse was trusted to use his or her own professional judgment in changing catheters and applying dressings. There was no system for tracking the causes of an infection or even for reporting a suspected cause.

All of that changed under the Toyota Way. The dressing kit for catheters was standardized, as was every step in the prevention, observation, and treatment of infection. Patients transferred from other facilities had to have a fresh catheter inserted under the new standardized procedures. Catheter lines near the femoral artery were to be avoided because a review of past infections revealed that lines in the subclavian artery had much lower rates of infection.

It was the job of every member of the clinical team to enforce the new standards. One day, when the busy radiology department refused to insert a new catheter in a patient according to the standard procedures, a nurse stopped everything and called Shannon on his cell phone. Within two hours, the chief of radiology installed the new line himself.

The effect of the Toyota Way on infection rates was profound and immediate. Within a month, the CLAB rate had plummeted and within 60 days, Allegheny General had achieved the impossible—zero infections for the month. In the first 12 months under the Toyota Way, there were just six infections and one death, compared with 47 infections and 19 deaths the year before. A follow-up study suggested that Allegheny General had averted $500,000 in medical costs and could save $1 million if the same infection controls were extended throughout the entire hospital. In the following three years, infections at Allegheny General's intensive-care units remained extremely rare. Zero was the new normal.

There are two very interesting things about the Allegheny General experience. The first is that there was no need to bring in new, more experienced, or more talented people to work in intensive care. That's usually the answer in most workplaces when a department is having problems. Shake up the personnel. Get some new leadership in there. But talent was not the problem. Shannon was able to produce world-class results with the same bright and highly trained people who, one year earlier and under different operating practices, had allowed 19 of their patients to die from infections.

The second interesting point is that the Toyota Way required little, if any, innovation in medical procedures. Shannon didn't ask the hospital to invest in expensive lasers, cameras, probes, or robotics. He standardized the way catheters would be inserted and dressed, but not in any way that was unfamiliar or required new training.

Think about that for a moment. These highly educated, highly skilled (and, in many cases, very highly paid) medical professionals were accidentally killing their patients at a rate of more than one a month. No amount of increased staffing, advanced training, or superior technology would have changed the death toll. All that was needed was the synergy of best practices, faithfully followed. The system they used in this case, the Toyota Way, is so elemental and easily understood that workers with the equivalent of eighth-grade educations use it to produce zero defect results in auto factories all over the world.

And which of the many steps taken by Allegheny General were the most important in saving lives? No one can say. That's the magic behind any synergistic system, whether it's the Toyota Way, Coach Gibbs's football brilliance, or the Business Brilliant principles in this book. By performing faithfully (not flawlessly) the proper set of everyday, replicable behaviors, the results you produce can be outstanding, unpredictable, and sometimes unimaginable.

➤ The Trouble with What Everyone Knows

In the past six years, household net worth in the United States has fallen by trillions of dollars. The Census Bureau estimates that Americans lost more than one-third of their net worth between 2005 and 2010. White-collar unemployment, meanwhile, has lingered around 6 percent, a number not seen since the 1983 recession, 30 years ago. Standing behind these ranks of unemployed white-collar workers are millions of employed workers who are worried about the stability of their jobs and wondering about the long-term viability of their professions and their chosen careers.

In February 2009, when we ran the Business Brilliant survey, Wall Street was in the midst of a meltdown. (The stock market was headed for what would turn out to be a 14-year low on March 9.) We really didn't know what to expect from the results, since everyone we knew was talking about how much money they were losing every day. Would such dramatic investment losses have any measurable effects on either group?

When the results came in, it seemed to Russ Prince and me that the two groups had moved even farther apart. The market meltdown of early 2009 seemed to have hardened both groups' positions and the middle class and self-made millionaires appeared to be more distant from each other than ever before. At the same time, the extraordinary results Prince continued to achieve with his clients through his coaching raised my level of urgency to share the principles of Business Brilliance. But before I could do that, I needed to study the evidence more deeply and test these survey results against reality. I wanted to reveal the signs of Business Brilliance among the greatest success stories of our time. I've been doing that for the past three years, and it hasn't always been easy, because, as you'll see, highly successful people often try to downplay or conceal the true secrets of their successes.

In the next chapter, I will take the saying "Do what you love and the money will follow" and stand it on its head. The chapter will show how the world's richest clown, the world's richest fine artist, and *Seinfeld*'s most successful bit player have all achieved enormous wealth by doing what they love while always, always *following the money.* The following chapter will show why self-made millionaires ignore the scrimp-save-and-invest mantra of the financial services industry and why three-quarters of all the people reading this book are underpaid. Subsequent chapters will explore principles of Business Brilliance such as "Know-Who Is Better Than Know-How," which reveals the virtues of taking a "heads I win, tails I don't lose" approach to any project, and "Imitate, Don't Innovate," which attempts to bury once and for all the myth that success requires a "big idea."

Every chapter in this book explodes a commonly held myth about creating wealth and reveals success secrets of self-made millionaires and billionaires that they're not always eager to discuss. Most founders of *Inc.* magazine's "Inc. 5000"—their list of the fastest-growing private companies in America—say that the ideas used in their businesses were more or less stolen from their previous employers, though you'll never see a news release to that effect. For years, eBay lied to the media about the "big idea" that led to its founding because its true origin, as one of many online auction imitators, wasn't very thrilling. Kinko's Copies never would have existed if its founder had been any good at holding down a regular job. Adam Mackay might never have produced and directed his movies with Will Ferrell if he hadn't listened to his manager and driven an impossibly hard bargain with Lorne Michaels at *Saturday Night Live*.

In the final chapter, I'll go out on a limb, offering my own four-point program for Business Brilliance, based on my interpretation of the best practices among self-made millionaires. I call this program LEAP, in part because following it requires a certain leap of faith in the *Business Brilliant* approach. It's also called LEAP because I believe that if you take all four points to heart and then execute on each of the accompanying 17 steps, you will enjoy a quantum *leap* in your income. As I wrote earlier, I can't promise that I know how to mint new millionaires. That's the stuff of late-night get-rich-quick infomercials. But I can promise that your outlook on making money will change fundamentally and your results will improve if you make the LEAP program a priority in your life.

At the same time, I accept that it's human nature to resist new information about any subject as familiar and powerful as money. Take, for example, the cold reception the medical establishment has given to the zero-infection phenomenon at Allegheny General. You would think that after Allegheny General produced those amazing results, every hospital administrator in the United States would be begging Richard Shannon to come in and teach their staffs how to stop killing patients.

You would be wrong.

The vast majority of hospitals still regard infections as unfortunate but inevitable events, despite the mounting evidence to the contrary. The Allegheny General example was followed by some other larger-scaled demonstrations of infection reduction through mastery of the mundane. But the medical establishment remains ambivalent about bringing the Toyota Way and similar quality-control systems into its clinics. Despite the dramatic zero-infection-rate examples set by Shannon and a handful of other pioneers, the rate of hospital infections and fatalities nationwide is moving downward very slowly, and only within the past several years.

It could be a question of motivation. Many industrial experts have noted that while the Federal Aviation Administration has a fairly easy time convincing airline pilots to cooperate with mandated checklists and other safety measures, hospitals must beg and cajole doctors to comply with even the simplest measures, such as washing their hands. Why the extreme difference when pilots and surgeons have so much in common? Both professions require quick-thinking, detail-oriented, take-charge personalities. The only obvious distinction between the two professions is motivation.

How can I put this delicately? Pilots are seated in the same planes as their passengers. Surgeons are not under the same knives as their patients. To paraphrase an old joke, surgeons may be interested in safety, but pilots are committed.

Which brings me to your motivation for reading this book.

You've probably never heard of Umair Haque, but the *Harvard Business Review* ranks the young London-based consultant as one of the world's 50 top management thinkers. In March 2012, Haque posted an unusual blog entry on the *Harvard Business Review* website. He wrote, "Lately, I've been in the middle of a full-blown omg what-the-hell-where-is-it-all-going-and-what's-the-point-anyways life crisis." Haque added that many of his colleagues are feeling the same way, which prompted him to wonder if we are living in an era marked by "titanic institutional failure."

"All around us," he wrote, "yesterday's institutions are buckling and breaking, creaking and cracking (markets, governments, universities, corporations)." We count on institutions to provide us with social stability and rules to live by, but Haque says it's obvious that the rules are all broken: "You know it and I know it. If you play by the rules today, you're probably going to end up broke, lonely, miserable, exploited and empty."

Even before the 2008 world economic crisis, it was already clear that the old rules of the baby boom generation were dying and would no longer apply in a new world of global communication and competition. In Haque's terms, the boomers grew up sheltered by stable workplace institutions that were "highways whose destination is prosperity: get on the highway, take the right exit, and *voila*." But now those highways are often roads to nowhere, and there is mass confusion about where to turn next. Many suspect there is nothing that can be done. For the first time in U.S. history, fewer than half of all adults believe it's likely that their children will have a better life than their parents. A Gallup poll found that this pessimism is greatest among people with more than $75,000 in annual income, of whom just 37 percent believe that the future will be a better place.

These observations, and many others like it, are why I see such an urgent need for this book. To me, the main issue for decades now has been risk. More and more financial risk has been heaped upon members of the educated middle class in the form of lost pension plans, reduced healthcare coverage, skyrocketing tuition costs, and the housing bubble. Big corporations and other institutional employers used to shelter us from these risks in exchange for our diligence, conformity, and loyalty. But that deal, common 50 years ago, is dead. Now the riskiest thing you can do is try to hold up your end of that bargain and hope that your employer will reciprocate. In other words, we are all now free agents. We are all entrepreneurs, whether we want to be or not.

One major theme that runs throughout the Business Brilliant survey results is that self-made millionaires, most of whom are already living entrepreneurial lives, are better suited to thrive in this new, freewheeling economy because they are more comfortable dealing with risk. I don't mean to say they are big risk-takers. As you'll see in chapters 5 and 6 in particular, they are much more proficient at controlling risks in their financial dealings than the middle class. But self-made millionaires have lived a long time with risk as a fact of life and a challenge that requires constant attention. As economic risk keeps growing for millions of people who might have thought just a few years ago that they were on that proverbial highway to prosperity, my belief is that the principles of Business Brilliance will provide the best and most attractive new route to affluence for any intelligent, educated person willing to practice them.

Convincing you will not be easy, I realize. Consider for a moment that most NFL football coaches have not adopted Coach Gibbs's groundbreaking method for testing football brilliance, even though it helped get Gibbs elected to the Hall of Fame. And most people running hospitals today still adhere to what Richard Shannon calls "a theory of inevitability" about infection deaths, even though Shannon and others have shown that infections can be all but eradicated through simple step-by-step processes. These two stories from very disparate fields demonstrate how easy it is for the majority of accomplished professionals to avoid rethinking their preconceived beliefs and habits—even if doing so would help them achieve their goals.

I see one common and inspiring quality that links Gibbs, the Hall of Fame coach, with Shannon, the eminent physician—and sets each of them apart from all their peers. Gibbs and Shannon were willing to question the received wisdom they had long relied upon. Their curiosity, their courage, to cast doubt on what everybody already "knew" to be true, to see the familiar with new eyes, allowed them to create breakthrough results for themselves and their teams.

So which are you? Are you the pragmatic airline pilot, willing to master some mundane methods in order to get where you want to go? Or are you the proud surgeon, too steeped in tradition, training, and privilege to contemplate change, even when the evidence says that new thinking is desperately needed? What is it that you "know" right now about money that just might not be true? What do you know about yourself, and your ability to sample a few new ideas? Are you ready to consider, like Coach Gibbs and Dr. Shannon once needed to do, that much of what you "know," what you've always known, might deserve a second look?

2

Do What You Love, but Follow the Money

MORE THAN 7 IN 10 MIDDLE-CLASS SURVEY
RESPONDENTS SAID "DOING WHAT I LOVE AND
ALLOWING THE MONEY TO FOLLOW" WAS IMPORTANT TO
THEIR FINANCIAL SUCCESS.

JUST 2 IN 10 OF OUR SELF-MADE MILLIONAIRE SURVEY
RESPONDENTS AGREED WITH THAT STATEMENT.

➤ The Billionaire Busker

If you had been one of Guy Laliberté's parents back in 1983, you probably would have been a little worried about your twenty-three-year-old son.

The French Canadian Laliberté had skipped college after high school and took off to Europe for a year. He supported himself hand-to-mouth as an accordion-playing street performer, or busker, to use the British term. When he first arrived in London, he had less than $1,000 in his pocket, and to preserve what he had, he spent the night sleeping on a bench in Hyde Park.

Laliberté's English wasn't very good and he soon moved on to Paris. There he fell in with other buskers, who taught him juggling, stilt walking, and "fire breathing," probably the most dangerous of circus-style street acts. Laliberté would first take off his shirt and tie back his hair for safety. Then he would swig a mouthful of toxic flammable liquid and, with a burning torch in one hand, spray a writhing plume of orange-yellow fire 10 feet into the air. Fire breathing became Laliberté's crowd-pleasing specialty.

Raised in a large middle-class family headed by a corporate executive father, Laliberté always expected to go on to college. But when he returned home from Europe, he instead joined a nonprofit collective of stilt walkers and acrobats called Le Club des Talons Hauts (the High Heels Club). His next several summers were spent living in a youth hostel while helping run Talons Hauts street festivals in the tiny Quebec resort town of Baie-Saint-Paul. Money and possessions never seemed all that important to Laliberté. Each winter he spent whatever cash he'd saved up by escaping to the beaches of Florida and Hawaii.

In early 1983, the Quebec government announced plans for a celebration of the province's 450th anniversary to take place the following summer. Money was set aside for festivities that would showcase Quebec's homegrown talent, and Talons Hauts received $1.6 million for a traveling circus that would visit 14 towns throughout Quebec over 12 weeks. Laliberté led the planning. He even dreamed up its name: Le Grand Tour du Cirque du Soleil.

The traveling circus was a chaotic mess that often flirted with disaster. The new "big-top" performance tent was almost impossible to set up. It collapsed in a rain storm one day during a preshow media event. Working conditions for the performers were so poor that there was a near-revolt by the European circus artists brought in to supplement the amateurish Talons Hauts regulars. The Cirque du Soleil show itself, however, won glowing praise from the press and the public throughout Quebec.

Le Grand Tour had been conceived as a one-year project, but Laliberté was determined to keep Cirque du Soleil going. He convinced the government to underwrite another season of shows in 1985. Outside of Quebec, however, the reaction was mixed. Shows in Toronto and Niagara Falls were poorly attended and the fledgling Cirque organization ended the year $750,000 in debt. A national tour of eight Canadian cities the following year fared much better, though, and ended with a showcase performance at the world's fair in Vancouver.

Cirque had an informal, collaborative style of organization in which Laliberté took on the de facto role of executive producer. He kept pushing the circus's creative staff to make the shows larger, more theatrical, and more visually lavish. Although the crowds kept growing through 1986, so did Cirque's debt. Laliberté seemed determined to spend money that Cirque didn't have. He went to France and brought back a gigantic new circus tent even though Cirque couldn't pay for it. For almost three years, the fiscal management of Cirque du Soleil involved bouncing checks, wheedling with creditors, and begging for government handouts.

Then, in 1987, Laliberté booked Cirque to open the Los Angeles Arts Festival. The finances at Cirque were so shaky at the time that some top members of the troupe quit over what they considered a reckless move. But Cirque quickly became the hottest ticket at the festival. All 30 performances sold out and the $19 seats were being sold by scalpers for $200. Elton John and Francis Ford Coppola were among the celebrities who counted themselves as fans. Jane Fonda said she saw the show seven times during its two-week run. Cirque returned to Quebec with $1.5 million, its money problems a thing of the past. Within five years, Cirque shows were touring Europe and Asia. Over the next 20 years, Cirque du Soleil grew into one of the largest, most profitable entertainment brands in the world.

Today, Laliberté heads a staff of 3,000 based at Cirque's ultramodern Montreal headquarters and training center. His management team develops and coordinates six different shows running year-round in Las Vegas, another permanent show at Disney World, and nine touring companies that perform all over the world. Cirque's $800 million in annual ticket revenue rivals the combined box office take from all the theaters on Broadway.

Thanks to his majority interest in Cirque's parent company, Laliberté's net worth is estimated at $2.5 billion. In 2009, he spent $35 million of that personal fortune on a 12-day ride in the International Space Station. Wearing a red bulbous nose and proclaiming himself "the first clown in space," Laliberté told an interviewer while in orbit, "I'm doing what every kid dreams about—running away and joining the circus."

Laliberté's story is often held up as a classic rags-to-riches triumph. His tremendous success suggests that anyone—even a street performer—who pursues a vision with hard work and determination, can end up falling into an enormous pile of money.

But there's more to this story than just passion and drive. After all, plenty of passionate, creative people work hard their whole lives and still struggle to make ends meet. Laliberté isn't a billionaire just because he followed his passion for more than 20 years. He's a billionaire because he's followed his passion *and* because he managed to hold on to a big equity stake in his business, even increasing it along the way at the expense of his other partners. That's why this chapter is titled "Do What You Love, *but Follow the Money.*"

I know it's far more common to see this equation put slightly differently: *Do what you love and the money will follow.* It sounds like a lot less work when it's put that way and it's a more attractive statement of faith. In the Business Brilliant survey, this compelling idea has achieved a high level of acceptance among the middle-class sample. More than 7 in 10 said that "Doing what I love and allowing the money to follow" was important to their financial success. Our self-made millionaire survey respondents disagreed, however. Just 2 in 10 had any faith that the money will follow when you do what you love.

Do What You Love, the Money Will Follow is not only a popular idea with the middle class, it's also the title of a classic self-help bestseller by Marsha Sinetar. The book has sold more than a million copies and remains in print today almost 25 years after it was first published.

➤ The "Do What You Love" Deception

Marsha Sinetar said the idea came to her in 1984 while on her way to work. She was a public school administrator in Los Angeles at the time, holding down a secure job that she no longer found challenging. What she really wanted to do was become an independent management consultant, write books, and live in the country. But she was afraid to take all the risks required to get there.

Then one morning while driving down Wilshire Boulevard, Sinetar had an epiphany: "Do what you love, the money will follow." The thought arrived in her mind fully formed, she said, "as if someone was speaking to me." By the time she got to work, she had resolved to start changing her life, although it would take her two full years to make a complete transition. Sinetar began taking consulting work on the side as a mediator in corporate contract disputes. She moved to a house in a quiet rural community outside Los Angeles. Once her consulting practice had built up enough clients, Sinetar finally quit the school district. By then she was collecting stories for the book she wanted to write. It would be about people who had made similar dramatic changes in their working lives.

Do What You Love, the Money Will Follow was released in 1987 by a small Catholic publishing house and became a surprise bestseller. Sinetar's premise was that in order to find happiness and prosperity by doing what you love, you need to overcome fears and self-doubt about where the money will come from. The book found a receptive readership among members of a sixties generation in the throes of their middle-age career crises.

Among the people she profiled was a teacher who quit the classroom to become a fine arts potter, a carpenter with an unused master's degree in English, a former secretary who took up wallpaper hanging, and another ex-secretary who went into the office-leasing business. One of her favorite subjects was a seventy-five-year-old man named Wayne who'd dropped out of grade school during the Depression and built a prosperous general contracting business.

"I always made a living because of me, not because I can build," Wayne told her. "During the Depression, with twenty people wanting every job, I was working. I'd just go to a place and convince them I could give them excellent service. They not only fed me, they paid me, too. . . . I earned 100 dollars a day during the Depression, cleaning roofs. It didn't have anything to do with the fact that I can do construction. It has to do with me."

Although Sinetar never explicitly pointed it out, the vast majority of people she cited as doing what they love were either small business owners like Wayne or self-employed and working from home. The satisfaction they expressed in doing the work they loved was drawn in large part from having an ownership stake in what they were doing. Sinetar herself was no different. She didn't seek another public-sector job she would love. She pursued the work she loved on the side, as a corporate consultant and author, where she owned a stake in her success and could flex her Business Brilliance.

Perhaps a more accurate title to Sinetar's book would have been *Do What You Love, but Follow the Money*. Almost all the people she profiled for her book were following the money and doing it gladly. It wasn't about chasing the almighty buck for them. It was about growing their livelihoods and creating services and things of value to other people. That was part and parcel of what they loved. There was a creative challenge in finding new things to love doing and new sources of income to make it happen.

And that was the case with Guy Laliberté. At almost every critical junction in the history of Cirque du Soleil, the entire enterprise might have collapsed or gone in a completely different direction were it not for Laliberté's personal devotion to following the money. It's not that he was driven by greed or profit. In fact, in a few situations, he resisted the allure of easy money because it threatened his creative control. For all his erratic management habits, the one constant in Laliberté's career was the nurturing and protection of his personal stake in the future prosperity of Cirque du Soleil.

When Laliberté took the lead in guiding Cirque through its early years, the troupe's nonprofit status was essential to its survival. This was how Laliberté got private donors and the government to foot the bill for all Cirque's early mistakes. The government was indulgent and creditors were patient because no one expected a lovable band of circus clowns to be good with money. At one point, Cirque's bank simply forgave $200,000 worth of bounced checks.

Laliberté would later say this was all part of a passing phase. "I told the government funding agencies that we'd be free of needing their support within five years," he was quoted in *Cirque du Soleil: 20 Years Under the Sun*, the official history of Cirque du Soleil. At one point he said he returned a subsidy check to the government because the circus had a profitable season.

Those years of spending beyond Cirque's means were dedicated to a very specific vision shared by Laliberté and the rest of Cirque's creative team. They wanted to present the circus arts as part of a theatrical experience, one that was more emotionally involving than the typical Ringling Brothers circus event. To do this, each new Cirque show required a unique set of costume designs, stage props, lighting effects, and an original musical score. Then the performers would also need to be paid more for extra weeks of rehearsals so all the acts can be shaped into a theatrical, storytelling whole.

It was an expensive vision, but Laliberté saw a pot of gold at the end of the rainbow. Theatergoers, he knew, are accustomed to paying much higher ticket prices than traditional circusgoers. Circus-as-theater cost a lot to produce, but it was also potentially very profitable.

Soon after the successful 1986 national Canadian tour, Laliberté and two other top Cirque administrators hatched their plan to turn Cirque into a private, for-profit company, with each one of them as one-third owners. Some members quit the troupe in disgust at the move, including Laliberté's longtime friend and mentor, Guy Caron, the artistic director of Cirque. But Laliberté assumed correctly that most members would stay because they were just happy to keep working.

The circus-as-theater vision for Cirque belonged as much to Caron as it did to Laliberté. But the two men had vastly different ideas about how to achieve it. Caron was a founder of Quebec's circus school, and held a deep belief in consensus decision making and nonprofit collective ownership. Laliberté, on the other hand, said that "I always had business goals, as much as I had goals to travel and have fun. . . . I always said that if Cirque makes it big, it will be because it succeeds at marrying art and business."

Under Caron, Cirque du Soleil might have developed into Quebec's national circus as an arm of the circus school. It might well have grown into a well-regarded regional performance group with a seasonal touring schedule, like the Los Angeles Philharmonic or the Mormon Tabernacle Choir. But Caron never would have led Cirque into becoming a global cultural phenomenon. Caron's Cirque would have never sold 10 million tickets a year, or employed more than 1,000 performers, teachers, and trainers.

Laliberté and Caron split on bitter terms, and by some accounts, Caron complained to others in Cirque that Laliberté would be better off selling used cars. If anything, the comment showed this poor understanding of Laliberté's true motives. At the time of this breakup, Laliberté passed up a potentially lucrative offer from Hollywood that any used-car salesman would have salivated over. It was a deal that would have solved all of Cirque's money problems with the stroke of a pen.

While Cirque was in Los Angeles for the arts festival, a team from Columbia Pictures came to him with a proposal for a Cirque du Soleil movie. The studio put a lot of money on the table and, after years of Laliberté's living so close to the edge of insolvency, it would have been understandable if he had grabbed at it. But as the negotiations proceeded, he believed that Columbia wanted him to sign over control over the Cirque du Soleil name. In exchange for one big payday, he and his management team might be reduced to working for Columbia, not as partners but as serfs. He rejected the offer.

There is a reason why I chose to open this chapter with a story from the performing arts. The seven principles of Business Brilliance are so basic and fundamental to creating wealth that I wanted to demonstrate they can apply to any job description on earth, even in fields where making money is far from the chief concern—like the arts. Even in the arts, where talent and artistry is supposedly valued above all else, the people who make the most money tend to be those who are most mindful of following the money. I discovered, for instance, that Laliberté's rise as the world's richest circus clown bears some striking parallels to the story of Damien Hirst, the world's richest artist.

Hirst was born into even less auspicious circumstances than Laliberté. He never knew his biological father, and his stepfather left the family when Hirst was twelve. His working-class adolescence in Leeds was marked by poor grades in school and a couple of arrests for shoplifting. "I grew up with quite an impoverished background," he told *Time* magazine in 2007. "I didn't see any possibility that I would ever get paid for doing anything I enjoyed."

Hirst always liked drawing as a boy, but he was rejected from the art college in Leeds. He moved to London and for two years he worked as a laborer on construction sites. Finally, on his second try, he was admitted to Goldsmiths' School of Art at the University of London.

There was a recession in the art world during Hirst's school years, and galleries weren't taking on new talent. So in 1988, Hirst curated and organized an independent show of Goldsmiths student works in London's desolate Docklands area. Hirst scraped up the cash to rent out a vacant warehouse, curated the show, and printed up the programs. Just as Guy Laliberté started out running the little street festivals in Baie-Saint-Paul at an early age, Hirst made his first mark in the art world in an organizing role, as a curator, not an artist.

The art show was called *Freeze* and it would become legendary for launching the careers of a new generation of British conceptual artists. Hirst's own contribution to the show was unremarkable, though. It was an assemblage of cardboard boxes glued together and decorated with house paint. Hirst was living in public housing at the time, and couldn't afford to actually produce some of the art he had designed on his computer. Thanks to *Freeze*, however, he met an art dealer who was willing to front him $6,000 to execute his first substantial work.

Hirst didn't pander. He did what he loved. He had always been fascinated by death and decay and had spent some time working part-time in a mortuary, where he sketched dead bodies. With $6,000 in hand, he produced *A Thousand Years*, a large glass case with the head of a slaughtered cow lying inside it. Also sealed inside the case was a colony of flies that bred maggots in the cow's rotting flesh. Above the severed head was an electric bug zapper. "In the rush to feed, they are massacred," wrote one London art blogger regarding the work. "To live is to die."

It was repulsive. It was disgusting. And when it was shown publicly for the first time in 1990, Charles Saatchi, the world's most famous art collector, stood before it with his mouth agape in awe. He gave Hirst a $60,000 commission to produce his next work, a 14-foot tiger shark suspended in a gigantic tank of formaldehyde. It was titled *The Physical Impossibility of Death in the Mind of Someone Living* and it became Hirst's signature artwork, an icon of 1990s British conceptual art. In 2004, Saatchi would sell Hirst's pickled shark to a New York hedge fund magnate for a rumored $12 million.

By then Hirst's reputation had been solidified as one of the richest, most successful artists of all time. In 2006, at the age of forty, he was worth an estimated $160 million, which is more than the net worths of Andy Warhol, Pablo Picasso, and Salvador Dali *combined* at the same age.

He achieved this with the help of 120 employees in a factory-style studio, where "original" Damien Hirsts are turned out under his supervision, but usually without his ever so much as touching them. He has paintings made of spin-art that take three minutes to produce and are priced at $10,000. He has a series of "dot" paintings—colorful dots on white canvas—that he admits he lacks the technical skill to do properly. His best ones, he says, are done by an assistant named Rachel.

And like Laliberté, some of Hirst's most masterful moves have been made at the juncture where art and commerce meet. In 2003, Hirst paid $15 million to buy back 15 of his own early paintings from Charles Saatchi in order to help control supply and demand of his seminal work. Experts could not recall any artist ever making such a wise and far-sighted investment maneuver.

Then, in September 2008, just a week after the debt crisis sank Lehman Brothers and shook financial markets all over the world, Hirst defied doomsayers and auctioned off $198 million worth of his own artwork at Sotheby's, exceeding even the high presale estimates. The auction was unusual because it was the first time any artist had managed the sale of his work directly to the public, cutting out the fat commissions normally enjoyed by his London and New York dealers. Hirst got the idea from his previous experience with Pharmacy, a London restaurant he partly owned. When the restaurant closed in 2004, Hirst personally oversaw auctioning off everything inside it, right down to the matchboxes. He raised $20 million that way, far more than the restaurant itself was worth.

Hirst's most controversial financial creation, however, is a small sculpture called *For the Love of God*. It is the most expensive work of art ever made. In 2006, Hirst had a platinum cast fabricated from an eighteenth-century human skull he bought in an antique shop. The cast was then coated with 8,601 flawless diamonds at a reported cost of $28 million. Hirst announced an asking price of $100 million and in August 2007 he claimed he'd gotten it, in cash, from an anonymous consortium. But critics speculate that he and his business manager are a part of the secret consortium, and that the actual price fell short of $100 million. If true, it would mean nonetheless, that Hirst still maintains an ownership stake in his most valuable piece, a stake he can always sell at a later date.

Around the time of that announcement, a *New York Times* editorial scolded that "Mr. Hirst . . . has gone from being an artist to being what you might call the manager of the hedge fund of Damien Hirst's art. No artist has managed the escalation of prices for his own work quite as brilliantly as Mr. Hirst. That is the real concept in his conceptualism, which has culminated in his most recent artistic farce: a human skull encrusted in diamonds."

It's curious that this *Times* editorial didn't register any disapproval of the crazed escalation of art-world prices in general. The article seemed to say that it's okay for art dealers and collectors to speculate and profit from rising prices, but if an artist excels in profiting from his own work, he somehow suffers a loss of artistic integrity.

It could be that the *Times* editorial reflects a certain ambivalence among the middle class about following the money. All Hirst has done is display typical middle-class millionaire interest in the wealth his work creates. The Business Brilliant survey found that 8 in 10 self-made millionaires have a substantial ownership stake in their work, while 1 in 10 say that although they don't have ownership now, they are seeking it.

There is a very wide gap of experience here between the middle class and self-made millionaires in this respect. Among the middle class, just 1 in 10 have an ownership stake in their work, and just 2 out of 10 say they are seeking it. But here is a survey result I find much more interesting. More than 6 out of 10 also agree that owning a stake in one's work is important. So, in simple terms, almost two-thirds of the middle class see the value of having an ownership stake in one's work, but less than one-third of the middle class is doing anything about it!

Why don't more middle-class people do what they love *and* follow the money? Why does one-third of the middle class acknowledge the value of having equity in one's work while doing nothing to pursue it? Is it really as Marsha Sinetar said, that you need to overcome your self-doubt and stop letting fear hold you back?

Certainly no one would accuse Laliberté and Hirst of suffering from self-doubt and trepidation. But self-confidence isn't everything, either. There are many bold, self-confident artists in the world who are also fairly rich and successful. How come none of them bought back their early works or run their own auctions, as Hirst did? Controlling supply and cutting out useless middlemen are fundamental business practices that are literally centuries old. Why was Hirst the first artist ever to apply such a time-tested strategy to his career?

And think about this. When Laliberté announced to the 60 or 70 members of the fledgling Cirque du Soleil that he and his two partners wanted to take over ownership of Cirque as a private for-profit company, he needed his performers and his creative team to go along with the plan. The ranks of Cirque had already been thinned somewhat by dissension at the time. Laliberté was in a vulnerable spot. Any one of the key members of Cirque could have asked him for a tiny slice of the pie—maybe a 1 percent nonvoting ownership stake in the new company—as a condition of staying. A few of them probably would have gotten it.

One percent of Cirque du Soleil would be worth about $20 million today. But none of them even asked.

Why?

➤ The Paralysis of the Paycheck

In the spring of 1969, a young psychology researcher named Ed Deci ran a series of experiments at Carnegie Mellon University that involved watching college students play the Parker Brothers puzzle game Soma. The results of Deci's experiments, which have been supported by dozens of other studies since then, challenged a lot of traditional ideas about how and why people work, learn, and play.

The experiments also cast an interesting light on why some people might have an easier time than others in finding work they love and following the money.

Soma is a deceptively simple three-dimensional puzzle. There are seven irregularly shaped plastic blocks that can be fitted into a perfect three-inch cube if they are put together the right way. The Soma puzzle can be solved by making other shapes, too, including a couch, an airplane, and a begging dog.

For his experiment, Deci put two sets of students in separate rooms and gave them all Soma puzzles. He asked them to solve the puzzles in as many different ways as possible within half an hour. The students in the first group were simply asked to try their best. The students in the second group were told they'd each get a $1 reward for each puzzle shape they solved. After half an hour, Deci announced to both groups that the experiment was complete. He asked them to wait a few minutes while he left the room to print out some questionnaires.

The students didn't know it, but the experiment didn't really begin until Deci left. He was absent for exactly eight minutes. During that time, another experimenter watched the students through a secret one-way mirror. He took notes on what they did with their eight minutes of free time.

The experiment revealed some curious differences in the behavior of the two groups. Many of the students in the first group, the ones who hadn't been paid, continued to try and solve the Soma puzzles during the eight minutes Deci was gone. But most of the students in the other group, who had been offered the $1 rewards, dropped the puzzles soon after Deci left the room. Deci hypothesized that for this second group of students, the monetary rewards had interfered with whatever intrinsic sense of challenge and enjoyment Soma might have provided them. The first group, having been offered no rewards, probably had more fun. That would explain why they kept playing with the puzzle even after they'd been told the experiment was over.

The students who were paid to play Soma likely experienced their $1 rewards as tools of control. Deci thinks this is why they stopped playing Soma once the money stopped. The dollar reward spoiled any sense of fun they might have had while solving the puzzles. "People experience [controls] as being antagonistic to their autonomy," Deci wrote. "So these events drain people's sense of enthusiasm and interest in the controlled activities."

Today Deci holds a psychology chair at the University of Rochester. He heads an academic center there devoted to the study of what is known as SDT, self-determination theory. Psychologists in the SDT field have cataloged more than 100 experiments that demonstrate how short-term rewards for behavior generate longer-term loss of interest and enthusiasm. Once blood donors were paid to give blood, they were far less likely to donate again for free. Kids rewarded with a certificate for coloring with magic markers lost their interest in coloring. Volunteer writers at a college newspaper quit volunteering after they'd been paid to write for a week.

"[This is] what millions of us—well-meaning parents, teachers and managers—are doing to the people we reward, whether we realize it or not," wrote Alfie Kohn in his 1993 bestseller *Punished by Rewards*. "[We are] killing off their interest in the very things we are bribing them to do." When a national pizza chain started offering free books for children who visit their restaurants, one prominent psychologist sourly predicted the end result as "a lot of fat kids who don't like to read."

Kohn points out that rewards themselves are not really the problem. It's how vividly we experience a reward as that "tool of control." Experiments with other common workplace controls such as being closely supervised, being evaluated on a task, or being placed in competition with others, all show diminished interest in the work as a result. This is especially true if the work demands some degree of creative thinking. Offering rewards and controls together—carrots *and* sticks—is worst of all. Work environments that are driven by monetary incentives and close supervision tend to sap worker enthusiasm for tasks that they might otherwise find interesting. Productivity can drop because employees feel an overwhelming need to reassert their personal sense of autonomy. So they get passive, withhold their input, or fail to give a full effort.

Deci and his colleagues at Rochester have found that these kinds of negative, self-doubting thoughts arise when we feel controlled and our autonomy is under attack. The emotional need for autonomy expresses itself more subtly than physical needs like hunger or thirst. You probably wouldn't say you're feeling "autonomy-deficient" after a week of working in a demanding job. You're more likely to wonder if you're getting sick of the business—a business you once felt sure you loved. At the end of the work week, you just want to do something different to make yourself feel better.

Deci hasn't coined a catchy name for what's going on here, although he commonly refers to it as the "undermining effect." For our purposes, I'd like to call it something else: Paycheck Paralysis.

You may have entered a career because you enjoy the work. As your skills develop and your capabilities expand, you should enjoy it even more, but the carrot-and-stick workplace environment undermines those pleasurable feelings. That's Paycheck Paralysis. Even as you keep getting better at what you do best, you're losing the passion you'll need to go out and get an ownership stake in it. Paycheck Paralysis can make you fall out of love with what you do—just enough so you never get to find the money while doing it.

Here's what's even worse: If you truly love your work, you're that much more likely to suffer from Paycheck Paralysis. The equation is pretty simple. People who feel real pride and passion in what they do have that much more to lose when workplace rewards and controls block their enthusiasm. The resulting feelings of lost autonomy, of being a pawn, would be much more grievous than if they'd never cared for the work to begin with.

I've noted before how more than 6 out of 10 middle-class respondents in the Business Brilliant survey think that it's very important to obtain an ownership stake in one's work, but most (8 out of 10) of survey respondents aren't even *trying* to get it. Why are so many of them essentially demotivated about something they say they consider very important?

Could Paycheck Paralysis partly explain why the English teacher never writes her book or the accountant never opens his own private practice? The butcher, the baker, the candlestick maker—some of them never follow the money on their own because they are under a kind of demotivating spell, one that they're not even aware of.

It was Deci's original Soma puzzle experiments that revealed a rare immunity to Paycheck Paralysis. A small percentage of the students who played Soma for money seemed to be impervious to feeling undermined. They were in the group that received $1 rewards for solving the puzzles but, when the half-hour period had ended, kept trying to solve the puzzles. To borrow a phrase from Deci, these students did not experience the rewards "as controls that were antagonistic to their autonomy." Instead, they seemed to experience the rewards as free money for doing something fun that they'd gladly do for free. Unlike everyone else in the experiment, they enjoyed the puzzles *and* the money.

Deci says now that these students would rank very high on what he and his colleagues at Rochester call "autonomy orientation." People who are considered highly autonomy oriented are more likely to seek out tasks because they are interesting and challenging. They are also more likely in general to take responsibility for their own behavior instead of blaming circumstances or other people. At the opposite pole are people who have a "controlled orientation," which suggests a dependency on rewards and what others demand, rather than on what they want for themselves. The controlled orientation (along with an anxious and fatalistic streak called "impersonal orientation") is at the root of Paycheck Paralysis.

On the website for the University of Rochester SDT program (www.psych.rochester.edu/SDT/questionnaires) there is a 17-point questionnaire that helps you locate where you fall on the General Causality Orientations Scale. For instance, if you've been offered a new job at a company where you've worked a long time, how likely is it that the first question to arise in your mind is, "What if I can't live up to the responsibility?" or "Will I make more money at this position?" Those are the impersonal-orientation and controlled-orientation responses. The autonomy-oriented first thought might be, "I wonder if the new work will be interesting."

If you take the test and score low on it, at least you'll know that you're prone to Paycheck Paralysis. That perhaps is the bad news. The good news is that, if you're like half the middle class and you want to follow the money but haven't, you can stop judging yourself for procrastination, risk-aversion, or laziness. You're having what is for you a natural reaction to feeling controlled. The first step for snapping out of Paycheck Paralysis and asserting your autonomy is to understand how and why you might be under its spell.

Adopting an autonomy orientation can help get you through a lot of situations that most people would consider controlling, primed for what I'm calling Paycheck Paralysis. The reason is that the actions you choose to take help create the social context in which you live. Certainly that was the case with Laliberté and Hirst. Rather than bemoaning the low pay and poor job opportunities for circus performers in Quebec, Laliberté has created thousands of circus jobs that never would have existed without Cirque du Soleil, and become a billionaire in the process. Hirst changed his life, and changed the art world in the process, by thinking about money with the same creativity he expends on his art.

Deci writes in his book *Why We Do What We Do*:

Rather than waiting for the world to give them what they want, people can become more proactive in making things happen for themselves. They can get the interactive process working on their behalf by behaving more autonomously. They can elicit from the social context more and more support for their autonomy. Their personality and the social contexts in which they operate are synergistic, *and together they affect people's experiences and actions.*

Synergistic. I added the emphasis in Deci's quote. To be autonomous, to do what you love and follow the money, you need to make choices most people are too afraid to make and ask for things most people are afraid to ask for. When you do these things, you impact your surroundings and help create a new reality. To see this kind of autonomous synergism in action, read on for the story of yet another artist, a Hollywood character actor named John O'Hurley.

➤ The Peterman Principle

On May 14, 1998, John O'Hurley bought a full-page ad in the entertainment trade newspaper *Variety*. It featured the following note addressed to the cast and crew of the recently ended megahit sitcom *Seinfeld*.

As I stand here knee-deep in the amber waters of the River Ganges, elbow-to-elbow with the fishwives of New Delhi, learning the gentle art of river laundering and putting a last-minute spit shine on a pair of baby-blue boxer shorts, I watch the slow parade of boats as it passes by me on the sunset of this never-ending river. I'm reminded how grateful I am to have docked at your port of call for as long as I did. For me the horizon will always be just a bit out of reach, and that is why I continue sailing. I wish you all extraordinary lives.

—*Jacopo Peterman*

For three years in the late 1990s, John O'Hurley appeared on *Seinfeld* as the clueless adventurer and pompous catalog company owner J. Peterman. It was a fairly small role. O'Hurley appeared in just 20 of *Seinfeld*'s 172 episodes, mostly in the final two seasons of the show's nine-year run.

Small as the role was, it was also extremely memorable. Fifteen years after the last *Seinfeld* episode was aired, it has been impossible for O'Hurley to walk anywhere without hearing people yell "Hey Peterman!" Most call out from behind his back or across the street, but others come right up and say it to his face. And it doesn't just happen when he's in the United States, since, according to O'Hurley's biography, *Seinfeld* reruns are broadcast in 85 countries around the world.

Many actors consider this kind of notoriety cancerous to their careers. It leads to typecasting, in which they become so completely identified in the public mind with one character that no one in the television or movie business thinks they're good for anything else. This is partly why the actors who played the two dozen or so best-known *Seinfeld* characters on the show have fled from the roles and tried to make everyone else forget them.

Patrick Warburton, who played the dumb car mechanic David Puddy in nine *Seinfeld* episodes, is typical. He told the *Los Angeles Times* in 2001 that "it's your responsibility as an actor to reinvent [yourself]." Typecasting, he said, is for actors who either want to do the same role or can't do anything else. "That's neither for me."

O'Hurley, on the other hand, seemed to think this was a false choice he didn't need to make. He was like the students in Ed Deci's Soma experiment who took the money *and* enjoyed the game. He began his post-*Seinfeld* career with that *Variety* ad promoting his Peterman identity. He popped up in TV commercials for Xerox, playing the Greek god Zeus with the Peterman voice. He did radio station voiceovers with the Peterman voice. An online video-tech company needed a spokesman and O'Hurley signed up, on the condition that he get an equity stake in the parent company. In 2006, O'Hurley told *Businessweek* that his

"Peterman-as-pitchman" character was worth seven figures a year as "that Mr. Magoo-type buffoon who can say anything for corporations."

So did typecasting as Peterman cause other work to dry up for O'Hurley? Not at all. O'Hurley made his Broadway debut in a production of *Chicago*. He played King Arthur in the touring company of the Monty Python show *Spamalot*. He won the 2003 *Dancing with the Stars* competition. He costarred with Loni Anderson that year in a short-lived sitcom called *The Mullets*. He hosted *Family Feud* from 2006 to 2010. O'Hurley even branched out beyond performing. He wrote a little book about life lessons learned from dogs, called *It's Okay to Miss the Bed on the First Jump*. It made the *New York Times* bestseller list. He composed an album of classical keyboard music. It made the Billboard charts.

The real-life J. Peterman didn't adapt to life after *Seinfeld* nearly so well as O'Hurley. The catalog company took up an over-aggressive growth strategy that landed it in bankruptcy in 1999. Then in 2001, in an irony of all ironies, O'Hurley met with the real John Peterman and made a deal to buy back from creditors the J. Peterman brand name. Today, O'Hurley is a top investor and board member in the resurrected J. Peterman company. The catalog now offers an $89 "O'Hurley golf shirt." O'Hurley told one interviewer that the J. Peterman character "has changed my life in ways that are inconceivable. And now that I own the company, I'm very happy to keep that franchise alive."

Until now, I've focused this chapter on people who come from fairly extraordinary circumstances and make the most of them—fire breathing, writing a bestselling book, or putting a rotting cow head inside a glassed-in artwork. This is a different issue. Why, given more or less the same opportunity as John O'Hurley, did all the other actors from *Seinfeld* flee from their associations with their characters? What made O'Hurley so different? The question leads back to Deci and his colleagues at the University of Rochester.

Much of Deci's work these past thirty years has surrounded the question of how workplaces can become more "autonomy supportive." The hope is that if organizations set up systems that allow employees to derive more intrinsic joy from their work, the employees would be more productive because they would feel as though the workplace was supportive of their autonomy.

The problem is, as shown earlier, that not everyone agrees on what an autonomy-supportive environment is. Some people are more prone to feeling controlled than others, so the same boss or circumstance that feels threatening to one person can appear challenging to another. One study showed how medical students who rank high on autonomy orientation are more likely to view their instructors as being very autonomy supportive, whether those instructors are or aren't. Some instructors might be extremely controlling, but the autonomy-oriented students don't recognize them as such.

Opportunity is truly in the eye of the beholder. Of the entire *Seinfeld* cast, O'Hurley was the only one to see how sweet it is to be part of the most watched, most successful comedy in television history. All the other actors on *Seinfeld* saw their characters differently, as threats to their freedom, as potential sources of control that could put straitjackets on their careers.

To O'Hurley, Peterman isn't a straitjacket at all. He is wearing the Peterman character comfortably—as he might an English Travel Jacket (page 22 in the J. Peterman catalog)—all the way to the bank.

3

Save Less, Earn More

ABOUT 9 IN 10 SELF-MADE MILLIONAIRES SAY "IT'S
IMPORTANT IN NEGOTIATIONS TO EXPLOIT WEAKNESSES
IN OTHERS."

AMONG THE MIDDLE CLASS, JUST OVER 2 IN 10 AGREED.

➤ The Wonder Bread Way to Wealth

When Suze Orman recalls her life before she became the nation's top financial guru and a media superstar, she talks about money the way recovering addicts or reformed sinners testify to their struggles with temptation.

In 1987, Orman was thirty-five years old and drowning in debt. She had her own small financial-planning practice in the San Francisco Bay area, and was leading what she admits was an overleveraged lifestyle. Her small house was mortgaged to the hilt. Her leased BMW cost $600 per month. Her credit card debt topped $100,000. At one point, Orman confesses, she dipped into her 401(k) retirement fund just to buy a $7,500 Cartier watch.

Since those days, Orman has made a fortune by scolding her millions of fans for indulging in far more modest excesses. Through nine bestselling books and repeated appearances on *The Oprah Winfrey Show*, Orman urges her followers to stop squandering dollars on frivolous luxuries and sock away that money by investing for retirement.

Orman's 1999 book *The Courage to Be Rich* provided five full pages of suggestions about how to save your way to wealth. Do you really need to eat French baguettes instead of Wonder bread? Is designer underwear a necessity or a luxury? Why not get rid of that fancy fragrant hand soap? "If you're not on a course of getting rich but want to be, you have to change course; it's that simple," Orman wrote. "To choose rich is to make every penny count . . . and to choose your luxuries very, very carefully."

Orman is so certain that saving is the path to prosperity that you would think she would have her own personal story to share, that she is living proof of what she preaches. You might be curious to hear how, by making every penny count, she completely turned around her own once-hopeless financial situation. But Orman can't tell you that because that's not what she did.

Orman dug her way out of debt not by saving more, but by earning more. She deployed her Business Brilliant skills, relied on the work that she loved and followed the money. While mired in debt in 1987, she landed a big new corporate client with a lucrative contract to provide re-tirement planning for its employees. Orman was paid $250,000 in a sin-gle month for her services, and all her spending sins and overindulgences were absolved. She didn't need to sell her house, trade in her BMW, or buy herself some cheaper underwear.

Orman commonly advises that it's not enough to cut back on spend-ing to get out of debt. Debt-ridden people, she says, should sell off their luxury items at a loss in order to start saving their way to wealth. So is that what she did with that $7,500 Cartier watch she bought with her plundered 401(k) funds? No. She gave it away to a friend.

Today Orman is only the most famous of a breed of personal-finance celebrities that has proliferated since the 1980s, when the popularity of IRAs began the rapid growth of households with stock holdings to 90 million today. These authors and media personalities all sermonize from the same fundamental gospel—that pinching pennies is a sure path to prosperity if you spend less, save more, and invest those savings in stocks and tax-advantaged mutual funds.

Newsweek columnist Jane Bryant Quinn was the queen of the move-ment until Orman dethroned her. David Bach and Robert Kiyosaki are the kings, while Ed Slott, CPA, has secured a lucrative niche in public television with his *Stay Rich Forever* infomercials in which he claims you can "parlay your IRA into a family fortune." (Full disclosure: I coauthored a book in 2001 called *The Armchair Millionaire* which extolled many of the same essential practices but with the aim of financial security, not a promise of riches.)

This message of personal frugality resonates deeply with the middle class. In the Business Brilliant survey, about 7 in 10 middle-class respondents agreed that "cutting back expenditures to help accumulate wealth" is important to their financial success. About the same number cited "cutting back on little luxuries" as being important. The 2008 financial crisis failed to shake middle-class confidence in these ideas, despite the devastating toll exacted on many retirement accounts. In fact, the surveys conducted before and after the crisis showed almost identical levels of support for the idea that you can save your way to riches.

Self-made millionaires, though, take the extreme opposite view. Only about 1 in 10 say that cutting back on little luxuries or reducing expenses has anything to do with accumulating wealth. To self-made millionaires, financial success is achieved by increasing what comes in, not restricting what goes out. Savings are a fine thing, but those who have gotten wealthy didn't get there by saving. Savings and investments only preserve what you've gained by other means, by working and following the money.

Anyone who has taken a serious look at self-made wealth knows this very well. When my old boss, *Worth* magazine founder W. Randall Jones, took two years to interview dozens of billionaires for his book *The Richest Man in Town*, he came up with twelve commandments of wealth drawn from what he learned in those interviews. None of those commandments involved thrift, saving, or investing. The British media mogul Felix Dennis can be a fanatical skinflint when it comes to running one of his start-up businesses. He brags about underpaying his employees and depriving them of company cars and cell phones. But Dennis spares no expense on himself. He writes in *How to Get Rich* that he has shelled out $790,000 on French wine alone over the past 20 years. "I spent a hell of a lot of what I made on sex and drugs and rock n' roll," he says. "The rest," he adds as a joke, "I wasted."

Despite all the evidence to the contrary, Orman has built her financial advice empire by convincing the middle class that cutting back expenses and hoarding the savings is some special discipline mastered by the wealthy. "Count every penny and make every penny count," she writes in *The Courage to Be Rich.* "How many of us do that? The rich do. I can promise you that."

Not to pick on Suze, but I don't know how she can make such an outrageous promise. My business brings me in touch with a lot of people who are rich by Suze's standards and all of them are too busy earning dollars to count pennies. Orman herself travels in fairly wealthy circles, so she must know better. In 2007, she told the *New York Times* that she spends at least $300,000 per year flying on private jets. That's probably a sensible expenditure, since her calendar is so crowded and her time is so valuable. But it's also an extreme example of why the rich don't count pennies. Their time is much better spent making money than saving it.

All the famous frugality gurus know this, as well, because they're all enriching themselves by earning more, not saving more. Quinn, Slott, and all the rest have made their money by applying their Business Brilliant skills to their careers. So when Orman claims that by scrimping and saving "this is how you get rich, financially speaking. Little by little," she's only half right. It's true enough that wealth accumulates in incremental stages. But those who achieve wealth do that by making opportunities count, not pennies.

On the other hand, this is a good place to acknowledge that a lot of people don't want to be in business for themselves. What about them? If your earning potential in the coming year is constrained by the size of a weekly paycheck, doesn't it make sense to cut back on spending and save what you can? Of course it does. It makes perfect sense. It just won't make you rich. Your savings are your savings. They're good to have but they are not the road to wealth.

From my perspective, the most damaging thing about the savings gospel is that it distracts people from where the action is—earning more money. Let's make the issue very simple for the moment. Let's pretend you have no interest at all in any of the other Business Brilliant principles described in the coming chapters. You want to earn more, but none of the strategies for doing it appeal to you. There is still one thing you can do to earn more money that doesn't take any special talent, new skills or effort.

You can ask.

The odds are that the sole reason you're not making more money at your job today is that you haven't *asked* for more money. It's true. By some estimates, about 3 out of 4 workers starting new jobs neglect to ask for more money upon taking their positions, even though 9 out of 10 hiring managers say they are ready to pay more if they're asked. Of the 1 in 4 employees who do ask, most of them ask badly and they don't ask for enough. Millions of people struggling to save nickels and dimes the Suze Orman way have passed up thousands of dollars in their places of work, dollars that were literally there for the asking.

But how many people bother to ask? Let's quote Orman for the answer: "The rich do. I can promise you that."

➤ The $1,000 Minute

In 1995, Linda Babcock was an assistant professor of economics at Carnegie Mellon University when a group of female students came to her with a complaint. A number of new courses were being taught by doctoral candidates in the coming semester, and all of the instructors were men. To the women, it felt like they had been denied the opportunity to teach because of their gender. They felt excluded, as though the department was being run like an old boys' club. They asked Babcock to look into it.

When Babcock broached the subject with the economics department head, she got the other side of the story. She learned that teaching positions had been awarded to doctoral students who had approached the department head with detailed proposals for new courses. All the students who did this happened to be male. There was no intent to discriminate against women. The men were granted teaching assignments because they asked for them. The problem was that the women *didn't ask*.

Following that conversation, Babcock and a few of her colleagues conducted a salary survey of recent graduates from the university's master's degree program in public policy. The results showed that despite having qualifications and credentials similar or identical to their female classmates, the men's salaries averaged 7.6 percent higher than the women's. Babcock and her colleagues weren't too surprised by that result, because for years salary surveys in all kinds of professions have shown similar earnings gaps between the sexes. These gaps are commonly assumed to be evidence of gender bias in hiring and compensation.

But Babcock had added another set of questions in the salary survey, questions that are rarely included in such studies. She wanted to know more about *asking*. How many of these graduates had tried to negotiate higher salaries for themselves before they accepted their job offers? Babcock knew that the career planning office at Carnegie Mellon strongly encouraged student job applicants to turn down their initial salary offers and ask for more money. She was curious to see how many students were actually following through on that advice.

Much to Babcock's surprise, more than half of the male graduates had asked for more money (57 percent) but only 7 percent of the female students had. Instead, 93 percent of the women (and about 4 out of 10 of the men) had accepted their initial salary offers with no questions asked, even though they'd been specifically advised to ask for more. The survey also revealed there was a significant reward for asking. Average pay for students who negotiated—men and women alike—was $4,305 higher, a 7.4 percent premium above salaries of the nonnegotiators. Almost all the pay disparity between men and women could be attributed to the fact that the men were *eight times* more likely than the women to ask for more money. The gender gap in Babcock's salary survey was actually a negotiation gap!

Babcock went on to coauthor a book called *Women Don't Ask*, in which she further explored the general aversion among women to negotiate on their own behalf. But the problem is hardly confined to women. Recall that nearly half the men in that survey suffered from the same aversion to asking. If you consider Babcock's survey results without regard for gender, you see that a meager 25 percent of all Carnegie Mellon graduate students asked for more money when they were offered their first jobs.

These were not unsophisticated people. All of them had earned master's degrees at a top university. They had been coached by the career planning office to ask for more money. They were offered tips on how to do it in a way that was reasonable and respectful. And yet, only 1 out of 4 of them followed through on that advice and asked for more money. Figuratively speaking, 3 out of 4 chose to walk out of the hiring office with $4,300 sitting on the desk. The money was theirs if they'd asked for it. They just didn't ask.

Other studies have shown similarly poor pay-negotiation habits among new hires in a vast number of fields. In their book, *Get Paid What You're Worth*, business professors Robin L. Pinkley and Gregory B. Northcraft write that only about half of all business executives—probably the most sophisticated job applicants around—report having negotiated their last job offer. Since that's a self-reported number, Pinkley and Northcraft suspect that in reality the share of nonnegotiators is probably much larger. Executive recruiters, for instance, told them that only about 1 out of 4 of their clients negotiate their salary offers. That's the same anemic negotiation rate that Babcock found at Carnegie Mellon.

In the coming year, 50 million U.S. workers will start new jobs. Most of them will accept the first salary offer they receive. For the simple want of asking, they will walk away from billions of dollars, and each of them will do it with a handshake and a smile.

If that seems unbelievable to you, consider the hiring process from management's point of view. Earlier in the chapter, I cited surveys that show 9 out of 10 hiring managers are ready to pay more money if they're asked. They deliberately keep their initial salary offers unrealistically low. A manager with a budget to control can't afford to start a salary negotiation with a "fair" offer if there's any chance that the new hire will accept a lower figure. More to the point, the manager making that initial offer needs to be prepared to raise the offer if the candidate asks for more. For that reason, the first offer needs to be very low as a precaution, in order to allow room for negotiation.

So with the possible exception of some civil service and union jobs, it is all but certain that every initial salary offer you have ever received in your life was deliberately unfair. Each one was significantly lower than what the hiring manager was fully ready to pay. And if you have ever accepted that first offer without even asking for more, you almost assuredly walked away from a significant pile of cash.

When Pinkley and Northcraft tried to probe the underlying reasons why so many highly professional and skilled businesspeople avoid negotiating salary offers, they discovered that most candidates feel vulnerable and afraid once they've been offered the job. It's that simple. The most common fear they express is that asking for more will displease the new boss. Negotiating, they say, might make them look "cheap, selfish, cocky [or] ungrateful." Another worry was that requesting more money would put the job offer itself in jeopardy. Asking for more, they feared, might prompt the hiring manager to withdraw the offer and try to find someone else for the job.

Both fears, however, are completely unfounded. When Pinkley and Northcraft surveyed employers on this subject, every one of them said they fully expected job candidates to negotiate initial salary offers. Negotiating doesn't harm your image, and in some cases it can actually help. When the researchers polled executive recruiters, 8 in 10 said that a candidate who negotiates in a professional manner will make a better impression on the new employer than the candidate who accepts the first offer right off the bat. It makes sense once you think about it. If you were hiring someone new, wouldn't you want that person to have a healthy level of self-worth and self-esteem? If a new employee is afraid to negotiate salary, what other difficult tasks will he or she prove too timid to handle?

Pinkley and Northcraft also found that job offers are almost never revoked, and in the rare instances when they are, the problem is usually that a résumé or application contained misrepresentations. Yes, they say, occasionally a candidate will negotiate himself out of a job. If you act unreasonable and drag out your salary negotiations too long, then it is possible that the company might withdraw its offer. But that's because you were a jerk, not because you negotiated.

Most hiring managers told Pinkley and Northcraft that they'd like their new employees to start out feeling satisfied about what they make. They don't want to bring in people who feel bad about their salaries and wish they'd asked for more. To test this idea, the researchers made up a chart of how a hypothetical top candidate for a job would react to various salary offers. Then they gave the chart to some hiring managers and asked them what would be their top salary offer if they knew that the best job candidate for the job would:

- Reject an offer of $35K.
- Accept an offer of $38K with dissatisfaction.
- Accept an offer of $41K with satisfaction.
- Accept an offer of $44K with pleasure.
- Accept an offer of $48K with great pleasure.

About 40 percent said they would make an offer of $44,000 if they knew the offer would be accepted with pleasure! The extra dollars, they figured, were worth it to ensure bringing in a happy new employee. About half of the managers said they would offer up to $41,000 to ensure that the job candidate at least felt satisfied. Only 10 percent said they would offer the minimum amount needed to gain the employee's dissatisfied acceptance. "In each case," Pinkley and Northcraft write, "they told us they would ultimately pay more to get this applicant if the applicant negotiated, but that they would be delighted to get the applicant for less."

What does this really mean? To me, it says that if you respond to an initial salary offer by telling your new employer the exact dollar amount that would make you happy, you have a 40 percent chance of getting it! You also have a 90 percent chance of getting a counteroffer that will at least leave you satisfied.

The differences in dollars in the above chart are significant. They fit right in with Linda Babcock's survey results and suggest that negotiating your salary might typically yield a 7 percent premium in pay. Other surveys have shown more modest results from negotiated salaries, more in the 4 percent range. But a pay raise of even 4 percent would mean an extra $2,000 to $4,000 in household income for the middle-class respondents to our surveys. In the words of one popular negotiating guide, your salary discussion may be the only chance you ever·get to make money at the rate of $1,000 *per minute.*

The financial benefits of that single $1,000-per-minute conversation can keep piling up for years to come. Once you start a job at a higher salary, the following year's salary bump will be calculated off that higher base. The total value of that one negotiation session will continue compounding each year for all the years you work at that job. It can even impact your base pay when you decide to change jobs.

Pinkley and Northcraft did some additional calculations to compare the career income trajectories of two hypothetical college graduates. Both start out with base salaries of $50,000. They each are given annual pay raises of 3 to 4 percent, and they each change jobs every eight years. The only difference between the two is that the first employee never negotiates salary when changing jobs. The second negotiates a 4.3 percent boost with each new employer. Over the course of their two 50-year careers, the employee who negotiates that minor 4.3 percent increase every eight years ends up earning $1.7 million more than the one who never negotiates.

After her first book came out, Babcock started giving workshops in negotiating techniques at Carnegie Mellon. She knew that despite the pay advantages enjoyed by job candidates who negotiate, it was also true that most of them conducted their pay negotiations poorly. They made more money than those who didn't negotiate at all, but most had failed to realize the full potential of their opportunities. Inept negotiators fare better than nonnegotiators, but they still wind up leaving money on the boss's desk.

Among the men and women who negotiated their salaries at Carnegie Mellon, Babcock discovered a secondary gender gap in outcomes that exposed one important point about negotiating: Higher goals always attract higher results. Even when women do ask, Babcock found, they usually start by asking for a more modest amount than the men, and they complete the negotiation too quickly. As a result, they end up with less. A famous study of MBA candidates who negotiated their first salaries showed that the men earned a 4.3 percent increase over the initial offer, while the women earned a 2.7 percent increase. The difference was explained by the fact the men went into the negotiation with higher expectations. They didn't get what they asked for, but they still got more than the women.

In her negotiation workshops, Babcock stressed how underselling yourself can be as costly as not negotiating at all. (The workshops were geared toward women, but men were welcome and some participated.) She encouraged the students to research the highest comparative salaries in their respective fields before discussing a salary offer. Then, when you get that initial offer, you should be prepared to respond with a number much larger than what you would reasonably want. If your first request far exceeds what you hope for, you're much more likely to end up with what you really want.

By 2005, after Babcock had been offering her negotiation workshops for about three years, the Carnegie Mellon annual salary survey revealed some big changes in behavior among the recent graduates. For the first time, female master's degree graduates negotiated their salary offers at a higher rate than the men (68 percent versus 65 percent). Even more impressive was the percentage gain in income. Women who negotiated increased their income by 14 percent, and men increased theirs by 16 percent. There was still a small gender gap, but everyone was earning more money.

Even if you don't want to change employers, you can use the same strategy to negotiate your current salary upward. The key is knowing your true current value in the workplace and in your industry and then "asking high" during salary review time. The Internet has made information about comparable salaries easier to find than ever. But you also need to ask around and network within your field to find out which of your skills and abilities are in highest demand, and then point to those in-demand abilities in the negotiation.

Babcock acknowledges that it is easiest to underestimate your value as an employee when you stay with one employer for a long time. In her second book, called *Ask for It*, she tells the story of a housekeeping manager at a luxury hotel in Bermuda. The woman was so good at her job that other hotels on the island were always trying to recruit her. The woman didn't want to leave her employer, but she used each competing job offer as leverage for requesting a raise. Her only question was, how much should she go in and ask for?

The woman's husband also worked in the hotel industry, so he was a useful adviser. He asked his wife to name a number that she would consider "outrageous." When she told him that she felt a $5,000 raise would be outrageous, he advised her to ask for $10,000. She did what he suggested and she got the $10,000 raise. When the next offer came along, she told her husband that a $6,000 raise would seem outrageous, so he suggested she ask for $12,000. And she got the $12,000. Every time she was offered a job elsewhere, she repeated this process. Within six years, she had raised her salary by $36,000, because she always requested twice as much money as what she personally considered to be outrageous.

Not everyone can get away with making salary demands like that. It probably helps to live in a tight labor market like Bermuda. But Babcock, like Pinkley and Northcraft, makes a pretty good case that most people could make a lot more money if they would just use a few simple techniques to get better at asking. Unfortunately, popular culture doesn't give much support to this idea. For whatever reasons, Orman's books sell much better than either Babcock's or Pinkley and Northcraft's. Orman appeared on *The Oprah Winfrey Show* many times while Babcock, Pinkley, and Northcraft never did—even though their ideas are better researched, and, as it turns out, much more reliable.

Of all the Business Brilliant strategies you'll read about in this book, asking is among the most powerful, if only because it costs nothing and it never hurts to ask. In the brave new world of work, in which regular raises and promotions have become things of the past, asking for more, asking well, and asking often are the only ways to ensure that you're earning what you're worth.

➤ The Wages of Fear

In her latest book, *The Money Class*, Suze Orman tries to acknowledge how the 2008 financial crisis has shaken her fans' faith in the frugality gospel. Orman's past advice echoed a lot of other financial advice, which assumed that a dollar saved and invested in stocks today would reliably earn a 10 percent rate of compounded interest for 30 years or more into the future. Since then, the stock market's volatility has soaked mutual fund returns and made the long-term outlook for savings very hazy. Orman has reduced her expectations for returns on savings to just 6 percent. The problem with 6 percent, though, is that you need to earn a lot more than the average American wage in order for a 6 percent return to amount to anything in the long term.

Suze admits, "We are long past the days when trimming the cable bill and stretching out the time between haircuts was enough." Now she recommends that we all downsize our idea of the American Dream itself. Don't buy a house. Take any job you can get. Send your kids to cheaper colleges. Suze has abandoned her past talk about following the example of the rich, because clearly, this is not what the rich are doing.

It's true that the working world for the average American is changing faster than most people realize. Not only is job security all but gone, but the future outlook for wages is stagnant. The Department of Labor estimates that there are 17 million Americans with college degrees who are doing jobs that don't require a college education, including 317,759 restaurant workers and 107,457 janitors. And with this poor outlook, the risks of retirement, uncovered medical expenses, and paying for college have all gone up. In 1979, about 28 percent of American workers in the private sector had defined-benefit pension plans at work. Today only 3 percent do. The management consultant Umair Haque, whom I quoted in chapter 1, assesses the current career picture this way: "It's one thing to offer a life of meaningless work in exchange for a huge paycheck. It's another to offer it for a stagnant median wage." Salaried employment looks like an increasingly challenging path unless you manage your career aggressively.

A recurring theme in this chapter is fear. It's the number one factor preventing people from earning more money. Most people won't ask the new boss for more money because they are afraid. Most people won't bring a competing offer to the boss for the same reason. And in those precious few moments when you've been offered the job and the hiring boss is sitting there, fully expecting you to ask for more money, it is fear that tells you—if you're like 3 out of 4 people—to accept that first lowball offer.

In the responses to questions about negotiating, the Business Brilliant survey reveals evidence of this general fear of asking among the middle class. The wide differences in negotiating styles between the middle class and self-made millionaires boil down to this: The middle class chooses conflict avoidance and being well regarded over earning more money. For self-made millionaires, it's the exact opposite.

For instance, about half of the middle-class respondents agreed in the survey that "when making business decisions, it's important to consider how the other side will view me." Just 2 in 10 self-made millionaires agreed with that. The middle class also seems to reject the essential clash of interests that every negotiation requires. Just 1 out of 3 middle-class survey respondents concur that "In negotiations, I expect people to try to take advantage of me." Among self-made millionaires, 2 out of 3 agreed.

Frankly, I'm surprised that this last result wasn't nearly unanimous. As Robin Pinkley and Gregory Northcraft showed in their research, every job offer you've ever gotten and will ever get represents an attempt to take advantage of you. Every hiring manager begins your working relationship by handing you a deliberately lowball salary offer. This is not because hiring managers are mean or selfish. It's because the job of a hiring manager is to secure your services at the lowest possible cost to the company.

What's your role? You're supposed to look after your personal interests. Hiring managers expect you to do this. They've started with a low offer in part to leave room for negotiation. And most of them will admire you if you negotiate well.

Looking after your interests has always been important in business, but the new, risky job environment makes sticking up for yourself an essential fact of life in every workplace. The frugality gospel of Orman and all the others doesn't really support this way of thinking, though. To me, their message seems to be, "You're average. Admit it. Hope for the best but prepare for the worst." It's a message that reflects the shame and self-denial I detect in some of the middle-class survey results, where most say they worry about what others think about them when they negotiate. Orman tells you to send your kids to cheaper colleges. A self-made millionaire would tell you to negotiate your compensation aggressively, as though your kids' futures depended on it.

The frugality gospel encourages you to see yourself as the vulnerable party in salary negotiations and overlook the vulnerabilities on the other side of the table. You want the job. That's a point of vulnerability on your part that your manager exploits by offering you less money than you want. But the manager also wants you to take the job. That's the manager's point of vulnerability, which you need to exploit by asking for the number of dollars that would make you happy. And to start, you ask for an amount that would make you *more* than happy, because you just might get it.

This is where the Business Brilliant survey reveals one of the biggest differences in attitude between self-made millionaires and the middle class. About 9 in 10 self-made millionaires agree that "It's important in negotiations to exploit weaknesses in others." Among the middle class, just over 2 in 10 agreed.

Exploiting the other side's weaknesses is an essential fact of negotiation. Nearly all self-made millionaires accept and understand this, while the vast majority of the middle class don't and can't. That's another reason why 3 out of 4 new hires respond to the first salary offer with a mere "Yes" and "Thank you very much."

The survey results show why earning more money is all about managing your natural unease with fear and personal rejection. Those unafraid to ask for more, like self-made millionaires, will always earn more than those who fear rejection. If a bunch of wet-behind-the-ears graduate students from Pittsburgh can use this knowledge to earn 14-point bumps in their salary offers, then certainly any adult with a proven track record in the workplace can make good use of the same skills. The trick is to not let "No" feel like rejection and failure, because it's not. Without the word "No," you can't be sure that you're earning all you can.

On this subject, I'll give the final word to Linda Babcock, who says, "If you never hear 'No,' you're not trying hard enough."

4

Imitate, Don't Innovate

ABOUT 7 OUT OF 10 OF THE MIDDLE-CLASS SURVEY
RESPONDENTS SAID THAT THEY BELIEVE IT TAKES "A
BIG OR NEW IDEA" TO BECOME WEALTHY.

ONLY 3 OUT OF 10 SELF-MADE MILLIONAIRES AGREED.

➤ The Man Who Could Have Been Bill Gates

Gary Kildall was a thirty-year-old Ph.D. in computer science at the Naval Postgraduate School in Monterey, California, when, in early 1972, he got a look at a new microchip produced by a local company called Intel Systems. The inch long Intel 4004 had been designed to work inside a desktop calculating machine, but Kildall and a handful of his fellow technophiles saw the 4004 for what it truly was: the nucleus of a revolution in microcomputing. For the first time ever, the entire central processing unit of a computer had been contained within a single inexpensive microchip. As one computer trade magazine announced at the time, Intel was selling "a computer for $25."

With 2,300 transistors packed into a chip smaller than a human thumb, the Intel 4004 could theoretically power a computer compact enough to sit on a desktop. Almost immediately, Kildall set out to prove it could be done. He worked nights and weekends on the project for more than a year, patiently developing dozens of laborious workarounds to cope with the 4004's pathetically limited memory. Kildall couldn't afford to buy many of the computer components he needed to complete the task, so he bartered with Intel for hardware by trading some of the new software code he was writing.

At the time, Kildall had a wife and young son at home and was living on a $20,000-a-year teaching stipend. He probably should have had other priorities. But Kildall was one of those people who gets a vision in his head and feels compelled to make it real. One day in 1973, he walked into the computer science department carrying a giant suitcase-sized box and plunked it down on his desk. It was heavy, ugly, and didn't do very much, but it was the very first personal computer. Kildall took it around the school, showing it off proudly to the amazement of hundreds of his fellow faculty and students.

Cobbling together the computer's hardware wasn't Kildall's greatest accomplishment, however. What mattered most was what he had done with writing new software code. Out of sheer necessity, and with no thought of the commercial possibilities, he developed a master program or control program so that his unique little computer could adapt itself to run useful software applications designed for much larger stand-alone machines. That's how Kildall developed the first operating system software for personal computers. After revising it further so it could run on the newer and faster Intel 8080 microchip, Kildall would call his operating system CP/M—Control Program for Microcomputers. Only when hobbyists started building their own 8080-based home computers did Kildall realize he'd created something of value. He put a small ad in a computer trade magazine and began selling copies of CP/M for $70, first to hobbyists, then to other small computer makers. In *Accidental Empires*, Robert X. Cringely wrote that within six years, hundreds of thousands of personal computers had been sold with CP/M running inside them. Kildall and his wife "made millions of dollars, essentially without trying."

When the personal computer revolution took off in the late 1970s, it launched on the wings of Kildall's CP/M operating system. Prior to CP/M, every computer manufacturer had to deal with the headache of writing machine-specific software for word processing, database management, and all the other things that people use computers for. But thanks to Kildall's invention, these companies could now simply license copies of the CP/M operating system and their customers could buy whatever CP/M-compatible software they liked. By 1980, there were an estimated

600,000 PCs in the entire United States, and about 90 percent of them were running on CP/M and using CP/M-compatible software. Popular software programs like dBase and WordStar worked *only* with CP/M. As Harold Evans wrote in his bestselling *They Made America*, "Kildall created the bedrock and subsoil out of which the PC software industry would grow."

With virtually no competition, CP/M earned Digital Research 85 cents of profit on every dollar of revenue that came in. Officials at Digital Research's bank once called to double-check some figures because they didn't think it was possible for any company to have such high profit margins. And, then, almost as suddenly as it began, the party ended. By the mid-1980s, Kildall and Digital Research were both on the road to oblivion and today Kildall ranks as a mere footnote in computer history. The reason lies with a few crucial miscalculations he made in 1980, part of a cautionary tale about how imitation so often trumps innovation when it comes to being Business Brilliant.

One of the first computer entrepreneurs to hitch his wagon to CP/M's rising star in the late 1970s was a precocious young programmer named Bill Gates. In 1979, when Gates was just twenty-four, he was running a software company called Micro-Soft. The company had secured an early, profitable niche in the personal computer industry by creating popular versions of BASIC and other common programming languages that communicate between a computer's hardware and its operating system software.

Gates and his partner, a high school friend named Paul Allen, didn't stumble into the software industry the way Kildall had with Digital Research. Since their teenage years, Gates and Allen had been looking for ways to turn their passion for code-writing into cash. The two originally wrote the Microsoft version of BASIC in 1976 because they saw a chance to get in on the ground floor with one of the earliest makers of homebuilt personal computer kits. After that, Gates often sought licensing deals that would pair Microsoft's BASIC with Kildall's CP/M, in the hope that Microsoft BASIC could ride CP/M's coattails and become an industry standard of its own.

Gates and Kildall had a lot in common. Both hailed from the Seattle area. They had even bumped into each other at a Seattle computer center years earlier when Kildall was still a graduate student at the University of Washington and Gates was a high school hacker sneaking some computer time. Both loved talking about software code as much as they enjoyed writing it. They also shared a passion for driving dangerously fast. When they weren't talking software, they swapped stories about speed traps, comparing the size of their most recent speeding tickets.

But their differences were much more pronounced than their similarities. Kildall was older, a family man, and a much more accomplished programmer. At heart he was an academic, a computer *scientist* with a Ph.D. Although he was nominally the head of Digital Research, he disdained making business decisions and preferred spending his time on complicated programming tasks that most CEOs would leave to their employees. Gates was the exact opposite. He was a businessman first and a programmer second. He started Microsoft while still a student at Harvard, and then he dropped out before finishing because he was so intent on getting his computer business going. At the age of twenty-five, he was still living like a college student in a disheveled one-bedroom apartment. And although Gates and Kildall shared a capacity for getting lost in days-long bouts of obsessive programming, their motivations were completely different. Bill Gates never would have spent a year building a microcomputer from scratch as Kildall did, merely out of intellectual curiosity. Gates's all-nighters were always driven by practical business objectives and deadlines, while Kildall had more of an artistic temperament. Some said Kildall designed computer code the way Mozart composed symphonies.

The stark contrast in the two men's personalities came to a head in 1980 when IBM contacted them about a new secret project. Big Blue, as IBM was nicknamed, was by far the largest computer company in the world at the time. It occupied such a dominant position in the industry that its seven main competitors were known collectively as the seven dwarfs. But by the late 1970s, IBM salespeople started seeing Apple II's and other personal computers popping up in the offices of their big corporate customers. IBM chairman Frank Carey, sensing a threat, decided that if IBM didn't move fast to produce a little machine of its own, the personal computer business would soon get too big for even Big Blue to dominate it. In early 1980, Carey signed off on a plan to rush an IBM PC to market by September 1981. The strategy was to cut out years of laborious development by using off-the-shelf hardware and by licensing existing software from other companies. Except for the logo glued to each unit, nothing about the new IBM PC would be unique to IBM.

An IBM engineer named Jack Sams was charged with setting up licensing deals for the IBM PC's software. Of all the personal computers then on the market, Sams was most impressed with the Apple II, which is why a product by Microsoft called the Softcard caught his eye. The one drawback to the Apple II was that its proprietary operating system prevented it from running popular CP/M-compatible software applications, including WordStar and dBase. The Softcard was a little translator card, created by Paul Allen at Microsoft, that snapped into the back of the Apple II and turned it into a CP/M-compatible machine. Even though the Softcard was a slight diversion from Microsoft's normal focus on computer language software, Gates embraced it because it represented yet another strategic opportunity to extend CP/M's market domination while also binding Microsoft BASIC to CP/M. Microsoft eventually sold hundreds of thousands of Softcards, which told Sams that it was a popular and reliable product. Sams started his software hunt by contacting Gates and proposing that IBM license the Softcard, along with all the other programming languages Microsoft offered.

What Sams didn't understand was that although Softcard was a Microsoft product, its most valuable feature was the CP/M operating system, owned by Digital Research. Gates told Sams that IBM needed to license CP/M directly from Kildall and offered to help Sams make the deal happen. At the time, Gates accepted his subordinate position in the software food chain. He had positioned Microsoft so that the company's success was dependent on CP/M's continued market domination. If CP/M were paired with Microsoft BASIC inside the new IBM PC,

Gates saw how the two complementary programs might be inseparable as industry leaders for years to come. So Gates arranged the initial meeting with IBM and Kildall. With Sams in the room, Gates called Kildall and said he was sending an important client Kildall's way and that Kildall should, according to several sources, "treat them right."

Gates's phone call, however, didn't do much good. Almost nothing went right when Sams and his team sat down with Kildall and his wife, Dorothy, who managed the business side of Digital Research. At first, Dorothy absolutely refused to sign IBM's strict, strongly worded confidentiality agreement. An entire day was wasted discussing what, if anything, the two parties could discuss. Once they got past that hurdle, Kildall was cold to IBM's insistence that Digital Research negotiate a flat licensing fee for CP/M and forgo Digital Research's usual per-unit royalty rate. It didn't help matters that Kildall was generally contemptuous of IBM because so many IBM products struck him as slow, unimaginative, and clumsily designed.

But the biggest stumbling block preventing a deal was Kildall's timing, or rather, his utter disregard for timing. IBM planned to build its personal computer around a new, faster Intel chip called the 8086, but CP/M would need an upgrade in order to run on it. Kildall already had such an upgrade in the works, called CP/M-86. But Kildall either wouldn't or couldn't guarantee to Sams that it would be delivered quickly enough to meet IBM's development deadlines. Sams tried to explain that IBM needed a schedule and a commitment by October 1980, but Kildall resisted. Perhaps Kildall assumed that IBM would bend to his schedule, since it appeared that IBM needed him and CP/M's 90 percent market share more than he needed IBM. But what Sams gathered from Kildall's attitude was that Kildall would never be a reliable partner and that the IBM PC project needed an alternative plan for an operating system. Not long after, he stopped returning Kildall's calls. Kildall's fate was sealed forever as "the man who could have been Bill Gates."

By giving up on Kildall and CP/M, Sams put himself in a tight spot. But Sams also knew that Gates, more than anyone, would be highly motivated to help him find a way out. During the time that Kildall was giving Sams the runaround over royalties and deadlines, Gates was back in Seattle bending over backward to accommodate IBM's development schedule. He had put almost all Microsoft's personnel to work on the IBM effort, shoving other projects to the side. Now Gates needed the IBM PC project to succeed, if only out of a sense of survival for Microsoft. So in the late summer of 1980, Sams told Gates that Kildall wasn't working out, and that the operating system issue was now Gates's problem to solve. Gates picked up Kildall's fumble and ran with it. He gave Sams the promise that Kildall would not—he would produce a detailed plan for an operating system by October. The difference was that Gates made the promise without having an actual operating system to work with.

Throughout 1980, Kildall's failure to set a hard release date for CP/M-86 fueled a rising sense of panic among manufacturers who needed the operating system for their new 8086 machines. In effect, Kildall's delays were holding the whole industry hostage. Across town from Microsoft, a little computer maker called SCP, Seattle Computer Products, came up with a stopgap solution. A programmer there spent months working from the CP/M technical manual (using it like a cookbook, as he would later claim) to write a new operating system so similar to CP/M that it would allow all CP/M-compatible software to work on the new 8086 machines. He called the operating system QDOS—quick and dirty operating system. The plan was to ship SCP's computers with QDOS until CP/M-86 was released.

When Gates and Paul Allen heard about QDOS, they figured they might be able to meet IBM's tight schedule by buying QDOS and then giving it a spit-shine and a new name. Paul Allen knew the owner of SCP fairly well, and he negotiated the rights for Microsoft to use QDOS for the grand sum of $25,000. The cash-starved owner at SCP took the money gladly, with no idea that IBM would be QDOS's ultimate customer. It took several months of around-the-clock programming to massage, tweak, and test QDOS before Microsoft presented a finished product to IBM's engineers under its new name: MS-DOS—Microsoft Disk

Operating System. Gates would later say that if Microsoft had tried to write an operating system from scratch it would have taken a year.

When IBM's programmers tried to run MS-DOS on their prototype IBM PCs, they could hardly believe how buggy it was. By one count Microsoft had left at least 300 bugs in the software, and IBM eventually chose to rewrite the entire program. But Gates had delivered on time, which kept the entire IBM PC project on schedule. The new IBM PC made its debut in August 1981, accompanied by a massive advertising and marketing campaign, the likes of which the personal computer industry had never seen. It only took a few years for Big Blue's new desktop machines to take over the entire PC market. By 1983, two out of every three new home computers were made by IBM and were running the MS-DOS operating system.

When Kildall got his first look at the IBM PC, he was enraged. He felt that MS-DOS was nothing more than a crude clone of CP/M and that Gates had stabbed him in the back. But he decided not to sue IBM and Microsoft, partly because software copyrights were a hazy area of the law, but also because he was so confident of CP/M-86's superiority. Once CP/M-86 was ready for release in early 1982, Kildall was certain that most computer users would switch over from MS-DOS. That's not what happened, though. CP/M-86 did prove to be a better and more reliable operating system, but it was also more expensive. Then IBM cautioned PC buyers that it would only offer technical support for computers running MS-DOS. In no time at all, Microsoft displaced Digital Research as maker of the industry standard in operating systems. Software companies responded to IBM's growing market dominance by pouring their resources into new applications for subsequent revisions of MS-DOS. They also stopped bothering to upgrade their existing CP/M-compatible products.

By the mid-1980s, Digital Research had entered a death spiral and Kildall waved the white flag of surrender. He approached Gates and asked him to consider buying Digital Research for what Kildall considered a fair price—$26 million. Gates rejected the offer and told Kildall the company might be worth only $10 million. A humbled Kildall had to look elsewhere to find a savior for his declining company.

Where did Kildall go wrong? One obvious answer is hubris. Having fathered a revolution in personal computing, Kildall assumed that all the other players would continue their childlike dependency on him. "In Gary's mind [CP/M] was the dominant thing and it would always be dominant," one close colleague of Kildall's told an interviewer years later. "And he really honestly believed that would never change." Kildall was blind to how the delayed release of CP/M-86 had pushed IBM, Microsoft, and Seattle Computer Products to their breaking points. He couldn't imagine that all three companies might work around him to steal CP/M's market. The irony is that the people at all three companies would have much preferred to help Kildall and CP/M-86 succeed. Instead, they were forced to go to the extreme lengths of launching a competitor to CP/M-86, solely because Kildall had left them no other choice.

Kildall's more fundamental mistake, however, was this: He didn't follow the money. He derided IBM's clumsy technology and overlooked its enormous market power, probably because technical subjects interested Kildall and marketing strategy didn't. Gates set his priorities in the exact opposite order. He was willing to hand IBM a shoddy product derived from other people's work because what mattered most to Gates was that the mighty IBM get its project done on time. Kildall, the innovator, followed his passion for technical excellence and was shocked that IBM wouldn't follow him. Gates, the imitator, took his cues from IBM every step of the way, because he *believed* that following Big Blue was the smartest way to follow the money. Gates guessed right, and became one of the richest men in the world.

➤ The Ride on the Back of the Bear

The rise of Bill Gates and the fall of Gary Kildall is a tangled tale, but it's also a strangely familiar one. Behind the development of any major invention you'd care to name—the telephone, the light bulb, the automobile, the television—there are legions of broken and disheartened men like Gary Kildall who might be considered the "true" inventors. Thomas Edison did not invent the light bulb. Joseph Swan had held the British patent for 18 years before Edison introduced his "improved electric lamp" in 1878. And Henry Ford did not invent the automobile. George Selden of Rochester, New York, patented the "safe, simple and cheap road-locomotive" in 1895, while Ford was still laboring as a mid-level engineer in Edison's electric company.

The names Swan, Selden, and Kildall are now largely forgotten because the myth of the lone inventor possessed by a brilliant idea is a powerful one in our culture. "We like to hear a good story about someone who's ingenious and comes up with a great idea and sees it through," says Stanislav Dobrev, a University of Utah professor who has studied the history of innovation. "[But] that's not true most of the time."

Dobrev researched the 2,197 car company start-ups in the United States between 1885 and 1981. The first 25 leading car companies were all defunct within 15 years, contributing to Dobrev's conclusion that it pays to be a latecomer, an imitator. Most people believe otherwise in part because vanquished innovators like Kildall and Selden tend to vanish from history. "You rarely hear about first movers who failed," Dobrev told the *Wall Street Journal* in 2011. "They don't exist very long. They don't leave a lot of records."

In *The Myths of Innovation*, Scott Berkun writes how innovators achieved their status as heroic figures in American history because "people preferred to believe, and tell, positive stories about them rather than the less interesting, and more complicated, truths." The notion that it takes a single bright idea to produce a great fortune is so widely held, Berkun points out, "that it's a surprise to many to learn that having one big idea isn't enough to succeed."

Most inventors who buy into the myth of innovation wind up sadly disappointed. A Canadian study from 2003 provides a vivid snapshot of how steeply the odds are stacked against inventors who expect to profit from their ideas. Of 1,091 inventions patented in Canada, only 75 of them ever made it to market—less than 1 percent. Of these, 45 lost money. Just 6 out of 1,091 patented inventions made significant profits for their inventors. By Berkun's estimation, inventors face such long odds because every innovation needs to overcome eight distinct development hurdles involving design, financing, and marketing before it can achieve financial success. When the odds of overcoming each hurdle are set at a somewhat generous 50-50, the chance of overcoming all eight is an infinitesimal *four-tenths* of 1 percent—amazingly similar to the success rate revealed by the Canadian study.

The other side of the coin is that while innovating rarely makes good business sense, most good businesses don't rely on innovation. Researchers who have studied small business find that the vast majority of start-up companies aren't innovative in the least. Studies by George Washington University researcher Paul D. Reynolds have shown that only about 2 percent of all company founders say they expect their businesses to have a major impact on the markets in which they operate. More than 9 out of 10 surveyed said they expect to have little or no impact at all. Hardly any of them plan to do anything particularly new or different. They plan to be successful without being innovative.

A survey of a far more elite group of business owners reveals the same general aversion to innovation. In 2005, Amar V. Bhide of the Harvard Business School interviewed 100 company founders from among *Inc.* magazine's 500 fastest-growing private firms in the United States. Only 6 percent of these company founders told Bhide that they started their businesses with unique products or services. Just 12 percent attributed their success to "an unusual or extraordinary idea." Instead, 88 percent cited "the exceptional execution of an ordinary idea" as the source of their high growth and success.

There are strong echoes of these results in the Business Brilliant survey. Only 3 out of 10 self-made millionaires agree that "Having a big or new idea is a critical factor to becoming wealthy." Nearly 9 out of 10 said "it is more important to do something well than do something new," which almost exactly mirrored Bhide's findings about "the exceptional execution of an ordinary idea" among *Inc.* 500 founders.

And yet, the enthusiastic belief in the "big idea" continues to cast its spell over the much larger middle-class population. About 7 out of 10 of middle-class survey respondents—people without any firsthand experience in becoming wealthy—said they believe it takes "a big or new idea" to become wealthy. About half think that doing something new is indeed more important than doing something well.

The notion that you can get rich from one brilliant idea is such a commonly held dream that whenever someone actually seems to have done it, the media eagerly embrace the story. Unfortunately, media coverage offers an extremely distorted view of reality. More people die from bee stings than shark attacks every summer, but you'd never know that based on the hysterical coverage devoted to occasional shark sightings. The same holds true with fatal lightning strikes, which always make the evening news, while many more people are killed each year by falling off ladders. Clever ideas are the shark attacks and lightning strikes of business success—they are dramatic, exciting, and very rare. You're more likely to make headlines with a big new idea, but you're more likely to succeed without one.

The media's appetite for tales of people getting rich off their out-of-the-blue brainstorms has provoked many successful companies to come up with media-friendly "creation myths." The most infamous case is that of eBay. For years, eBay pushed the story that founder Pierre Omidyar had been inspired to create the online auction site because his fiancée wanted to use the Internet to grow her collection of PEZ dispensers. *Businessweek*, the *Wall Street Journal*, and the *New Yorker* all seized on this delightful story of how a fortune was built when one man in love wanted to please his bride-to-be and help her trade in the most frivolous and useless objects imaginable—PEZ dispensers. For years this story was repeated and played up by eBay's top executives. They even posed for news photographers while holding the goofy little toys that had supposedly made them all multimillionaires.

It wasn't until 2002, eight years after eBay's founding, that a book about the company revealed how the PEZ story was a complete fabrication. It was made up by a young employee who was failing in her job of drawing media attention to the company. In truth, Omidyar had started something called AuctionWeb as a hobby, and his first sales involved all sorts of drab, uninteresting items. Yes, Omidyar's girlfriend did eventually buy and sell some PEZ dispensers on the site, but only after it had been up and running for more than two years.

Even without such corporate spin, the media can usually be counted on to promote the myth of innovation on their own. Look up the first long *New Yorker* profile of Bill Gates and you'll find no mention of Gary Kildall. The article opens its segment on Gates's dealings with IBM this way: "In 1980, I.B.M. approached Gates to write an operating system for the personal computer it was designing." That's not really true, but if the writer had included the story of how Gates had sent IBM to see Kildall, he would have undermined the premise of his article, that Gates was a software visionary whose speculations about the future were worth reading about in the pages of the *New Yorker*.

If there is any harm done by creation myths like eBay's PEZ story or media puffery like the *New Yorker's* Bill Gates profile, it's that they offer the public badly distorted ideas about what it takes to be successful. In 2004, a pair of University of California, Berkeley, business professors attempted to explore the power of what they termed "the garage belief"— the common notion that most entrepreneurs start out by tinkering and innovating in garages, basement workshops, or even dorm rooms. Pino Audia and Chris Rider surveyed business school students and found that on average the students believed about half of all start-up businesses begin this way, while a more accurate count is much closer to 25 percent.

When Audia and Rider then studied a group of 96 new businesses that received venture capital funding, they found that most hadn't

counted on garages or innovations to get started. The distinguishing feature most commonly shared among almost all of these companies was
that they started out by relying on knowledge, partners, and funding
sources that their founders had identified *in their previous jobs*. As Dan
and Chip Heath would write, "companies aren't born in garages. Companies are born in companies."

Audia and Rider concluded that "by misrepresenting the process by
which many individuals become entrepreneurs, the garage belief may
lead to seriously misinformed employment choices by individuals, ill-
advised resource allocation decisions by companies, unsuccessful course
offerings by business schools, and/or ineffective program offerings by
governments."

Bhide came to a similar conclusion after his survey of *Inc.* 500 founders. These successful startup entrepreneurs weren't lone-wolf inventors
pursuing big ideas. They were imitators working from their areas of expertise, borrowing or stealing what they learned from their former employers. "The *Inc.* founders we interviewed typically imitated someone
else's ideas that they often encountered in the course of a previous job,"
Bhide wrote. "Any innovations were incremental or easily replicated.
They were too obvious to qualify for patent and were too visible to protect as a trade secret."

Gates's true role as imitator, not innovator, was always assumed
among his Silicon Valley rivals. Larry Ellison, the billionaire founder of
Oracle Corporation, has been particularly outspoken in his criticism of
Gates's business practices. "Bill goes out and methodically searches for
good ideas to steal," Ellison told an interviewer. "That's perfectly rational behavior. That's made him very successful. But then, one by one, Bill
starts to claim credit for the stolen ideas. He actually starts believing that
they really were his ideas in the first place. . . . He can't bear to see himself
as Rockefeller; he sees himself as Edison."

The passage of time, however, has revealed Gates's terrible track record as a visionary. Gates's first book, published in November 1995, was
called *The Road Ahead*; it devoted just a few pages to the Internet, paying

it lip service as a "beginning" step toward a true information superhigh-way. "Seeing far into the future is not what Mr. Gates does best," the *Economist* groused when the book came out. "Naturally, he has a vision; but the vision is disappointingly similar to that of so many pundits who have tried to look ahead." Within six months of the book's publication, Internet usage had exploded and Gates and his coauthors had to rewrite almost half of *The Road Ahead* prior to its paperback release in 1996. "No matter how much Bill Gates may claim otherwise," Netscape founder Jim Clark has said, "he missed the Internet, like a barreling freight train that he didn't hear or see coming."

My point here is not to take anything away from Bill Gates. I think that the true Bill Gates story, the one that never gets told, is a valuable one. For example, the game plan that Gates relied on, the one that con-sistently yielded results for him, is a sound business strategy that anybody can learn from and imitate: find the field that interests you the most, work with the biggest and richest player willing to partner with you, and then do everything you can to help that big, rich partner succeed.

For Gates, who started out in the fast-growing software industry, it took just three steps within about seven years for this strategy to take him from college dropout to multimillionaire. First, Gates and his partner, Paul Allen, wrote Microsoft BASIC with the sole intent of partnering with the leading maker of personal computer kits. Then they developed the Softcard in order to wed Microsoft BASIC with CP/M, the leading operating system at the time. The third step was more a function of luck, but luck, as they say, always favors the prepared mind. The Softcard is how Microsoft gained the attention of IBM. When Kildall faltered in helping IBM with its operating system, Gates pounced.

As a growth strategy for little start-ups, this is a business approach that could be applied to just about any industry. (It can even be adapted as a career strategy inside any large organization: just seek out and offer help to the most powerful patron or mentor who will have you.) It's a proven recipe for success, but it's hardly a magic formula. The difficult part of the recipe, one frequently encountered by Microsoft in its dealings with IBM, is executing in the face of adversity. In the computer industry, IBM was notoriously difficult to partner with and was well known for its arrogant treatment of small vendors. During the development phase of MS-DOS, IBM's insistence on secrecy and strict security measures strained both Microsoft's meager resources and the patience of Microsoft employees. It didn't help that IBM's buttoned-down corporate engineering culture chafed against the high-energy nonconformist atmosphere at Microsoft. But Gates endured every challenge, not only because he appreciated IBM as a source of tremendous opportunity, but also because he saw firsthand the peril of underestimating Big Blue's power, the way Kildall had.

Steve Ballmer, now Microsoft's CEO, was one of Gates's chief lieutenants in the 1980s. He has compared working with IBM in those days to being at the mercy of a dangerous animal. "We used to call it, at the time, riding the bear," the excitable Ballmer once said in a filmed interview. "You just had to try to stay on the bear's back. The bear would twist and turn and try to buck you and throw you but darn, we were going to ride the bear! Because the bear was the biggest, the most important—you just *had* to be with the bear! Otherwise you'd be *under* the bear!" In the computer industry, IBM was the bear. Riders on the bear got rich. The rest, with few exceptions, got eaten.

➤ The Egg of Columbus

It was the summer of 2004, and weekends were killing Stuart Frankel's business. As the owner of two Subway franchise sandwich shops inside a Miami hospital complex, Frankel was growing frustrated with the way his sales dropped off every Saturday and Sunday. The two-day lull in foot traffic to his stores was eating into whatever profits he made on weekdays. It left his employees with little to do and good food was going to waste because his inventory wasn't turning over fast enough to keep everything fresh.

So Frankel did what every cash-strapped shopkeeper does. He ran a sale. He decided to advertise cut-rate weekend prices for Subway's popular Footlong sandwiches. On weekdays, Footlongs at Frankel's shops remained at $5.95 plus tax, but he reduced the weekend price to $4.67, so that the total after tax came to a flat $5. Frankel put up signs in the windows: "Five-Dollar Footlongs!"

As ideas go, this was hardly a big one or a new one. Cutting prices to generate revenue is a pretty basic, commonsense business practice. One little twist was Frankel's choice of a $5 sale price. Conventional wisdom says that a $4.99 sandwich will sell much faster than a $5 sandwich. There are even brain theories, backed by clinical research, suggesting that we appraise value by reading prices from left to right so that $4.99 *feels* like a much better bargain than $5.

But Frankel had his own reason for calling it the Five-Dollar Footlong. "I like round numbers," he said.

On the first weekend of Five-Dollar Footlongs, sales volume doubled at Stuart Frankel's two shops, and although his food costs went up, so did employee productivity. Even at the cut-rate price of $5, Frankel found he was making money on the increased volume. It took a few months, but other Subway owners in the Miami area took notice. A failing Subway shop in Ft. Lauderdale copied the $5 idea and sales instantly doubled there, too. Then the largest Subway franchisee in South Florida, the owner of three dozen shops, ran Five-Dollar Footlong promotions in stores where sales had been flagging and saw a 35 percent increase in revenue. By 2006, Subway franchise holders in other cities all around the country were imitating the Five-Dollar Footlong and getting good results.

Most franchise companies are based on ordinary ideas, and Subway ranks among the most ordinary of all. There is nothing innovative about making sandwiches from cold cuts, so each Subway shop owner needs to constantly hone his or her execution skills and stay on the lookout for little ideas that have worked well for fellow operators. As the Five-Dollar Footlong spread to other markets around the country, Frankel and some other franchisees tried to get national advertising dollars behind the effort. But when Frankel made a proposal before Subway's franchisee marketing board, it was voted down. Too many owners feared that cut-rate Footlongs would drive up food and labor costs, despite Frankel's evidence to the contrary. For two years, the Five-Dollar Footlong promotion languished at Subway's national level, even as more and more shop owners reported glowing success when they ran the promotion on their own. Finally the marketing board relented and gave the go-ahead for a four-week campaign in 2008. By then, the Five-Dollar Footlong had been tested at so many Subway shops that there was no need for any formal market research. It was the first ever time that Subway made such a large investment in national marketing and advertising dollars without spending a dime on research.

Subway rolled out its national Five-Dollar Footlong promotional campaign on March 28, 2008. The "irritatingly addictive" TV jingle, coupled with hokey hand signals signifying "five" and "foot-long," became a campy cultural phenomenon as thousands of teenagers recorded their own renditions and posted them on YouTube. Subway even spoofed its own jingle by putting an extended-play dance remix on its website. In the Five-Dollar Footlong's first year as a national campaign, Subway's sales rose 17 percent, while revenues sagged everywhere else in the fast-food industry. Subway estimated that the promotion boosted sales nationally by $3.8 billion. Other fast-food players responded, with Domino's, KFC, and Boston Market all coming up with $5 promotions of their own. One restaurant consultant told *Businessweek*, "Five dollars is the magic number now."

I tell this story because it shows how imitation, which sounds like it should be a simple process, is actually very difficult to do because even proven ideas can face an uphill struggle for acceptance. Paul Orfalea, the founder of Kinko's Copies, encountered a similar battle in the 1980s. It took him three years of coaxing and cajoling to get his independent store-owners just to try moving to a 24-hour schedule like other successful convenience businesses. Kinko's owners objected that staffing the stores all night would be too difficult and they worried about keeping their employees safe. When the first Kinko's stores that tested a round-the-clock schedule saw revenues jump by as much as 50 percent, most other owners remained unconvinced. At one annual meeting when the subject was being debated yet again, an exasperated store owner stood up and said, "If you like money, then do it." Eventually, 24-hour operations became the norm, and today anyone looking back would wonder what the fuss was all about.

A legend called "The Egg of Columbus" illustrates how simple ideas like the Five-Dollar Footlong or the 24-hour copy shop are commonly undervalued because they seem so ordinary and obvious in retrospect. When Christopher Columbus first set sail, most educated people already knew that the Earth was round and accepted that the Far East could be reached by sailing westward. So when Columbus returned from his first voyage, not everyone was impressed. Over a late-night dinner with some Spanish gentlemen, Columbus was confronted by the question of whether he'd done anything special, or if he had merely been the first to follow through on an ordinary idea. Columbus responded by handing the men a hard-boiled egg and asking each of them to attempt to stand the egg on its end. One by one, they tried and failed. When the egg was returned to Columbus, he tapped it gently on the tabletop, cracking and flattening the shell just enough to allow the egg to stand up. "What is easier than to do this which you said was impossible?" Columbus asked his dinner mates. "It is the simplest thing in the world. Anybody can do it—*after he has been shown how.*"

Damien Hirst, the conceptual artist profiled in chapter 2, often hears people react to his work by telling him that anyone could do what he does. In 1995, he told the *New York Times*, "It's very easy to say, 'I could have done that.' After someone's done it. But I did it. You didn't. It didn't exist until I did it. It's like me saying I could have written 'She Loves You.'" In similar ways, the Five-Dollar Footlong and the 24-hour copy center might seem in retrospect like natural, obvious business tactics that any company in a similar situation might have made. But that interpretation is no different than the criticism Columbus faced. It overlooks the persuasive efforts, the commitment, and creative problem solving it takes to deliver on any idea, even an ordinary one. In the cases of Subway and Kinko's, their shop owners realized billions of dollars in new revenue thanks to the determination of Stuart Frankel with his Five-Dollar Footlong and a few forgotten Kinko's owners who took the lead in staying open all night. Just as society so often exalts innovation, it often denigrates or dismisses the significant challenges posed by executing on ordinary ideas. And since ordinary ideas are, by definition, much more common than *extra*ordinary ideas, executing on them has a far greater impact on most companies' profits.

When Paul Orfalea sold off his remaining interest in Kinko's to a Wall Street buyout firm for $116 million in 2003, the stories in the business press often emphasized that Orfalea had been the beneficiary of a great social and technological wave. Kinko's, the media decided, had emerged as the McDonald's of copy centers during a period when millions of Americans began working for themselves from home and needed places like Kinko's to get their reports and presentations bound and reproduced. It's true that, even by Orfalea's own estimation, 42 million Americans were working out of their homes when he left Kinko's in 2003, compared with just 7 million when he opened his first store three decades earlier. But attributing Orfalea's great success to social trends would suggest, similar to the Spanish gentlemen in the Egg of Columbus story, that anyone could have done what Orfalea did. It ignores the question of how Kinko's managed to far outperform its competitors, all of whom presumably stood to benefit just as much from the same changing trends in American work habits.

Kinko's began as a one-man operation in 1970 when Orfalea, then twenty-two, opened a tiny photocopy and stationery shop near the University of California, Santa Barbara. The 100-square-foot store was so crowded that when he leased a second copier, he had to move the machine out onto the sidewalk every morning. A friend of Orfalea's called him "Kinko" in reference to his mop of curly red hair, so "Kinko's" is the name Orfalea put on the shop.

It was while working alone behind the counter at his first store that Orfalea had the insight that would make him a multimillionaire. It had nothing to do with technology or innovation. (The truth is that the founder of Kinko's has never learned how to service a copy machine.) Instead, Orfalea's insight involved his customers and human nature. One by one, as students and professors came into his shop with their science papers or test forms, Orfalea noticed that almost all of them were in some kind of agitated emotional state. "The customer walks into a store stressed out and confused," he wrote in his autobiography, *Copy This!* "She doesn't know what she wants and she wants it done yesterday." Orfalea came to realize that "we weren't so much selling copies as we were assuaging anxiety."

As Orfalea grew the business by taking on partners and opening new stores near college campuses all over the country, his chief concern was that copy centers might become a commodity industry with very low profit margins. Any competitor could lease a few photocopiers and compete with Kinko's on price, driving down profits to the point where no one could make any money. But Orfalea also knew that customers in a fragile emotional state will tend not to concern themselves with price, *as long as you assuage their anxieties.* It became Kinko's chief guiding strategy to charge more than competitors, but also to offer better service.

Throughout *Copy This!* Orfalea details the many ways he executed on this very ordinary idea. For instance, a casual conversation with a convenience store operator led to Orfalea's fervent conviction that Kinko's should stay open 24 hours a day. The store owner told Orfalea how surprised he was to see overall revenue go up by 50 percent once he started keeping the store open all night. Late-night foot traffic was fairly light and couldn't possibly account for the increase in sales. It was a mystery to him, until he realized that his regular customers were now coming in more often at all hours of the day. The man reasoned that the customers had become more loyal to his store, perhaps without even knowing it, because they liked the feeling that the store was always there for them. Staying open around the clock had relieved them of *worry*. After that, Orfalea wrote, "I became possessed, absolutely possessed, with the idea that this was a change we had to make."

Orfalea always tried to look at a Kinko's location from the standpoint of a stressed and anguished customer. People should feel soothed when they walked in the front door, he decided, and that meant nice pale blue walls, clean carpeting, and orderly spaces for people to work. "We wanted them to see more than a copy shop," Orfalea insisted. "We wanted them to see a sanctuary where they could come to solve their problems." Orfalea even consulted with an uncle who owned a tavern about how to make the Kinko's environment more welcoming and comfortable. He got angry when he caught store managers failing to leave out little freebie items like liquid paper, pens, and paper clips in the work areas. The managers complained, reasonably, that too many of these items were disappearing. But Orfalea had to explain that if Kinko's wanted to keep charging higher prices, managers had to stay focused on their customers' anxieties. Panicked customers who needed pens or a few paper clips on the way to their meetings would never forget they were able to snag these items for free at Kinko's.

At a place where copying documents was the main source of revenue, Orfalea made sure that copying ideas became the main source of inspiration. He was manic about far-flung store owners sharing bright ideas with each other. In the years before e-mail, Orfalea installed a voicemail system that allowed each store owner to broadcast observations and ideas to hundreds of colleagues all over the country. It wasn't unusual for owners to get 30 such messages a day. Once, Orfalea persuaded the local owner of a McDonald's to give him a tour behind the counter so he might pick up some tips about efficient workspace design. "I often told our coworkers, 'everything has a place and everything in its place,'" Orfalea wrote. "McDonald's really taught us how this principle looked in action." Fast service, supported by an orderly workplace, was just another way for Kinko's to take care of its customers and their emotions.

"In retail there are few secrets," Orfalea likes to point out. "Ninety percent of what we do . . . is obvious." It was his company's mastery of the obvious, of the mundane, that inevitably attracted the attention of the investment community. Why would a New York private equity firm spend hundreds of millions of dollars to enter a low-profit commodity industry like copy centers? The reason lies with the unique culture Orfalea built at Kinko's, which kept profits high through the exceptional execution of an ordinary idea, and through imitation, not innovation.

➤ The Blinding Flash of Genius

Losing out to Bill Gates and IBM was personally painful for Gary Kildall, but it hardly left him a pauper. In 1991, he sold Digital Research to Novell for $120 million—almost five times as much as the $26 million asking price Bill Gates had rejected six years earlier. Kildall moved to Texas, where he kept a collection of 14 sports cars at a lavish lakeside ranch. A licensed pilot since his teenage years, Kildall could now afford to fly his very own Lear jet.

Throughout the 1980s and into the 1990s, Kildall never stopped innovating toward his vision of a world made better by personal computers. Digital Research remained about ten years ahead of Microsoft with its pioneering work on desktop networking and application multitasking. In a separate venture, Kildall led the first effort to put an entire encyclopedia on a single laser disc (this was years before CD-ROMs). He founded another company, called Prometheus Light and Sound, that came up with many of the earliest innovations in wireless technology.

But Kildall never managed to make peace with certain facts of life in the computer industry. For instance, he hated how BASIC continued to be the most common programming language taught to children. Kildall's complaint was that BASIC didn't help children to think in a way that would solve programming problems, so he personally wrote a superior program based on an educational language called Logo. But Digital Research's Logo, nicknamed Dr. Logo, didn't sell very well. Kildall was disappointed to discover that since BASIC was the language computer teachers had learned when they were young, they preferred not to switch to Dr. Logo. For all its inadequacies, BASIC was the language they felt most comfortable teaching.

"I expected too much of educators," Kildall wrote in a personal memoir that has never been published. "It was then that I learned that computers were built to make money, not minds." Paul Orfalea might have counseled Kildall to try and figure out ways of making teachers feel more comfortable with Dr. Logo. Stuart Frankel might have suggested price-cutting, loss-leader giveaways, and a promotional campaign so children and parents would demand Dr. Logo. But Kildall, for all his genius, preferred to blame the entire computer industry for Dr. Logo's failure rather than seek out ways to improve the product and its marketing.

Maybe Kildall's obstinacy was a by-product of how easily his first success had come to him. Kildall had created CP/M with no thought of ever selling it. His simple devotion to excellent code-writing had made him a millionaire. Then, having profited so handsomely from this first flash of innovative genius, Kildall kept expecting the same relatively effortless success to arrive with each subsequent innovation. He never accepted that executing on any idea can be just as difficult an intellectual challenge as developing the idea itself. Instead, with each setback, Kildall got more frustrated and resorted to blaming the entire computer industry for having its priorities out of whack.

Disappointed inventors often suffer from this kind of debilitating sense of injustice. The 2008 movie *Flash of Genius* starred Greg Kinnear in the role of Robert Kearns, a garage inventor who designed the first intermittent windshield wiper, only to see his creation stolen and copied by the auto industry. Based on a true story, the movie shows how Kearns's lawsuits against the carmakers yielded prompt settlement offers worth millions of dollars, all of which Kearns refused. Kearns wanted the manufacturers to admit their thievery and return all manufacturing rights for the wiper to him, even though lawyers cautioned him that these demands were unrealistic.

By the time Kearns finally won several of his lawsuits, his legal costs and other debts had consumed almost all the money the courts awarded him. Although the movie provides a gauzy bittersweet ending to the story, in reality Kearns died alone and on the verge of madness. His dream had been to employ his children and grow rich in a family business manufacturing windshield wipers. Instead, his obsession destroyed his family. When he died, his wife had been long gone and he was estranged from most of his children.

Kildall's final years, though not so desperate, were also clouded in bitterness and disappointment. He and his wife Dorothy divorced in the 1980s. Kildall remarried, and then that marriage failed. He was diagnosed with a heart condition, so his private pilot's license was revoked, cutting him off from one of his greatest personal passions. As both the wealth and myth of Bill Gates grew ever larger, Kildall started drinking more and obsessing about his nemesis.

One particularly galling moment for Kildall came when he was invited to attend the 25th anniversary celebration of the computer science department at the University of Washington, where Kildall had studied and had been among the first computer science Ph.D.'s. The invitation stated that the evening's featured speaker would be one of the department's most generous donors—Bill Gates. That was almost too much for Kildall to take. He called to complain to the head of the computer science department, who hung up on him.

As recounted in the Harold Evans book, *They Made America*, Kildall wrote bitterly in his unpublished memoir about the irony of Gates being honored at the university where Kildall got his computer training. "Gates takes my work and makes it his own through divisive measures, at best. He made his 'cash cow,' MS-DOS, from CP/M. So Gates, representing wealth and being proud of the fact that he is a Harvard dropout, without requirement for an education, delivers a lecture at the twenty-fifth reunion of the computer science class. Well, it seems to me that he did have an education to get there. It happened to be mine, not his." This reference to Gates was the last line that Kildall wrote.

One evening in 1994, during a visit to Monterey, Kildall was discovered lying unconscious on the floor of a biker bar, under a video game machine. No one could say whether he'd fallen or if someone had hit him. Twice that weekend Kildall visited a local hospital to complain of headaches. Three days after sustaining his injuries, he died in his sleep of a brain hemorrhage at the age of fifty-two.

Although Kildall didn't live long enough to see it, the day eventually came when a successor company to Digital Research got the best of Gates. The company, Caldera Systems, did it by beating Gates at his own game—imitation.

Even before Kildall sold his interest in Digital Research, the company had hit on a strategy of cloning MS-DOS and then adding some superior features while undercutting MS-DOS on price. Since MS-DOS itself was a clone of Digital Research's own CP/M, the company had Microsoft in a bind. Gates could hardly sue Digital Research for copyright infringement without opening up the whole can of worms over where he had gotten MS-DOS in the first place. Digital Research's MS-DOS clone, called DR-DOS, drove Gates nuts. In e-mails since made public, Gates whined to Steve Ballmer that competition from DR-DOS was cutting into MS-DOS profits by 30 or 40 percent.

In 1996, Novell spun off ownership of DR-DOS into a small private company called Caldera Systems. Caldera promptly sued Microsoft for $1 billion, claiming that Gates had personally engaged in restraint of trade and other illegal monopolistic behaviors, including making a public threat to retaliate against IBM if Big Blue dared to start doing business with DR-DOS. The lawsuit dragged on for almost four years before Microsoft settled out of court for what the *Wall Street Journal* calculated was $275 million. According to *They Made America*, some estimates say Microsoft settled for as much as $500 million.

Fourteen years earlier, Gates could have bought out Kildall for a mere $26 million. But Gates never foresaw how buying CP/M outright would insulate Microsoft from the legal troubles that would end up costing the company hundreds of millions of dollars years later. Gates was never any good at seeing around corners or intuiting the future, despite all the myths to the contrary. His prediction record about most things was always very poor, because Gates was an imitator, not an innovator. He achieved his vast fortune not by chasing after vague visions of a better world but by seizing on concrete opportunities to follow the money. And that should be inspiring news to most of us, who aren't innovators or visionaries, either.

5

Know-How Is Good, "Know-Who" Is Better

NEARLY 9 IN 10 MIDDLE-CLASS SURVEY RESPONDENTS BELIEVE THAT FINANCIAL SUCCESS REQUIRES PUTTING ONE'S OWN CAPITAL AT RISK.

LESS THAN 4 IN 10 SELF-MADE MILLIONAIRES BELIEVE IN THE NEED TO RISK ANY OF ONE'S OWN CAPITAL.

➤ The Ogre of Omaha

In 1951, a twenty-one-year-old stockbroker we'll call "Ed" bought a Sinclair gas station in a 50-50 partnership with a buddy from his National Guard days. The two friends didn't know much about running a gas station, but they had a good location near a busy intersection in eastern Nebraska and America's love affair with the car was taking off. It seemed like a can't-miss proposition.

Ed and his buddy worked evenings and weekends, pumping gas and cleaning windshields, only to watch most cars pull into a Texaco station across the road. It took a while for them to realize that this rival station was owned by someone who was a pillar of the local community. This man had built up a great deal of customer loyalty over the years and no amount of hard work and service with a smile would change that. Losses at the Sinclair station continued to mount, and the two partners finally gave up. Ed lost his entire $2,000 investment. A big chunk of what had been $10,000 in life savings was gone.

The main reason Ed had taken such a costly gamble on buying a gas station was that he was miserable in his stock brokerage job. He liked analyzing stocks, but he was shy and hated selling. He especially disliked his firm's dependency on brokerage commissions. To Ed, the whole brokerage business seemed dishonest. He felt like a doctor who gets paid according to how many prescriptions he writes, regardless of how sick his patients get.

The postwar economy was booming in the early 1950s and Ed managed to build up a nice portfolio of stocks for himself by investing on the side. But this was a source of frustration, too. Most of Ed's stocks were doing well, thanks to a value-investing strategy he'd learned from a book, but his gains were limited by his small pool of capital. Ed often faced the wrenching choice of selling one stock before its time, just because he needed cash to buy a better one. And all the while Ed knew that every stock boom ends with a bust. In 1955, the Dow Jones industrial average hit a historic high, beyond the peak that preceded the Great Crash of 1929. Older men in the brokerage business were cautioning him that the stock market was bound to fall.

With his limited capital and the prospect of a down market looming, Ed realized that his personal financial goal of retirement at age thirty-one was impossible for him to reach all by himself. He needed to get others to invest with him. So even though he was painfully shy and not a natural salesman, Ed started an investment partnership so he could use other people's money to leverage his market smarts. He raised $70,000 from a handful of close friends and family members. Seven people each kicked in $10,000.

Ed limited his own financial contribution, however, to exactly $100. He wanted to make sure this venture would not become another money-losing debacle like the Sinclair station. The deal was this: Ed would charge a flat annual 4 percent fee for managing the money. And even though he had contributed just $100 of his own capital, he would be entitled to keep *half* of all annual returns from the partnership's holdings above 4 percent. If the partnership's investments should lose money over the year, Ed would share in only one-quarter of the paper losses. But as it turned out, there were no losses. The stocks in Ed's new partnership rose by 10 percent in 1957, even though the stock market dropped by

8 percent. The next year, when the Dow recovered and rose 38 percent, Ed's partnership holdings grew by 41 percent.

This early record of success enabled Ed to start a second partnership, and then a third. By the time Ed organized his fourth and largest investment partnership, he structured it so that the table was tipped entirely in his favor. Now Ed was entitled to one-quarter of all the gains above his 4 percent management fee, and *none* of the losses. He could place bets on the market without the fear of risking a dime of his own capital. It was as though he were playing a coin-flip game called "Heads I win, tails I don't lose."

With millions of dollars under his management, Ed went on to ride one of the greatest bull markets in Wall Street history. The DJIA climbed by 74 percent between 1957 and 1961, while Ed's partnership holdings grew by 251 percent. Ed managed to achieve his goal of independent wealth by the age of thirty-one. Eventually, he became richer than he ever imagined was possible. But in 2011, on his eightieth birthday, Ed still hadn't retired.

Ed, if you hadn't figured it out by now, *is* Warren Edward Buffett. The native Nebraskan, a self-made billionaire, is the third-richest man in the world. He controls assets worth $411 billion as chairman of Berkshire Hathaway, the holding company descended from his original investment partnerships. Buffett's personal net worth peaked at $62 billion in 2008 before he started moving billions of his money into a charitable foundation. In 2010, Buffett was granted the Presidential Medal of Freedom, in recognition of his status as a "legendary investor" and for his pledge to donate 99 percent of his wealth to philanthropic causes.

Buffett has been lionized as the Oracle of Omaha for his seeming ability to foresee the direction of the stock market over the past 50 years. Investors have pored over Buffett's stock-picking methods for decades, trying to emulate his famed strategy of buying stock in cheap, out-of-favor companies. The Buffett name has become a brand, invoked by countless self-help books and seminars that promise to teach value-investing "the Warren Buffett way." All of them promote the notion that with hard work and careful study, individual investors can learn from Buffett's example and stock-pick their way to their own personal fortunes.

The problem with this notion is that it assumes Buffett's investing success is entirely due to his stock-picking know-how, when the truth is that Buffett's billions would have been impossible without his adeptness at know-who. It is a myth that Buffett's fortune was built on a series of crafty, well-timed buy-and-sell decisions. The true secret of Buffett's success from the beginning was that he used the brute strength of his investors' dollars to squeeze profits from the companies he invested in. He earned outsized returns for himself and his investors via bareknuckled boardroom tactics that no individual investor could ever even attempt. To the management teams of some undervalued companies in the late 1950s, Buffett wasn't the Oracle of Omaha. He was the Ogre of Omaha.

Back in 1958, Buffett was managing just over $1 million in his partnerships. That year he poured 35 percent of this money into a sleepy little enterprise called Sanborn Maps. The company's main line of business was declining, but Buffett had discovered that Sanborn's stock price was nonetheless trading far below its true value. The reason was that Sanborn had invested its cash in a portfolio of stocks in other companies, a portfolio that was growing right along with the Wall Street bull market of the 1950s.

That little bit of know-how allowed Buffett to put his know-who to work. He persuaded a number of wealthy people he knew outside his investment partnership to also buy stock in Sanborn. Eventually, Buffett was the leader of a force of allied stockholders who controlled a big enough stake to secure a seat on Sanborn's board of directors. Then Buffett began pushing Sanborn's management to realize its portfolio gains and lift the company's stock price. The management hemmed and hawed about tax liabilities, but Buffett persisted. He was not shy at all about asserting his rights as a board member. Buffett threatened to force a stockholder vote and take over the company. The frightened management agreed to buy back existing shares of the company at a premium price. Sanborn essentially paid Buffett to go away by giving him and his friends a fast 50 percent return on their investment.

Not long after this victory, the Ogre of Omaha bought a $1 million stake in another tired Midwestern company, called Dempster Mill Manufacturing. Again, Buffett's know-who enabled him to rally wealthy friends and colleagues to put their own money behind his strategy. Buffett eventually controlled the entire board and then set the company on a course that maximized profits for himself and his friends. He fired the CEO and hired a cutthroat replacement who shut down factories, laid off workers, and liquidated inventory. Buffett milked Dempster for everything it was worth, taking stock dividends out of the company and reinvesting the proceeds in more promising companies. Then Buffett sold off what was left of Dempster at a price that nearly *tripled* his partnership's initial investment.

These are not the actions of some oracle who foresaw rising stock prices in Sanborn's and Dempster's futures. They are the actions of a well-financed, well-connected corporate raider. True, Buffett's skilled analysis identified Sanborn and Dempster as ripe victims for raiding in the first place. But Buffett never would have been able to unlock the value of his shares in these moribund little companies without the clout of his partnership and his wealthy allies.

Pretend for a moment that some small investor in 1958 had arrived at the exact same insight about Sanborn's potential value and bought a hundred shares of underpriced stock in the company. That lone investor might have hung onto Sanborn stock for years to come, waiting and hoping for the stock to achieve its potential. Meanwhile, in the space of 18 months, Buffett bullied the management, took his profit, and ditched the company. That's the crucial difference between the mythical "Warren Buffett way" and the actual methods Buffett used to amass his fortune. The power to pull off these moves, and to do it with other people's money, is why young Warren Buffett gave up on investing the Warren Buffett way as soon as he could.

Over his lifetime, Buffett has uttered a series of witticisms that are repeated avidly by his fans. One favorite is: "Rule No. 1: Never lose money. Rule No. 2: Never forget rule No. 1." Most people assume that this is Buffett's playful way of saying, "Never make a bad investment." But that's ridiculous. Buffett would be the first to admit he's made many bad investments. What Buffett hasn't done for the past 60 years is lose money the way he did in 1951, by sinking 20 percent of his savings into a Sinclair station. Buffett jokes to this day that the Sinclair station was the worst investment he ever made. It also happens to be the last time Buffett put such a large share of his own capital completely at risk, with no protection from other people's money.

Buffett's Rule No. 1 is really a warning to not go all in with your own money. You want to invest if you can in ways that limit your risk, so you won't lose your money even if your partners lose theirs. Warren Buffett has been playing this game of "heads I win, tails I don't lose" ever since he started his first partnership. It's a game that requires a little know-how and a lot of know-who. Buffett is a multibillionaire because he has played the game better than anyone else.

➤ The Premier's Mistress

The idea that it takes other people's money to get ahead financially is not very popular among middle-class survey respondents in the Business Brilliant survey. Less than 1 in 5 said that "getting others to invest with you" is important to financial success. An overwhelming middle-class majority—nearly 9 in 10—believe that financial success *requires* putting one's own capital at risk. That's 90 percent of the middle class doing the one thing that Warren Buffett advises against.

Self-made millionaires, on the other hand, think a lot more like Buffett. About 6 out of 10 self-made millionaires reported that it's important to get others to invest with them. Less than 4 in 10 believe in the need to risk any of one's own capital at all. People who have already achieved significant financial success understand that self-made does not mean self-financed. This is why know-who is more important than know-how.

Chapter 2 showed how Guy Laliberté, the billionaire founder of Cirque du Soleil, and Damien Hirst, the world's richest fine artist, both made their fortunes by doing what they loved while following the money. Look a little closer at Laliberté's and Hirst's stories, however, and we see that following the money for these two wasn't really about money at all. It was about people. It was about know-who.

During its first four seasons, Cirque du Soleil was constantly pitched at the brink of insolvency. It was Laliberté's skills at know-who among government funders and private donors in Quebec that kept the troupe going. During Cirque's inaugural summer tour of the province, Laliberté ingratiated himself among as many government officials as he could, plying them with special VIP treatment at the shows and arranging publicity events with supportive politicians. Laliberté especially cozied up to Quebec's premier, René Levesque, and Levesque's inner circle. According to an unauthorized biography of Laliberté, he even exploited the happy coincidence that Levesque's mistress was a trampolinist who was friendly with several Cirque performers.

Although Cirque was founded as a one-year project, Laliberté's savvy know-who secured Cirque's government funding for four successive years, which was long enough for Cirque to build a following and take off as a profit-making concern. But Cirque was hardly a government welfare case. It required indulgent private sector friends, too. In 1985, when a failed national tour left Cirque $750,000 in debt, Laliberté was able to turn to Quebec's more conservative business community, cultivating a friendship with a prominent insurance mogul who helped raise funds to keep Cirque's creditors at bay. Cirque's bank overlooked $200,000 in bounced checks. "Guy was a master networker," one Cirque executive recalled. "He gave circus tickets to everyone he thought he could use for future purposes. He treated them like kings. He knew that it would be well worth it down the line, and he turned out to be right."

Laliberté did these things because he had to. He had no other way to keep his pet project and his sole source of income alive. In that sense, he and Hirst encountered similar problems and came up with similar know-who solutions. As first discussed in chapter 2, Hirst in his youth faced meager prospects for personal success as an artist, so just like Laliberté, he distinguished himself instead by becoming an organizer and a showman.

Hirst took on the curatorship of the *Freeze* exhibition out of desperation. He was living in public housing and had no money to produce any of his conceptual artwork designs. Like so many entrepreneurs, all Hirst had was his desire to create something from nothing, and, very much like Laliberté and Gates, to follow the money by following the people with money. Hirst knew, for instance, that there was a rich real estate firm with land holdings in the desolate Docklands area that probably would like having the biggest names in art come through the area for a visit. So Hirst went to the firm and raised the $10,000 in seed money he needed to get things going. During the exhibit's run, Hirst knew that VIP dealers might be wary of venturing into the unfamiliar industrial area, so he made arrangements to be helpful. He offered to pick them up at the nearest train station and drive them to the station personally, winning himself some valuable face time with some of the biggest names in the field.

Finally, his role as curator of *Freeze* sparked the one conversation that got his career on its feet. A dealer he met at the exhibit commissioned Hirst's $6,000 piece with the rotting cow's head sealed in the glass case. Revolting as it was, Charles Saatchi, London's most famous art collector, fell in love with it. Saatchi became Hirst's prime patron for the next dozen years, commissioning subsequent pieces and helping Hirst become a multimillionaire before the age of thirty.

Both Laliberté and Hirst figured out at an early age that achieving their career goals required them to follow the money, which in turn required them to follow people with money. Hirst took on the role of curator of *Freeze* because he had no other avenue for stirring interest in his work among people who mattered. Laliberté needed years of generous backing from public and private funders because Cirque shows were expensive to produce. They were more Broadway than Barnum and Bailey, and that was a big part of what made Cirque so special. Laliberté never could have worked his way up from fire-breathing street performer to $1 billion in annual ticket sales without his know-who, without other people and their money.

About 750,000 new small businesses open up in the United States every year, and another 750,000 small businesses shut down. About 90 percent of the closed businesses report no losses to creditors because the companies were in debt only to their founders. Like most small businesses, they were run by sole proprietors who relied only on their credit cards and other personal resources for cash reserves and capital.

The irony is that many of these small businesses fail because the sole proprietors run out of funds just as they reach the brink of success. This may sound counterintuitive, but when a business begins to grow, expenditures almost always climb more quickly than revenues. Fast growth, which should be a good thing, often causes undercapitalized companies to overextend themselves, make clumsy mistakes, and fail. This is why so many small business owners become slaves to their creations. They are overworked, underpaid, in debt, and teetering at the edge of insolvency—and this is especially true of those whose businesses are succeeding and *growing*.

Paul Green is someone who once fit that description exactly. Today Green is possibly the richest guitar teacher in the world, having founded the national School of Rock franchise chain. But he might be just another struggling small businessman if he didn't know the right dentist, someone willing to be his first investor.

Back in 1998, Green was twenty-five years old and scratching out a living in Philadelphia by teaching one-on-one electric guitar lessons to small children and teenagers in a music store attic. Most music instructors are very poorly paid, but money wasn't Paul Green's main source of frustration. It was how slowly his students were learning. Most of them didn't practice enough and Green, who loved rock and roll with a passion, found it hard to hear them play so badly, week after week.

One day he hit on the idea of getting some of his students to start playing together in a rock band's rehearsal space. He found they sounded better because they'd been rehearsing more often, thanks to peer pressure. They hated playing badly in front of each other. Their progress persuaded him to open his own for-profit school of rock music so that all his students could rehearse with each other and then put on live performances for parents and friends. He rented a rundown three-story building and invited a few of his guitar-teacher friends to join as faculty. By 2003, he had 80 kids enrolled at the Paul Green School of Rock. Tuition barely covered salaries and expenses, though, and Green had to take a restaurant job on the side to make ends meet.

On October 3 of that year, a new movie called *School of Rock* opened in cinemas nationwide. It starred Jack Black as a manic, impulsive electric guitar teacher who behaved a lot like Paul Green. Green was enraged and felt he'd been ripped off. Two years earlier, a camera crew from the cable channel VH-1 had shot footage for a documentary about Green's school, but nothing had ever come of the project. The new Jack Black movie was released by Paramount, a sister company to VH-1, but the filmmakers denied they had conceived their movie with any help from VH-1. Green briefly considered suing, then dropped the idea. As it turned out, Jack Black's *School of Rock* would be the best thing ever to happen to Paul Green's School of Rock.

Enrollment at Green's school doubled within a few months of *School of Rock*'s opening. There wasn't enough space in the old building to accommodate everyone, and Green opened a second site in the suburbs. Expansion and new tuition dollars were positive signs of success, but they also marked the beginning of Green's troubles. He started to run himself ragged trying to manage two separate schools located miles apart.

Green was complaining one day during a visit to Joseph Roberts, his dentist. Roberts had a son in Green's school, so he already knew quite a bit about the enterprise. As a successful private practitioner on Philadelphia's high-rent Rittenhouse Square, Roberts also knew a lot more than Green about running a business. His expert diagnosis was that Green needed to register his School of Rock as a corporation and take on investors. It wouldn't be possible for Green to expand to a third site or a fourth without them. Roberts went on to become Green's first investor and the first chairman of the Paul Green School of Rock, LLC.

Investor money raised by Roberts and Green allowed the school to expand to five sites around Philadelphia while Green started scouting locations in other cities. Then a private-equity firm bought a minority stake in the business and installed a management team to roll out an ambitious nationwide franchise expansion plan. By 2010, there were 50 School of Rock branches across the country, with nine in the greater New York City area alone. Annual revenue hit $10 million. That year, Green was able to cash out his interest in the company and leave to pursue a few things even closer to his heart. He is music coordinator for the Woodstock Film Festival and is working with Adam Lang, co-creator of the 1969 Woodstock Festival, on starting a music college in the Woodstock, New York, area.

Until Paul Green started taking on investors, he had been playing a game of "heads I win, tails I lose" with his business. The result was lots of glowing press and some degree of success, but always in the shadow of catastrophe, always one bad quarter away from collapse. Failure at any point along the way would have left Green much worse off than when he started. He would have been jobless and stuck with a pile of debt. That's the way hundreds of thousands of businesses die each year, with a whimper and with some sole proprietor holding the bag.

Know-who got Green into Warren Buffett's game: "Heads I win, tails I don't lose." In *The Origin and Evolution of New Businesses*, author Amar Bhide uses this expression at least five times in four chapters to describe how the most successful entrepreneurs identify and pursue their opportunities. Smart entrepreneurs are always trying to set up deals in which success will be well rewarded while failure will exact only a minimal cost. In Bhide's view, the "heads I win, tails I don't lose" approach dispels the popular image of the entrepreneur as "an irrational, overconfident risk-seeker." Bhide's studies showed that most founders of *Inc.* 500

companies had put less than $10,000 into their businesses at the start-up stage, an amount small enough so they could bounce back easily even if everything went wrong. Buffett has some sage words of advice of his own on this score: "In order to succeed," he says, "you must first survive."

Nonetheless, most new business owners never obtain outside investors to help finance growth and protect themselves from risk. The main reason is that most never ask for it. One study says that fewer than 4 in 10 businesses look for external funding during their first two and a half years in existence. One reason for this is that many new businesses are either too small or not growth-oriented enough to be attractive to outside investors. But another reason might be that owners don't know how to seek out a common but little-known source of business investment, the informal investor.

Paul Green's dentist was an informal investor. Damien Hirst's first patron was an informal investor. They were not friends, not family, nor were they in the investment business, like angel investors or venture capitalists. They were just people who had a bit more money than Green and Hirst, who liked what they saw in them, and were willing and able to make what might be considered a modest gamble. The most famous informal investor of this kind was a Scottish car salesman named Ian McGlinn. In 1977, McGlinn gave a friend of his girlfriend's about $7,000 to expand her little retail store in Brighton, England. In exchange, McGlinn got a half-share in the business, which was called The Body Shop. In 2009, McGlinn sold all his stock in The Body Shop for more than $200 million.

By some estimates, informal investors like Roberts and McGlinn contribute eight times more money than venture capitalists to new small businesses in the United States each year. Scott A. Shane, an Ohio professor who studies business start-ups, says that informal investors have a low profile because they're not very interesting to the media. "The typical [informal] investor looks too much like you and me," he writes in *The Illusions of Entrepreneurship*, "and his investments are mundane at best." More than half of all informal investments are for about $15,000 or less, and many informal investors have incomes below $50,000. But together they are a deceptively large force. Shane cites estimates that about 1 percent of all households in the United States have some ownership stake in a private business managed by someone outside the household. That's 1 million informal investors.

Shane says that most informal investors are different from angel investors and venture capitalists in another important way: They're not looking for huge returns on their investments. "In fact," Shane writes, "one study found that more than one-third (35 percent) of informal investors expected no return (that's zero, nada, zilch) on their investments in start-ups. Clearly the typical informal investor is investing in start-ups for non-financial reasons, such as to help out a friend."

The message to take from that statistic should be pretty simple. Go out and make more friends.

➤ The Success Contagion

Few people who have met Bill Gates would consider him "a people person." One of his Harvard professors deemed him someone with "a bad personality and a great intellect." Gates always seemed bored with small talk and generally incurious about people. His social awkwardness, as well as his poor personal hygiene habits, became the stuff of legend. "Even after spending a lot of time with him," Walter Isaacson once wrote in a *Time* magazine profile of Gates, "you get the feeling that he knows much about your thinking but nothing about such things as where you live or if you have a family. Or that he cares."

But if Gates seemed uninterested in people personally, during Microsoft's formative years he never stopped obsessing over what they were thinking and doing within the computer industry. As one computer executive said about Gates in the early 1990s, "If you talk to Bill about any software company or any hardware company, there's a very high probability that he will be able to tell you who the CEO is, what their software is, what their problems were." Gates wasn't a glad-hander or a schmoozer, but he was unquestionably a networker.

Entrepreneurs succeed when they function as bridges between different kinds of networks. Gates, for instance, ended up acting as the bridge between IBM and the personal computing community. Gary Kildall might have been that bridge if it weren't for his indifferent attitude toward his networks of customers and strategic partners. When IBM decided that Kildall was too difficult to deal with, the company asked Gates to produce its new PC operating system. Gates knew he couldn't possibly build such a product from scratch on IBM's tight deadline, but he accepted the challenge anyway. Then he relied on his network of Seattle computer contacts to find an obscure operating system, Q-DOS, which he purchased and repackaged for IBM as MS-DOS.

The word *entrepreneur* comes from the French terms for "between" and "to take." Entrepreneurs take profits by brokering the relationship between players and filling so-called structural holes that ordinarily prevent disparate groups from working together. In this sense, Guy Laliberté brokered a relationship between his network of circus performers on one hand, and his network of Quebec business and government leaders on the other. Neither group had the independent means to create Cirque du Soleil. Only Laliberté knew enough people in both worlds to bring them together. Paul Green and his dentist filled the structural hole between the thousands of parents willing to pay for their children's music lessons and the investors who bankrolled the School of Rock.

If networks are so critical to business success, it should stand to reason that the most successful people would have the greatest number of close personal contacts. But the Business Brilliant survey and other social research show that this isn't the case. Middle-class survey respondents, for instance, said that on average they have 9 people with whom they "extensively/closely network in order to source more new business." Among self-made millionaires, however, the average number is just 5.7. This number actually gets smaller as wealth levels increase. It's 5.1 among self-made millionaires with net worths between $10 million and $30 million. Those above $30 million net worth average just 4.8 members in their close networks.

How can this be? Why wouldn't the wealthiest people report the largest number of immediate contacts? To answer this question, we have to look at what social science tells us about the nature of friendship itself. Although even a teenager can compile 5,000 friends on Facebook these days, it seems to be an immutable fact of human nature that no one can maintain more than a handful of true "best friend" relationships. Surveys continue to show that the average American, for instance, has about four close social contacts with whom that individual can comfortably discuss very important matters. The majority of Americans have between two and six close social contacts of this kind, making up what has been called a "core discussion network."

The smaller numbers in the core business networks of the Business Brilliant survey's wealthy and very wealthy respondents suggest that effective networking requires a very tight, very close group of this kind. When the middle-class survey respondents say they network "closely and extensively" with nine people on average, the way they define the phrase "closely and extensively" comes under suspicion. If survey research tells us that hardly anyone can maintain "close" ties to nine different people, then maybe what most middle-class respondents regard as "close and extensive" networking isn't very close and extensive at all.

The Business Brilliant survey has some evidence that supports this possibility. It shows that self-made millionaires are on more intimate terms with members of their core networks, particularly regarding crucial matters of motivation and money. For instance, 7 out of 10 self-made millionaires said, "It is essential I understand the motivations of my business associates." Fewer than 2 out of 10 members of the middle class said the same. When asked how they evaluate prospective business associates, a majority of self-made millionaires said that, among other details, they want to know how much these prospects earn and the size of their net worth. Fewer than 1 out of 6 respondents in the middle-class sample said they wanted to know these things. It seems that self-made millionaires succeed by networking with small core groups of people they know and understand very well. Middle-class business networks are more likely to consist of larger groups of casual acquaintances.

Researchers who have studied social networks say that network size alone does not predict your capabilities as a connector. It is the structural makeup of your core discussion group that can best predict how successful you will be as a bridge or a connector, someone who can broker relationships and profit by filling those "structural holes" between networks. What matters most is how many people you know in your networks *who don't know each other.*

In their book *Connected*, Nicholas A. Christakis and James H. Fowler say that within the average American's social network, there is a 52 percent chance that two of his or her contacts will know each other. This factor in networking is called transitivity. A transitivity rate above 52 percent suggests that, more than most people, you are deeply embedded in one type of network where many people know each other. You are so deeply embedded that it is not likely that you will serve as an effective bridge to other networks. On the other hand, if you have a low-transitivity network, one in which lots of the people you know don't know each other, then you are much more likely to occupy a central position in your network, one in which people commonly ask you to recommend contacts that they can't reach easily on their own.

"If you are happier or richer or healthier than others, it may have a lot to do with where you happen to be in the network," Christakis and Fowler write. Connectors and bridges are said to have a lot of "friends of friends" relationships, called "weak ties," in diverse areas of activity, which is advantageous for the connector. "People who have many weak ties will be frequently sought out for advice or offered opportunities in exchange for information or access. In other words, people who act as bridges between groups can become central to the overall network and so are more likely to be rewarded financially and otherwise." This is true inside large organizations, too. We've all known one or two connectors at work who seem to know lots of people in different parts of the organization. These people tend to have a lot of influence in the workplace precisely because they know so many people who don't know each other that they can be the bridge to getting things done in some cases.

One thing I notice about Gates, Laliberté, Hirst, and Green is that all of them started out deeply embedded in their respective networks—computer programmers, circus artists, art school graduates, and music teachers. What set them apart was how they reached out and made networking inroads into somewhat alien worlds of superior wealth and resources—IBM, the government of Quebec, patrons of the arts, and private equity investors. Christakis and Fowler point out that the care and tending of your social network requires this sort of deliberate action because "social networks tend to magnify whatever they are seeded with." By seeking stronger ties to people with greater wealth and resources than your own, you are seeding your network for future triumphs, even if your networking efforts don't meet with *any* immediate measurable success.

Chapter 4 described how Gates progressively sowed the seeds of his tremendous success by always seeking partnerships with the strongest computer industry players who would partner with him. Laliberté seized the opportunity to make contact with Quebec government officials during Cirque's first summer as a part of the province's 450th anniversary celebration. Hirst's solicitation of a $10,000 grant from a real estate company for the *Freeze* exhibit opened the way for his vast wealth in conceptual art. Green owes everything he has to that initial partnership with his well-to-do, financially savvy dentist.

Networking of this kind isn't easy. It goes against certain natural instincts that dictate how "birds of a feather flock together." What's more, studies reliably show that the vast majority of people are uncomfortable in situations that necessitate their being the least-affluent member of any group. One famous experiment, repeated many times, shows that most people say they would feel happier earning $33,000 in a workplace where everyone else makes $30,000 than if they were earning $35,000 in a workplace where everyone else makes $38,000. They would be happy to sacrifice $2,000 a year in salary just to enjoy being top dog in a lower-paying workplace. For most people, it's not enjoyable to be at the bottom of the pecking order, even if the reward is greater net income.

The tiny minority of people who function as connectors between disparate networks either do not feel bothered by socializing from the bottom, or, if they *do* feel bothered, they don't let the feeling stop them from serving as connectors. One thing connectors can count on, however, is that connectors in any station of life enjoy connecting with fellow connectors. There is a measurable tendency of people with many connections to be connected to others with many connections. It is also true that if you are not a connector, you are more likely to socialize with fewer people, and the few people you do socialize with will likely *not* be connectors, either. In this way, networking produces a rich-get-richer, poor-get-poorer effect in society. Christakis and Fowler wonder if this helps explain in part why the income gap between the rich and everyone else in America keeps growing, aided by online social networking.

Another explanation is that there is also a well-documented "friend-of-a-friend" network effect in which people's moods, behaviors, and other conditions are marginally affected by people they don't even know. These effects can be good or bad, depending on what a given network is seeded with. Christakis and Fowler found, for instance, that you are 15 percent more likely to be happy if a friend of yours is happy, but you are also 10 percent more likely to be happy if a friend of a friend is happy, and 6 percent more likely to be happy if a friend of a friend of a friend is happy. Loneliness has an even more powerful network effect. You are 52 percent more likely to feel lonely if a close friend feels lonely, 25 percent more likely to feel lonely if a friend of a friend feels lonely, and 15 percent more likely to feel lonely if a friend of a friend of a friend—someone you have never even met—feels lonely. This same three-degrees-of-separation effect can be found among binge drinkers, smokers, and people suffering from obesity. If you become obese, it triples the chances of your close friend becoming obese, and it may even have an effect on the weight gain experienced by people two and three degrees separated from you.

The authors of *Connected* admit that these findings run counter to people's perceptions of their own free will. "Particularly in the United States," they write, "we are accustomed to seeing our destinies as largely in our own hands: we 'pull ourselves up by our own bootstraps' and believe that 'anyone can strike it rich.' We see our society as a meritocracy that rewards sound choices and creates opportunities for the well-prepared." But we are also social creatures and our habits and emotions have been proven to be as predictably communicable as the flu.

So is success contagious? Does it help you to follow the money if the people within your network are also following the money? The answer to both questions is probably yes, since so many of the behavioral differences found between the middle class and self-made millionaires are highly social habits such as seeking equity, negotiating higher pay, imitating success in others, and finding investors. It makes sense that self-made millionaires with these habits of mind will gravitate toward and influence others with similar habits, especially because they share a common belief in the power of know-who.

Imagine for a moment that your core discussion network is made up of about five successful connectors, each of whom has his or her own core discussion network of about five successful connectors, each of whom in turn also has a core discussion network of about five successful connectors. That's roughly 150 people within at least three degrees of you who are actively looking for chances to be bridges between networks, eager to fill those "structural holes" that normally prevent productive relationships from happening. The contagious effect of a network of 150 connectors, most of whom you will never meet, might produce opportunities for you in such roundabout ways their sources might seem just as random and mysterious as that of a head cold. You would be apt to feel very lucky, even if you've made a conscious effort to seed your core network with successful connectors.

The network effect suggests that this is how you can make your own luck. Self-made millionaires like luck. They believe in it. The Business Brilliant surveys show that 8 out of 10 consider luck as important to their financial success. In fact, they value luck far more highly than "getting a good formal education," which only 3 out of 10 consider important. Among the middle class, however, the ratio is reversed. About 6 in 10 believe education is important while just 4 in 10 say the same about luck. The middle class tends to favor know-how over know-who, which seems unfortunate. The research shows, and the experience of our self-made millionaires seems to back it up, that if you don't tend your network, if you don't seed it so your opportunities are magnified, then when it comes to becoming Business Brilliant, you are literally out of luck.

6

Win-Win Is a Loser

ABOUT 7 IN 10 SELF-MADE MILLIONAIRES SAID "I CAN EASILY WALK AWAY FROM A BUSINESS DEAL IF IT'S NOT JUST RIGHT."

TO THE MIDDLE CLASS, IT'S NOT THAT EASY. JUST OVER 2 IN 10 SAY THEY CAN DO THE SAME.

➤ The Least-Interest Principle

Adam McKay had been the head writer at *Saturday Night Live* for three years when he decided in 2000 that it was time to move on. He was tired of the long late-night hours and the thankless creative tussles with producer Lorne Michaels, who had founded the show in 1975. When you are the head writer at *SNL*, McKay told an interviewer in 2010, "What you learn pretty quickly is that it's Lorne's show. . . . There's only so much pushing and shoving you can do."

What McKay really wanted was to move from New York to Los Angeles. He thought he might pitch a sitcom there, write screenplays, and maybe, eventually, he would direct movies. But when he told his manager, Jimmy Miller, about his plans to quit *SNL*, Miller asked him to wait. Miller was an experienced Hollywood operator who had managed Jim Carrey from stand-up comic to stardom. Since McKay had already decided to leave the show, Miller figured his client had nothing to lose by asking Lorne Michaels for better contract terms. So Miller advised McKay to go to Michaels and, as McKay remembers it, "make some unreasonable demands."

McKay presented Michaels with five conditions for staying on the show. "I said that I want a raise, I don't want to ever go to a production meeting," McKay recalls. "I won't be head writer anymore, but I want to name my on-screen credit, and I want to make short films. And [Lorne] said yes."

The next season, McKay's *SNL* on-screen credit was "coordinator of falconry." McKay managed his own filmmaking budget and hired a small crew, including a professional producer and cinematographer. He started directing stars like Steve Buscemi, Willem Dafoe, and Ben Stiller in a string of short movies about "every crazy thing I could think of," including a pawn shop for food and a woman who shoplifts dogs from pet stores. "It was an amazing experience," McKay said. "It ended up being the greatest thing ever, because I learned how to make movies."

Over the next two years, McKay shot more than two dozen comedy shorts for *SNL*. Then he left the show and moved to Los Angeles, just as he'd planned two years earlier. But he arrived in Hollywood as an experienced filmmaker, not just another gag writer with a screenplay to pitch. He and his friend from *SNL*, Will Ferrell, went on to make a series of feature-length comedies together, including the cult hit *Anchorman: The Legend of Ron Burgundy*, which McKay wrote and directed. In a span of just four years, McKay was writer, director, and producer for *Talladega Nights*, *Step Brothers*, and *The Other Guys*, each of which starred Ferrell and grossed more than $100 million. Today McKay is one of Hollywood's top five comedy filmmakers.

The turning point in McKay's career was the moment he took his manager's advice and deployed what is known in negotiation as the "least-interest principle." In any relationship, especially a business relationship, the person with the least interest in continuing the relationship is the one with the greatest power for setting its terms. The weaker your interest, the stronger your leverage. As G. Richard Schell puts it in his bestselling *Bargaining for Advantage*, "The party with the least to lose from no deal generally is the party that can afford to insist that critical deal terms break its way." All other factors aside, being ready to walk away from a deal is your best guarantee that the deal will work for you.

The Business Brilliant survey suggests that a preference for the least-interest principle is very closely related to financial success. About 7 in 10 self-made millionaires said, "I can easily walk away from a business deal if it's not just right." To the middle class, the benefit of the least-interest position is not so clear. Just over 2 in 10 say they can easily walk away. In a sense, McKay and his manager, Jimmy Miller, embody these two contrasting attitudes. McKay, a writer and stage performer with a middle-class upbringing, was not a natural negotiator. He wasn't even aware of the bargaining power he had attained the instant he decided to quit *SNL*. Miller, however, owed his entire livelihood to deal making. Having risen from humble Pittsburgh roots to become a Hollywood player, Miller saw McKay's situation in a completely different light. From his perspective, McKay was ready to squander a golden opportunity. In the end, McKay took Miller's advice, and his subsequent two-year tenure at *SNL* turned out to be much more than a golden opportunity. It was priceless.

There is an alternative interpretation to the Business Brilliant survey results, one that might also explain the deal-making differences between self-made millionaires and the middle class. What if self-made millionaires have an easier time walking away from deals precisely because they are millionaires? Doesn't their superior wealth give them the upper hand in most negotiations? Don't members of the middle class have less wiggle room and a greater need to make a deal work, at whatever terms are available?

That's probably true in some cases, but the full set of data from the Business Brilliant survey suggests that most members of the middle class have a lot in common with McKay—they don't always recognize when they have the upper hand, nor are they inclined to exploit their least-interest position when they have it.

Recall in chapter 3 how the vast majority of people who are offered new jobs never try to negotiate their salaries beyond the first offer they are given. At the moment of the job offer, it is you, the candidate, who are in the least-interest position. The manager offering you a position has named you the top applicant. With the manager's cards on the table, there is virtually no risk at all in asking for more money at that point. It would be very difficult for any manager to justify hiring the second-best candidate, simply because the top candidate asked for a few more dollars. And yet, three out of four job candidates fail to see this situation in these terms. They accept the first offer they are given with gratitude.

The crucial point to understand about the least-interest strategy is that it is often more a matter of approach than an actual objective position, as it was with Adam McKay. The best negotiators always project an appearance of least-interest, indicating that they could walk away at any minute, even on deals they would really like to close. You can sweeten the terms of any deal just by acting like you are less interested in closing than the other party. And sometimes, even if you privately feel you really need a particular deal to succeed, the *only* way to make it work is to put up a least-interest facade. Desperation, even when it's disguised as an eagerness to please, can be a deal-killer.

In the fall of 1983 in Silicon Valley, a Frenchman named Philippe Kahn had a problem that his American friends might have called a classic catch-22. Kahn had a software product for computer programmers called Turbo Pascal that he was selling for $50 per copy. Microsoft had a competing product priced at $500 that was also slower and bulkier. With its superior performance and low cost, Turbo Pascal should have been selling like crazy, but Kahn couldn't afford to promote it. If he had more money for advertising, he could sell more copies, but he needed to sell more copies before he could afford to buy advertising.

A Paris-born math teacher, Kahn arrived in California the previous year with $2,000 in his pocket, along with an early version of Turbo Pascal. He had hoped to land a job in Silicon Valley or sell Turbo Pascal to one of the many software companies there. Neither of these plans worked out, so he started up his own company, calling it Borland International because he assumed it sounded better than "Kahn International." When Borland failed to attract any venture capital investment, Kahn was forced to run the company on a shoestring, selling copies of Turbo Pascal and another product mostly by word of mouth. This was years before the Web, blogs, online advertising, and even e-mail spam. The only practical way to advertise a computer product in those days was to buy ads in the computer trade magazines, and those magazines were unwilling to extend credit to little companies that lacked venture capital backing.

Kahn desperately needed to advertise, and he needed to do it with little or no money down. He was hardly in the least-interest position. But Kahn knew that if he appeared as desperate as he really was, no magazine would ever run his ad without demanding full payment upfront. So he targeted *Byte*, the favorite magazine of computer programmers at the time. He invited a *Byte* sales representative to visit Borland's office, and once the appointment was set, Kahn went about planning a least-interest dog-and-pony show.

Some temporary workers were hired to show up in the Borland office that day, just to help the company look busier than it really was. Kahn made up a phony advertising budget chart that included the names of *Byte* and all its competitors. Then he drew a heavy black line through *Byte*'s name and left the chart out on a desk so the *Byte* sales rep could see it. "Here was this chart he thought he wasn't supposed to see," Kahn told *Inc.* magazine years later. "So I pushed it out of the way. He said, 'Hold on, can we get you in *Byte*?' I said, 'We don't really want to be in your book, it's not the right audience for us.' 'You've got to try,' he pleaded. I said, 'Frankly, our media plan is done, and we can't afford it.' So he offered good terms, if only we'd let him run it once."

The flip side of the least-interest principle is that when you put up a show of indifference about whether a deal succeeds or not, you provoke the opposite party to envision what it might lose. Suddenly, the opposing party sees risk where previously it had seen none. Kahn's lack of interest in *Byte* and the line drawn through *Byte*'s name on the chart put the *Byte* sales rep back on his heels. It would be embarrassing if his boss saw Borland buying ads from every magazine except *Byte*. And what if Borland succeeded and grew without ever running an ad in *Byte*? Word might get around that *Byte* didn't matter very much, all because of this one blown sale. Most people in Kahn's position would have flattered the sales rep, praised *Byte*'s importance to the industry, and begged for advertising credit, probably in vain. By doing the opposite, by doubting *Byte*'s value to Borland, Kahn had the *Byte* sales rep eating out of his hand, pleading with him for just one chance to extend Borland credit for a full-page ad.

The full-page ad ran in the November 1983 edition of *Byte*. Kahn hoped the ad would bring in at least $20,000 in revenue, enough to pay for the ad. Instead, his company sold $150,000 worth of software that month. Within five years, Borland International had annual sales of $82 million.

➤ The "Wish, Want, Walk" Formula

In hindsight, Adam McKay's five demands for staying with *Saturday Night Live* produced an ideal "win-win" outcome. Lorne Michaels got to keep McKay at *SNL* for two more years, during which McKay made his films and also continued to supply ideas and scripts for live sketches. McKay, in turn, got a well-paid apprenticeship in filmmaking. During his final months with the show, McKay created "*SNL* Digital Shorts," a genre of funny four-minute videos that were shot and edited quickly with digital equipment and then put online following their broadcast debut. Years after McKay left *SNL*, Andy Samberg and other cast members stepped in and produced wildly popular digital shorts like "Lazy Sunday," "I'm on a Boat," and "Natalie Portman's Rap." The short videos drew millions of online viewers and helped keep the show relevant among Web-savvy young adults—just one legacy of McKay's and Michaels's "win-win" deal.

Most people think that a "win-win" happy ending of this kind should be the ultimate goal in any negotiation. The Business Brilliant survey found that more than 8 out of 10 middle-class survey respondents agreed with the general statement that "Win-win solutions are best," as did 6 out of 10 self-made millionaires. But when we looked at our data more closely, a slightly different picture emerged. We found that as the level of personal wealth goes up, the level of enthusiasm for win-win goes down. Among self-made multimillionaires, those with net worths exceeding $30 million, the Business Brilliant survey showed that fewer than 2 in 10 believe that win-win is a winner.

Why would that be? What do the very rich know about win-win that most of us don't? It turns out that win-win has a dubious reputation among almost everyone who has seriously studied the art and science of negotiation. The win-win goal can be a dangerous trap, especially for anyone who goes up against an experienced negotiator. If you attempt to make a deal from a win-win perspective with someone who assumes a more aggressive "I-must-win" posture, you're liable to be the only party surrendering concessions in the name of preserving the deal. Once you make it your priority to achieve a reasonable compromise on a win-win basis, then what appears to be a win-win outcome might actually be "wimp-win"—with you as the wimp and the other guy as the winner. I suspect this explains why just a very small minority of self-made multimillionaires agrees with the middle-class consensus that "win-win solutions are best." You don't become a multimillionaire by playing wimp-win.

The term "win-win" has such a favorable popular image that skilled and cagey negotiators have learned how to employ positive-sounding win-win "happy talk" as a cudgel to beat concessions out of weaker parties. A professional negotiation coach named Jim Camp tells how big companies skillfully invoke friendly win-win bromides such as partnership, fairness, and problem solving in order to squeeze painful price reductions from their smaller suppliers.

In his book *Start with No*, Camp describes a General Motors effort called PICOS, or Price Improvement for the Cost Optimization of Suppliers. The advertised idea behind PICOS was to work with GM's parts suppliers to help them hold down their costs of production. "That's win-win, isn't it?" Camp writes. "It sure was—for GM, because when the rhetoric was stripped away, 'cost optimization' was a politically correct euphemism for bludgeoning suppliers into submission. . . . If a supplier went belly-up or couldn't deliver under the negotiated terms, there was always another supplier who believed that it could somehow live with those prices. PICOS, and its win-win rhetoric, sounded good in theory, but it was and is devastating in practice for many businesses." Camp complains that it is common today for business schools to teach "the win-win mantra" in their negotiation courses, while also offering "right across the hall, a course in 'supply system management' that's expressly designed to destroy the win-win model!"

This skepticism about win-win is not confined to professional hardball negotiators like Camp. Few have done more to advance the idea of ethical win-win deal making than Stephen Covey, whose *Seven Habits of Highly Effective People* is one of the bestselling business books of all time. And yet, even Covey says that the popular conception of win-win can easily make you a loser if you're not careful.

Covey tells the story of a client who complained that his best efforts at win-win had failed him. The man ran a large chain of retail stores and his recent experience renegotiating some leasing agreements had left him bitterly disillusioned. "We went in with a Win/Win attitude," he explained to Covey. "We were open, reasonable, conciliatory. But they saw that position as soft and weak, and they took us to the cleaners."

Covey had to point out to the retailer that if he felt he'd been taken to the cleaners, then he hadn't been involved in a win-win deal at all. Instead, he had let himself lose and he'd let the other guys win. "When he realized that what he had called Win/Win was really Lose/Win, he was shocked," Covey writes. In Covey's view, the retailer's mistake was that he didn't have the courage to say "No deal" when the negotiation started to go against him. "With No Deal as an option, you can honestly say, 'I only go for Win/Win. . . . And if we can't find it, then let's agree that we won't make a deal at all." Covey believes that win-win is a perilous misnomer. It should really be understood as "win-win or no deal," which Covey regards as a "higher expression" of win-win. Without saying as much, this is Covey's way of paying tribute to the least-interest principle. Unless you are willing to walk away—and 80 percent of the Business Brilliant survey's middle-class respondents are not—then there can be no win-win.

Many hundreds of books have been written about negotiation and its various strategies. Most include some variation on the same essential three-step negotiation preparation process—three steps that have very little to do with win-win. The first step involves identifying and writing down a specific goal or set of goals for the negotiation. The second is making a thorough study of the other party and its bargaining position. The third step is determining in advance the point at which you will walk away, also known as a BATNA, or best alternative to a negotiated agreement. Negotiation guru Michael C. Donaldson sums up the three steps as "wish, want, walk." You set the goal for what you wish for, determine what you want to know to get it, and then draw the line at which you'll walk. Negotiating is not so much a battle of wits as it is a contest of psychology. Our surveys tell us that when it comes to succeeding in each of these three crucial negotiating steps, self-made millionaires are much better prepared psychologically than the middle class.

I touched on goal setting earlier, in chapter 3, when we explored the evidence that those who ask for higher salaries tend to get paid much more than those who don't ask. Numerous studies have shown the same thing about all negotiating and goal setting. Those who start with a high opening bid rarely get what they ask for, but they almost always get a lot more than those who start out by being more reasonable. The studies also show that there is little risk in asking, even for a set of outrageous goals, as long as you ask in a way that is courteous and respectful. Ask nicely enough and you can ask for the moon.

Identifying ambitious goals is just the start, though. The most critical part of goal setting seems to be the simple, fundamental act of writing down the goal or goals on paper. The Business Brilliant survey finds that having written financial goals correlates almost exactly with financial success. One in three middle-class survey respondents have established financial goals. For self-made millionaires, it's about 5 out of 10. For self-made *multi*millionaires, it's well over 8 out of 10.

Negotiation experts say that the pressures of bargaining can make even the smartest people forgetful, so it's all the more important to have a written reminder of what you want, in your own handwriting, sitting in front of you. Dominick Misino, a former hostage negotiator for the New York Police Department, approached every hostage standoff while holding a sheet of paper with a line drawn down the middle. On the left side he'd write NEGOTIABLE and on the right side he'd write NON-NEGOTIABLE. Then he'd fill in both sides. "It's not exactly high-tech," according to Misino. "But I have to tell you, it's saved many a negotiation. The simple rules are sometimes the very best rules, and this simple one works for everything from hostage negotiation to buying a car or a refrigerator."

When you have your goals in writing, there are also psychological factors that make you more likely to defend those goals. Research shows that writing makes you feel more committed and less likely to change your mind later. Salespeople in high-pressure fields like real estate and used cars know this, which is one reason why they so often ask sales prospects to fill out so many forms by hand. They know that the more you write down on paper while closing on a time-share condo or a rusty Chevy, the less likely you are to back out of the deal during the three-day cooling-off period. You can use the same technique on yourself if you want to improve your chances of sticking to your goals. By writing them down, you make it psychologically more difficult for you to forget or betray them at some later time when you may be feeling stressed or pressured to compromise.

The second common step in negotiating—learning about the other party's motives and desires—is also a habit that we find tracks very closely with other aspects of Business Brilliance. As we saw in chapter 5, self-made millionaires make a much greater effort than the middle class in finding out about their business associates' lives, including how much they make, how much they are worth, and how much they want to make. Less than 2 out of 10 middle-class survey respondents said that

"It is essential that I understand the motivations of my business associates," a statement that 7 out of 10 self-made millionaires agreed with. Among self-made *multi*millionaires, the verdict was almost unanimous. They always want to know as much as they can about the people they are dealing with.

Negotiators who expend extra effort in discovery about their opposing parties tend to produce better outcomes. A well-known study in Britain revealed that highly skilled negotiators with proven levels of success dedicated four times as many hours as less-skilled negotiators in investigating opponents for areas of potential common ground. All told, these top-ranked negotiators spent 40 percent of their prep time on opposition research, compared with just 10 percent of prep time among the lower-skilled, less-successful negotiators.

The more you understand about what is important to the opposite party, the more likely it is that you can arrive at a true win-win result with minimal sacrifice on your own part. One famous illustration of this idea was the story of how an Arizona-based trash hauler rescued its failed bid for a municipal waste contract with a small California coastal town. The trash hauler's bid was $5 per ton higher than the winning bid, but instead of giving up, a consultant for the trash company discovered a unique deal sweetener. The consultant was a surfing enthusiast who knew that the California town had a serious problem with beach erosion. Since the trash hauler's trucks regularly dumped all their waste 230 miles away in Arizona landfills, it wouldn't cost that much extra if the trucks made return trips filled with tons of Arizona sand. The hauler got its price and the town got its beaches replenished.

Misino, who often faced dangerous half-crazed individuals in his job, says he always tried to see the situation from the hostage-taker's viewpoint, but only so that he could anticipate the disturbed man's vulnerabilities and drive a harder bargain. "Empathy," says Misino, "is not sympathy." The trick, he says, is to understand the other person's position thoroughly without feeling sorry for him. A negotiation experiment undertaken at Northwestern University showed that negotiators primed to understand what their opponents were thinking produced much better results than those who were prompted to understand what their opponents might be feeling. The results suggest it really is better to grasp what's in the heads of those on the other side of the table, but not what's in their hearts. "You want to understand what the other side's interests are," a researcher told the *Economist*. "But you don't want to sacrifice your own interests. A large amount of empathy can actually impair the ability of people to reach a creative deal."

This last point underlines another advantage in knowing all about the other party, an advantage that doesn't involve win-win at all. It involves searching for the other side's weak points, and here, also, we find that self-made millionaires are more likely to be psychologically poised for success. About 9 out of 10 self-made millionaires reported in the Business Brilliant survey that "It's important in negotiations to exploit the weaknesses in others." Only 1 out of 4 members of the middle class said the same. If that seems a little cold, consider that most self-made millionaires see it as a matter of fair play, since they count on getting the same treatment from the other side of the table. About 7 in 10 said that "In negotiations, I expect people to try and take advantage of me." Most of the middle class takes a more benign view. Only about 1 in 3 expect the other negotiating party to try and take advantage. And yet, as we saw in chapter 3, every first salary offer you've ever received was an attempt to take advantage of you, since every first salary offer is deliberately low in order to allow room for potential negotiation. This simple fact of workplace life seems to be unrecognized by two-thirds of the middle class, and it probably costs them billions of dollars in lost salaries every year.

We opened this chapter with a discussion about the importance of being ready to walk away from a deal, which is the last of the three critical points in negotiating. To recap, about 7 in 10 self-made millionaires told us that "I can easily walk away from a business deal if it's not just right." For the middle class, only 2 in 10 say they can easily walk away.

But what if you really do need the deal you're negotiating? Even then, a willingness to be compliant and an eagerness to please during negotiations is no guarantee of closing the deal. Eagerness can look like desperate neediness, which will make the other party suspicious and reluctant to commit. According to Camp, "More bad deals are signed and more sales are lost because of neediness than because of any other single factor." He advises his clients to absolutely never exhibit need and coaches them in learning how to never *feel* need either. " 'Need' is death, 'want' is life," he writes. "Believe me, this different attitude will be instantly perceived by the folks on the other side of the table. Confidence and trust go up across the board. Control and discipline go up for you."

Camp tells a story about a new client who had hired him after blowing a big deal with a major multinational corporation. The client felt that his company had offered the big corporation superior technology, superior service, and excellent terms right from the beginning. Then during negotiations over the contract, he compromised in every way possible in order to land the deal, including throwing in a lot of expensive equipment at no charge. The negotiators from the big corporation broke off their talks anyway.

It wasn't until much later that Camp's client discovered that the CEO of the multinational had nixed the deal. His eagerness to close the deal by making costly concessions had backfired. Rather than cultivate goodwill, his concessions aroused suspicion that his company was either incompetent, untrustworthy, or unable to deliver. The CEO of the larger company felt certain that something must be wrong for this small company president to be so agreeable and accommodating.

➤ The Reciprocity Trap

An apocryphal quote, often attributed to Bill Gates, says, "You don't get what you deserve in business. You get what you negotiate." The discipline of negotiation can be considered a synergistic system for producing financial gain. Its three fundamental principles—stick to high goals, understand the opposing party's perspective, and set a point at which to walk—function in a way very similar to Toyota's quality-assurance system discussed in chapter 1. You don't have to know which part of the three-step negotiation process is working each time, but all the parts work together well enough and often enough that they can combine to create the unpredictable results, which are the hallmark of synergy. Recall Linda Babcock's story in chapter 3 about the negotiating success of the housekeeping manager at the hotel in Bermuda. The woman had never dreamed of making a six-figure income until she decided to "wish, want, walk."

So with literally hundreds of books and programs of every kind available on negotiating, why are so many people so bad at it? G. Richard Shell gives three simple reasons, and each one dovetails with wish, want, walk. He says that most people set goals that are too modest, they fail to prepare, and they lack desire. Above all, novice negotiators avoid Donaldson's "wish, want, walk" because executing on these steps often makes people feel bad. A set of social customs and psychological traps are at the root of all negotiating success and failure.

Shell is a professor at the Wharton School of the University of Pennsylvania, where he gives seminars and workshops on negotiation. He has found that as students and executives learn to set higher, more ambitious goals, they improve their objective results, but in the process they also report feelings of dissatisfaction and discouragement. Aiming high can get you better results and leave you feeling worse at the time. This is why, in psychology, there is a phenomenon known as "preserving self-esteem though reduced expectations." The old slacker credo of "Aim low, succeed often," is funny because it contains a grain of truth about human nature. There is some evidence that people feel better when they ask for $50 and get $50 than if they ask for $100 and "only" get $60. Materially, you're better off with $60, but missing your goals leaves a bad feeling not present when you achieve your low goal.

Shell says that most of the psychological foundations of negotiations can be described in terms of these kinds of common psychological binds, known as biases, that must be overcome in order to excel at negotiating.

It is hard for most people to set high goals because they fear the bad feelings that come when they fall short. Most people also feel uncomfortable snooping around to find the other party's weaknesses. And it feels particularly rude and ill-mannered for most people to draw a line and say "no deal." Consider for a moment that all of the people who take Shell's course at Wharton are students and executives studying at a world-renowned school of business. If they report having bad feelings accompanying their negotiation successes, how should the rest of us feel?

From a negotiating perspective, the most pernicious of these psychological biases might be what is called the "norm of reciprocity." Most people reflexively try to return a kindness with a kindness. Say something nice to them, and they will feel an emotional pull to return the favor. This is why flattery and gift giving are such successful social behaviors. The offering of a compliment or a gift incurs a feeling of psychological indebtedness in the receiver. If you've ever gotten fundraising junk mail that has "free gift enclosed" printed on the outside of the envelope, the sponsor of that mailing is trying to exploit your instinct for the norm of reciprocity. Mailings that include token gifts, such as a cheap set of personalized mailing labels, have been proven to raise more donations than envelopes without them.

The norm of reciprocity is a nice thing. It is a central feature of our humanity. But in a business negotiation, your natural inclination toward reciprocity can be easily used against you. Every negotiation coach will point out the many ways in which skilled negotiators attempt to engender feelings of camaraderie, friendship, and partnership, all with the sole intent of gaining the upper hand over you. The opposite party in a negotiation will tell you that you've been very fair and reasonable and then in the same breath propose an unreasonably low settlement offer. In that moment they are hoping you will yield to your basic human instinct to repay their nice words by submitting to their unfair bid.

If we return once again to the subject of hiring and salary negotiation, many people say they accept the first salary figure they are offered because responding with a request for more money feels somehow ungrateful. That's exactly how the hiring manager expects you to feel. To save money in his or her budget, the hiring manager will flatter you and welcome you to the team with a rock-bottom salary offer, knowing that human nature will make it difficult for 3 out of 4 people to do anything but shake hands and accept gladly.

The right move in such a circumstance is to turn the tables psychologically. You express gratitude for the offer, talk about how you can't wait to get to work, *and* you say that you would be very happy to accept the job offer with a salary of so many thousands more. Now whose instinct for reciprocity is being challenged? For the manager to do anything but give you at least a portion of what you want is to risk making you unhappy, and no one wants to have a brand-new unhappy employee. As we discussed in the studies by Pinkley and Northcraft in chapter 3, about 40 percent of all hiring managers are willing to pay what it takes to make their new employees happy—*if* those employees ask for it. A full 90 percent of managers said they are willing to negotiate a high enough pay level to ensure that a new employee at least feels satisfied, but only if the employee offers them a number.

Ultimately, the norm of reciprocity is all about the innate human desire to be perceived as a nice, considerate person within one's social setting. The new hire accepts less money than he wants because he fears appearing ungrateful for the job offer. The weaker party in the negotiation agrees to a deal he instantly regrets because he would feel like a jerk if he stood up and announced that there's no deal. However, according to Stephen Covey, selling out the goals you've set for yourself doesn't mean you are reasonable or considerate. It means that you lack courage. Negotiators who worry too much about the other side's judgments of them are setting themselves up for disastrous "lose-win" deals in which, as Covey puts it, "I'll be so considerate of your convictions and desires that I won't have the courage to express and actualize my own."

Susceptibility to this lack of courage varies greatly from person to person. The people who are least susceptible, according to the Business Brilliant survey, are called multimillionaires. Almost 97 percent of self-made multimillionaires agree that "in business dealings, it's not my responsibility to 'look out' for the other person's interests." Among all self-made millionaires, over 85 percent agree. But for the middle class? Less than 25 percent agree. Just 1 in 4 believe in this fairly fundamental fact of negotiation, that the other side needs to look after itself, with no help from you. As the hostage negotiator Dominick Misino might say, empathy makes for smart negotiating, but sympathy does not.

A series of results in the Business Brilliant survey reveals that self-made millionaires in general are far more comfortable than the middle class when it comes to advancing their interests over those of other people. About 75 percent of self-made millionaires agreed with the statement that "Coming out on top in business dealings is paramount." Just over 30 percent of the middle class agreed. About 9 out of 10 self-made millionaires said "I am always looking for a way to gain advantage in my business dealings" and "It is important in negotiations to exploit weaknesses in others." For the middle class, just 4 in 10 are looking to gain advantage, and a little over 2 in 10 see the importance of exploiting weaknesses in others. Self-made millionaires seem much more willing than the middle class to accept that following the money is a competitive sport with winners and losers.

In fact, almost 8 in 10 self-made millionaires believe that "Being Machiavellian is essential to becoming wealthy." Among self-made multimillionaires, people who have attained great wealth, the belief in Machiavellianism is found in nearly 9 out of 10 survey respondents. The middle class, however, rejects the idea. Fewer than 2 in 10 believe that being Machiavellian is essential to becoming wealthy. As we've observed many times before, our survey reveals that middle-class perceptions about how to achieve wealth are grossly out of step with the perceptions of those who have actually done it.

Machiavellianism has been described by psychologists as a cool, rational, detached, and opportunistic attitude. People who score high on tests for Machiavellianism are more able than most to identify optimal strategies for getting what they want and they tend to behave in a self-interested manner if it is to their advantage. They are not as emotionally affected as others by social norms and social pressures, which is why they tend to be more upset by inefficiency than injustice. But it's not as though Machiavellian personalities can never be trusted. They understand, perhaps more than most, that reciprocation is vital in building long-term trusting relationships. On the other hand, if there is little or no consequence for taking advantage, Machiavellians tend to take advantage.

In one clinical experiment, individuals with "high Mach" test scores were found to be about twice as likely to take advantage of a weaker party than those with low to average Mach scores. Each test subject in the experiment played a simple two-step game on a computer screen with another player in a separate room. When this invisible player trusted the test subject with $40, the rules of the game gave the test subject two options. The test subject could either reciprocate the act of trust and split the $40 with the other player, or the test subject could keep the entire $40 with no negative consequences. In this test environment, those with low to average Mach scores shared the money 55 percent of the time. Individuals with high Mach scores, on the other hand, reciprocated trust and shared the money only 27 percent of the time. In almost 3 out of 4 instances, the high Machs took the money because it was there for the taking.

Many successful businesspeople are known for their Machiavellian streaks. Go back over the tales of billionaires we've told so far, and it's not hard to pick out the sharp Machiavellian moves that helped them secure their fortunes at critical moments. Warren Buffett never worried much about the managers at the tired little companies he bought up and then blew up during his earliest partnerships. Guy Laliberté did not share any equity in the newborn Cirque du Soleil with his creditors or his fellow performers, even though many had made great personal and financial sacrifices to help Laliberté's circus succeed. Bill Gates, who had acted like Gary Kildall's loyal buddy when Microsoft sales were dependent on Kildall's computer operating system, turned on Kildall once Gates had jumped into bed with IBM. At that point, Gates determined that in order for Microsoft's new operating system to win, Kildall's company had to be run out of the business.

Stories of this kind raise the question of whether following the money is an instinct one is born with, or whether it can be learned. At the margins, of course, the negotiation courses taught by Linda Babcock, Richard Shell, and others demonstrate that increased focus on proven techniques can improve just about anyone's negotiation results. But the experience of disappointment and frustration over bad deals can also build resolve in an individual to stop being a sap and take a page or two from Machiavelli. The retailer in Stephen Covey's story had to negotiate a lot of bad deals before he could learn how to say "no deal." The small company owner coached by Jim Camp had to learn a painful lesson about appearing desperate, a mistake he's not likely to repeat. It's important to remember, too, that Buffett, one of the richest men to ever live, started his first investment partnership only after he'd failed in his determined efforts to grow rich by investing alone. Buffett had no inborn drive to get hold of other people's money and use it to raid other people's companies. His career as a corporate raider was merely a means to an end, after his first preference—to remain a shy, solitary investor—hadn't panned out.

One of the best stories about a once-burned, twice-resolved entrepreneur can be found in *The New New Thing*, the biography of Internet mogul Jim Clark, written by Michael Lewis. Clark is best known as the founder of Netscape, the first commercially marketed Web browser. Clark was an engineer by training who founded a company called Silicon Graphics in 1983. He was so enamored with his company's unique three-dimensional imaging products, that he found himself desperate for the cash necessary to develop the products to their full potential. He courted venture capitalists as investors, and kept selling off pieces of Silicon Graphics in order to secure precious working capital. The strategy worked well for Silicon Graphics, but not so well for Clark. As the company grew larger and more successful, Clark's stake in Silicon Graphics had shrunk so small that he found he no longer controlled his creation. By the time he sold off his final stake in the company during a feud with the CEO, Clark had become a millionaire, but he had made other investors in the company much, much richer than himself. Clark deserved better, having founded the company, but, to restate the axiom attributed to Bill Gates, you don't get what you deserve in business. You get what you negotiate, and Clark had negotiated badly.

Embittered by the experience, Clark began Netscape in 1991 with a completely different approach. This time around, when it came to raising cash to fund the start-up, Clark did not go begging. Instead he behaved as though he was in the least-interest position. First he announced that he would decide who would be invited to invest with Netscape, and he excluded some investors who he felt had screwed him over during his years with Silicon Graphics. Then Clark laid out his terms. Equity shares in the company would be sold on a 3-for-1 basis. Netscape was valued at $18 million, but in order to buy a 10 percent share of Netscape, it wouldn't cost you $1.8 million. It would cost three times that much: $5.4 million.

Until then, it had been customary for computer company founders to sell equity on a dollar-for-dollar basis. No one questioned it. That was the social norm of reciprocity in Silicon Valley culture. If you want to enjoy the fruits of venture capital investment, you should accept certain customary practices regarding equity. But Clark was fed up with Silicon Valley convention. It had burned him once before, and he resolved that this time would be different.

The result was that although some venture capitalists turned up their noses on principle at Clark's outrageous 3-for-1 offer, others bought in eagerly. One venture capitalist who had been an early investor in Silicon Graphics begged Clark for permission to invest in Netscape, but to no avail. Clark blamed the man for his problems at Silicon Graphics and refused to let him have a piece of the new company. On the day that Netscape was formally incorporated, the man killed himself with a gunshot to the head. He had been suffering from paranoid delusions in the weeks before his suicide, but some speculated that he could not live with what he knew he had missed out on.

When Netscape made its first public stock offering in 1995, the stock price rose in a matter of months from $28 to $140. The astonishing success of Netscape stock marked the beginning of the Internet investment bubble, and Clark was one of many people who would become very rich from it. From his initial Netscape investment of just $5 million, Clark made a reported $2 billion—not because that's what he deserved, but because that's what he negotiated.

7

Spread the Work, Spread the Wealth

NEARLY 9 OUT OF 10 SELF-MADE MILLIONAIRES SAID THAT WHEN IT COMES TO TASKS THEY ARE NOT EXCEPTIONALLY GOOD AT, THEY ARE VERY LIKELY TO DELEGATE THOSE TASKS TO PEOPLE WHO DO THEM BETTER.

BY CONTRAST, 2 OUT OF 3 MIDDLE-CLASS RESPONDENTS SAID THAT WHEN FACED WITH SUCH TASKS, THEY WOULD LIKELY "DO THOSE TASKS ANYWAY."

➤ The Disability Advantage

For someone who had barely graduated from high school, fifty-six-year-old Jay Thiessens was doing pretty well for himself back in 1998. He had a beautiful home in Sparks, Nevada, in which he and his wife had raised three children. He owned a fishing boat and a motor home, and his small custom manufacturing company, B&J Machine and Tool, was pulling in $5 million a year.

Thiessens achieved this level of success by making a number of very typical self-made-millionaire moves. He gained an equity stake in his employment at an early age. He broke away and started his own company as soon as he was able. Then he grew the company over the years by plowing cash back into it, instead of saving money for retirement. There was nothing innovative about B&J's products and the company had no sales staff because it relied on networking and word of mouth to build its clientele. When Thiessens launched B&J in 1971, he put up only $200 of his own money. In a bit of clever deal making, Thiessens persuaded one of his former employers to take on all the risk of financing B&J's initial equipment and property rental costs.

For most of his life, though, Thiessens harbored what he called "a little secret." The secret was that Thiessens was illiterate. Thanks to a few lenient teachers and a lot of vocational classes, he was handed a high school diploma in 1962 that he could not read. Over the ensuing years, he developed a kind of mental block about reading and, by the age of fifty-six, he still could not make his way through a children's book.

Like a lot of illiterate adults, Thiessens was very good at covering up his secret. He had an open and assertive demeanor, mainly because he couldn't function at work without getting help from his employees. "I could never handle a situation right as it happened," he told one interviewer. "I had to wait to act on it until the right people were around me." Most of his workers considered him a good listener with an excellent memory for details, so his aversion to reading and writing seemed to be a mere matter of personal style. They assumed he was too busy during the day to deal with paperwork, when in fact he carried business correspondence home with him each night so that his wife could read it to him in bed.

It was in 1998 that Thiessens finally shared his secret with his employees at a company retreat. Afterward, he found a reading tutor and went public with his news, in hopes of encouraging other adults faced with the same embarrassing problem. An Associated Press report spread Thiessens's story in newspapers all over the country, *People* magazine ran a pictorial, and he was even profiled on a cable television reality show called *Courage*. Most stories about Thiessens at the time remarked how he had built a profitable company with a 50-person payroll *in spite* of his inability to read. But it was also true that many of Thiessens's best management practices came about precisely because he could not read.

Thiessens, for instance, admitted to being something of a control freak by nature. His illiteracy forced him to let go and delegate more tasks to his managers and workers. The general manager at B&J recalled how "[Jay] would bring legal stuff to me and say, 'You're better at legalese than me.' I never knew I was the only one reading them." Thiessens also lightened his burden by instilling a strong culture of teamwork in the company. Various employee committees were used to resolve problems that otherwise would have been dumped on him. The resulting esprit de corps at B&J was so strong that when a flash flood filled the main plant with three feet of water, the employees pitched in and saved the company by working around the clock for four days disassembling and cleaning all the machinery.

Thiessens's story is an extreme example of a very commonly observed fact: A lot of entrepreneurs were poor students when they were young and had particular difficulties with reading and writing. A 2007 study concluded that about 35 percent of U.S. small-business owners suffer from some form of dyslexia, compared with about 10 percent of the general population and just 1 percent of corporate managers. Business professor Julie Logan, the author of the study, concluded that in order to overcome their learning deficits, successful dyslexics become proficient at getting help, which happens to be an absolutely crucial skill for anyone building a business.

"I know that sounds very strange," Logan told National Public Radio. "But one of the things that we found in the study is that people who have dyslexia, actually, at a very early age, learn how to get other people to do things for them. They learn how to delegate to compensate for their weaknesses. So they learn to trust other people to do things. This is a great advantage in business because if you start a business, you get good people around you and you delegate. You actually can keep your eye on where that business is going and be very strategic."

Logan's research showed that companies headed by dyslexic owners tend to grow twice as fast as other companies and that dyslexic owners are twice as likely as others to be running two or more companies at once. Presumably, the nondyslexic business owners fall behind because they can't resist the temptation to micromanage. As Logan explained, "The willingness to delegate authority gives [dyslexics] a significant advantage over non-dyslexic entrepreneurs, who tend to view their business as their baby and like to be in total control."

The most successful dyslexic entrepreneur in the United States is probably self-made billionaire Charles R. Schwab, founder of the brokerage company that bears his name. When Schwab was applying to colleges as a young man, he had miserable verbal SAT scores and was accepted at Stanford only because he was recruited for the golf team. Schwab did well in science and math during his freshman year, but he almost flunked out because he failed the same introductory English course twice. "It was a very debilitating, depressing thing for me to do that," Schwab recalls, "because I was thought of as pretty bright and I didn't realize how incompetent I was at the skill of writing." To get by, he charmed his teachers and leaned on other students for help. Even in science and math classes, he had to ask friends and roommates to take notes for him during lectures because he found it impossible to listen and write at the same time.

Business school was somewhat easier for Schwab, but he was still nowhere near the top of his class. He recalls jealously watching classmates get hired by Fortune 500 companies as "General Motors Scholars, Merit Scholars, Baker Scholars." Schwab decided to skip the corporate ladder, where reading and writing skills are essential, and took the entrepreneur route instead. He partnered with two friends from business school and the threesome started an investment newsletter that Schwab could neither edit nor even read very easily. "A lot of people who are brilliant entrepreneurs think they can do everything," he once observed. "They don't develop the team that they need to have in order to accomplish the various levels you're going to reach in your growth curve as a successful company." Schwab never had a problem developing teams with skills that complemented his own. He'd been doing that out of necessity since he was eighteen. His team-building abilities helped make him a billionaire several times over, and he has far surpassed the career achievements of his more bookish business school classmates.

The Business Brilliant survey reveals that the desire to delegate tasks is found most commonly among those who have had the most financial success. Nearly 9 out of 10 self-made millionaires said that when it comes to tasks they are *not exceptionally* good at, they are very likely to delegate those tasks to people who do them better. By contrast, among the middle-class respondents, two-thirds said that when faced with such tasks, they would likely "do those tasks anyway." This approach is often a mistake that you can end up paying for twice. The final result is probably not as good as it could have been, and even if it is, you've expended time and energy that would have been better spent on the things you do well. Self-made millionaires—and dyslexics—seem to know this better than most members of the middle class.

Chapter 5 described how Paul Orfalea, founder and CEO of Kinko's Copies, improved the service levels at his stores by studying and imitating McDonald's and other companies he admired. At the root of Orfalea's penchant for borrowing bright ideas was his extremely debilitating dyslexia. Orfalea's office at Kinko's had no computer and was almost completely devoid of paper. He reviewed his mail with his assistants each day and gave them verbal suggestions about how they should respond in his name. Then he'd race out the door and go visit some stores. "Anybody can sit around an office thinking about what people were doing wrong," he wrote in his autobiography. "My job was to get out and find out what people were doing right—and exploit it. Then I tried to spread those practices throughout the Kinko's network."

Orfalea squeaked through college at the University of Southern California the same way Schwab survived Stanford—by getting other people to take lecture notes and rewrite his papers for him. When assigned to a big group project, Orfalea proposed that if the other group members would do all the writing, he would do all the duplicating the project required. Ironically, his visits to the university's copy center for that project inspired him to open up a retail copy shop of his own. As he expanded Kinko's from the one shop to 800 all over the United States and Europe, Orfalea claimed he managed his time by repeating the mantra, "Anybody else can do it better." Looking back, he says that "every major success I've had in my life has come about because I knew that somebody, often anybody . . . could do something better than me."

After selling his interest in Kinko's for hundreds of millions of dollars and leaving the company in 2000, Orfalea started teaching an unusual economics course at the University of California at Santa Barbara.

Naturally, he gave infrequent writing assignments and limited them to a single page in length. Discussions in class were punctuated by exercises in which Orfalea would sometimes pick out a male student at random and challenge him to ask one of the young women in the class for a date—right there in front of everyone. "They get a chance to learn to talk to each other," Orfalea explained. "They get to see someone asking for something he wants or needs from another person. Sometimes that's all we need to do in life."

When Kinko's expanded to Great Britain during the 1990s, Orfalea found a business partner and kindred spirit in the eccentric businessman-adventurer Richard Branson, another amazingly successful dyslexic. Sir Richard (he was knighted in 2000) may be the richest high school dropout in history. With the Virgin Group, he has built a vast business empire in which responsibilities are delegated on a uniquely grand scale, if only to accommodate the contours of Branson's dyslexic brain.

Throughout his upbringing in British boarding schools, Branson was physically beaten by headmasters who assumed he was either too stupid or too lazy to complete his assignments. In 1967, at age sixteen, he started up a magazine for London-area college students. Like Schwab, he couldn't edit or read the publication he was running, but he excelled at selling advertising, usually from a pay phone at his boarding school dormitory. When Branson quit school for good that year, his headmaster predicted that he would either end up in prison or become a millionaire.

Today Branson's wealth is estimated at $4.2 billion thanks to the hundreds of products and services bearing the Virgin brand name, including Virgin Atlantic Airways, Virgin Megastores, Virgin Hotels, Virgin Mobile phones, Virgin Money, and even Virgin wine. Virgin has become one of the best-known brand names in the world, even though Branson freely admits he's not good at details. He is now in his sixties and hasn't held day-to-day responsibilities in any business since he was a teenager. He's never even learned how to read a financial spreadsheet. Once, at a board meeting, Sir Richard kept mixing up the terms "net revenue" and "gross revenue" until a staff member took him aside and drew a picture of a net catching fish to illustrate the difference for him.

If Virgin were organized like Procter and Gamble or any other large, diversified corporation, Branson would be hopelessly lost as CEO. But Virgin Group's modus operandi is the ultimate in delegated responsibility. Every one of its 200 or so product lines is a separate stand-alone corporation, controlled by Virgin but run by a team of entrepreneurs who hold significant equity stakes. Branson has explained that he never wanted Virgin to have "a vast head office and a pyramid of command from a central board of directors. I am not saying that such a structure is wrong. . . . It is just that my mind doesn't work like that."

Freed from poring over spreadsheets and five-year strategic plans, Branson has promoted Virgin's renegade image through headline-grabbing stunts such as around-the-world balloon flights and a record-setting Atlantic Ocean crossing in a powerboat. To publicize the U.S. introduction of Virgin Cola, he showed up in Times Square astride an army tank. Although Virgin has suffered a good number of failures (Virgin Cola and Virgin Money both flopped in the United States) the Virgin brand remains so appealing to investors that the Virgin Group can often launch a new company with zero risk on its books. According to one report, Virgin Money was financed in Britain with $500 million worth of investor cash, while "Virgin retained a 50 percent stake without coughing up a penny."

Branson is likely to pass on any proposal that fails to excite him right away. He's well known for sizing up people and ideas within 30 seconds of being introduced to them. "I rely far more on gut instinct than researching huge amounts of statistics," he wrote in his book *Losing My Virginity*. "This might be because, due to my dyslexia, I distrust numbers, which I feel can be twisted to prove anything." He once told *60 Minutes*, "If I could read a balance sheet . . . I wouldn't have done anything in life."

What excites Branson most is the chance to play David against industry-dominating Goliaths. He looks for companies willing to go up against what he calls "a big bad wolf" that has been overcharging and underserving the public. Whether the wolf is British Airways or Barclays bank, Virgin's simple formula is to steal a small, profitable piece of the market by offering better service at a lower cost and with a sense of style and fun.

By those criteria, Branson has boasted that there is no limit to how far the Virgin brand name can be extended. Already you can zip through London's traffic gridlock on the back of a taxi-motorcycle called Virgin Limobike, or you can put down a 10 percent deposit on a $200,000 Virgin Galactic spaceship ride (blastoff date as yet unknown). Rock star Peter Gabriel once joked with Branson that Virgin should offer total cradle-to-grave services, beginning with Virgin Births and ending with Virgin Funerals. Branson's response, in under 30 seconds, was that he wasn't sure about Virgin Funerals, but he rather liked the sound of Virgin Births.

➤ The Strength Test

If a reading disability, or any disability, might be considered a gift, it's because some disabled people learn to accept their personal limitations at a young age. They give up trying to fix their weak points and instead they seek opportunities to show what they do best. By the time he was twenty-two, Paul Orfalea had already accepted that he would have to start a business of his own because he knew he was a miserably inept employee. Charles Schwab has noted, "I've been able, I think, to recognize my strengths and my deficits. . . . I think that probably has been the single most important benefit I received from having this learning issue early on in my life."

There is a great deal of common sense in focusing on your strengths and getting others to cover your weaknesses. But common sense doesn't always make for common practice. Most people say they feel a much greater pull to mend their weak spots before they develop their strengths. A Gallup poll found that 87 percent of working Americans agreed with the question "Is finding your weaknesses and fixing them the best way to achieve outstanding performance?" When asked to choose between building on their strengths and fixing their weaknesses, 59 percent preferred to fix their weaknesses.

The Business Brilliant survey shows similar results, but mainly among the middle class. About 7 out of 10 middle-class survey respondents said that when it comes to tasks they are not exceptionally good at, their most likely response is to "work hard to get good at those tasks." Among self-made millionaires, just 2 percent said the same. A sizable minority of the middle class, about 4 in 10, also agreed that "I try new, unfamiliar activities in order to expand my capabilities." Fewer than 1 in 10 self-made millionaires said they were interested in attempting the unfamiliar. If they're not exceptionally good at something already, the millionaires would rather not start learning now.

For more than a decade, Marcus Buckingham at the Gallup Organization studied how people choose to work with their strengths and weaknesses. He thinks that the oversized concern with weakness is rooted in the way we're raised and how we're taught in school. When Gallup asked parents how they would react if a child brought home a report card with an F in algebra and A's in English and social studies, 77 percent of the parents said they would spend the most time talking to the child about the F, not the A's. Buckingham asked in *Now, Discover Your Strengths*, "Despite the demands of today's education system, does the most time really deserve to be invested in the child's weakness?" The schools also devote more time and attention to weaknesses. A child with this report card is far more likely to get remedial help with algebra than special enrichment classes in English and social studies.

Gallup has uncovered a number of common and potentially destructive myths about the relative importance of workplace strengths and weaknesses. For instance, 61 percent of workers say they need to focus on their weaknesses because that's where they feel they have the most room to grow. In follow-up interviews, they said that shoring up their weak areas makes them feel more responsible, more well rounded, and less vulnerable to embarrassment and risk of failure. What's missing from this equation is any desire to attain expertise, excellence, or mastery—capabilities that produce real value in the workplace and are only achieved by working from your strengths. And, as Buckingham points out, working from your strengths is always a more meaningful and rewarding experience, because "you will be the most inquisitive, most resilient, most creative and most open to learning in your areas of strength."

In previous chapters we explored any number of beliefs about financial success that give self-made millionaires a decided edge over the middle class. This difference in attitudes toward strengths and weaknesses may be the most important edge of all. Each day, middle-class employees dutifully take up certain tasks that require them to engage their weaknesses. They feel conscientious about working with their weaknesses, and hope that the practice will shield them from future reproach and failure. Meanwhile, self-made millionaires are spending each day *avoiding* their weaknesses in order to stay focused on their strengths—where distinction, fulfillment, and profits are found. Hour by hour, day by day, the middle-class people protect themselves by becoming more well-rounded and ordinary, while the millionaires enrich themselves by becoming more specialized and extraordinary.

To be fair, self-made millionaires probably have more opportunities to delegate responsibilities in their weak areas, since 9 out of 10 respondents are business owners who call their own shots. By contrast, 3 out of 4 middle-class respondents are employed by someone else. They probably have job duties that are not so easily handed off to others. But is that really true? Buckingham has a commonsense prescription for becoming more strengths-oriented at work: He advises that you have a "strong conversation" with your boss about your job responsibilities. Give your immediate supervisor a proposal detailing how it would help the company if you worked at your strengths more often and had some other duties reassigned. Most people have never done such a thing and I suspect most are afraid to try. As chapter 6 showed, most workers are a lot like Adam

McKay at *Saturday Night Live* before he talked to his manager. They don't recognize when they have the boss over a barrel. And even if they did recognize it, they would be reluctant to exploit the advantage.

But before you can even consider requesting a change in duties at work, it's important to know what your strengths really are. (A strength, according to Buckingham, can be simply defined as something that makes you feel strong when you're doing it.) Self-made millionaires are more certain about their strengths than the middle class. Among self-made millionaires, 85 percent said that "I know what I'm exceptionally good at that makes money." Just a little over half of middle-class survey respondents said the same. What's more, the millionaires' strengths have been battle hardened through painful trial and error. About 7 in 10 self-made millionaires agreed that "Setbacks and failures have taught me what I'm good at." Fewer than 2 out of 10 in the middle class agreed.

Norm Brodsky was pretty sure he knew his strengths back in 1987. In eight short years he had taken Perfect Courier, his New York–based messaging and trucking company, from zero to $120 million in yearly sales. Growing the company that fast required Brodsky to put a lot of faith in his own judgment. Other people's ideas didn't appeal to him, because no one knew his business better than him. Whenever something went wrong, he relied on his own ingenuity to devise rules that would prevent it from ever happening again. As the company grew, Brodsky rewarded his most loyal employees with promotions, sometimes giving them roles they weren't fully qualified to fill. And it all worked. Perfect Courier was one of the fastest-growing small businesses in the country. Brodsky took on debt and started buying other companies, hoping to spread his Midas touch.

Then, on October 19, 1987, stock markets crashed all around the world. The Dow lost 22 percent of its value in a single day, and Perfect Courier got hurt in the fallout. Wall Street's financial printing business dried up overnight, costing one division of Perfect Courier almost all its revenue and putting the whole company in a cash squeeze. Then Perfect Courier's banks, spooked by the financial collapse, called in their loans, demanding cash that Perfect Courier didn't have. Perfect Courier had to file for bankruptcy and pare itself down to almost nothing. Even Brodsky's personal checking account was seized. Everything he had built over eight years unraveled in the space of just a few months.

"The shock of firing four thousand people was overwhelming to me," Brodsky recalls now. "That was the first time I really sat down and asked myself what went wrong." Besides the crash and the called-in loans, there were other causes beyond Brodsky's control. Competition in the messaging business had doubled in recent years, putting pressure on prices. And newly affordable fax machines, regarded as "electronic wonders" by *Time* magazine in August 1987, had begun to take a huge bite out of the demand for delivery services.

But Brodsky decided that it wasn't enough to blame the crash, the banks, the competition, and the fax machine. "There was a whole bunch of processes that I could have used to stop those four things from destroying the company," Brodsky says. "There were a number of decisions I made that were really bad decisions." Foremost among them was that he didn't listen. The same self-confidence that enabled Brodsky to take Perfect Courier so far also proved to be his downfall. "When things started falling apart, my advisers, my lawyer, my accountant, they all said to me, 'Look, there's a way to save this. You better look at this method, or that method.' They told me a whole bunch of things. And I said, 'No, no, no. I can save this company.' This [crash] is b.s., I told them. This is temporary. I created a god like atmosphere around myself."

Brodsky didn't recognize the soundness of the advice he'd been offered until after Perfect Courier had collapsed into bankruptcy. If he had listened to his lawyers and accountants sooner, the fall might not have been so hard. "Sure I would've been hit," he says. "I would have lost 30 percent of my sales, but I would have survived. Instead I thought that only I could save the company, that I was invincible, that nothing bad could ever happen to me."

Since then, Brodsky has become a small-business guru and sage, mentoring and guiding young entrepreneurs on the subject of wise business management. He is a columnist for *Inc.* magazine and wrote a book called *Street Smarts: An All-Purpose Tool Kit for Entrepreneurs.* The bankruptcy of Perfect Courier is something he wears as a badge of honor now. It was an experience that taught him lessons he could not have learned any other way. His chief observation is that most people go wrong by trying to do all the work themselves and blaming bad results on others. The trick, he says, is to do the exact opposite. Trust others to do the work for you, but keep all the blame and responsibility for yourself.

As he picked up the pieces of his broken company, Brodsky managed his shrunken staff in a very different way. He realized that he'd been promoting loyal employees beyond their capabilities because he wanted people around him who would do what he said. That's not what he needed to pull Perfect Courier out of bankruptcy. Instead, he hired extremely capable people who could work without his direct instruction. These were people who could contribute to the company in ways that complemented Brodsky's own strengths. For the first time, Brodsky stopped trying to control his employees. He allowed himself to learn from them.

"When I walk into a meeting with a yellow pad," he says, "I open it to the middle and I write down three words: 'stupid stupid stupid.' I do that to remind myself that maybe I'm not the smartest person in the room. And to remind myself that even the least-smart person in the room may still have a really good idea." Without that kind of disciplined humility, a lot of managers and business owners are so busy acting in command that they shut down their employees' ideas and observations.

Brodsky illustrates the point by telling how Perfect Courier got started in the document-storage business. After declaring bankruptcy, Brodsky decided to rebuild with a culture of listening—listening to customers and listening to each other. A key part of that culture was a commitment to never say "no" to anyone. So when someone called to ask if Perfect Courier was able to store boxes of documents, she didn't hear "no," even though that was the truthful answer. Instead, the Perfect

Courier employee took down her information and promised to get back to her. Then he passed along the information to Brodsky.

The inquiry made Brodsky curious. He made some calls, pretending to be someone who needed a place to store boxes of documents. Brodsky discovered that the big local players in the storage industry offered lousy service at exorbitant prices. In Richard Branson's terms, they were the "big bad wolves" that signified opportunity. Brodsky also discovered that the market was growing. Manhattan law firms and other corporations desperately needed low-cost locations where their documents could be reliably stored and retrieved on a day's notice. Brodsky envisioned his courier drivers zipping back and forth with document boxes between Manhattan's office towers and some cheap warehouse space across the East River in Queens.

"From that call grew a business that I just sold for $110 million," Brodsky says. "Here was a customer service guy earning a few hundred bucks a week. He's not the smartest guy in the room, but if you trust him to do what's right and follow through, you can build a whole business around it."

There are certain inevitable risks involved in delegating, which is why so many people shy away from it. The most obvious issue is that when someone takes a task off your hands, that task will not be done the way you would have done it. Delegating responsibility involves trust and acceptance. You need to trust that the task will be handled well and you also need to accept that sometimes it won't.

The reluctance to delegate can have deep psychological roots. In his book, *The Decision to Trust*, Fordham University professor Robert F. Hurley tells of his consulting experience with a brilliant and talented senior executive whose inability to trust his subordinates ended up ruining his career. The executive was a well-known control freak. He wouldn't allow even his most reliable employees to proceed on a project without his approval at each stage. Projects slowed to a crawl as a result, but the executive responded angrily to any suggestion that he needed to give his people more running room.

A "contagion of distrust and anxiety" spread throughout the executive's business unit, Hurley writes. The employees felt so controlled and devalued that they stopped trying to contribute creative ideas. The unit's financial results began to lag, and Hurley was brought in as a consultant. Over time, Hurley learned that the executive's upbringing had made him a miserably insecure individual. Life had been tough on the man's parents, so they taught their son that the world is a threatening place in which even the smallest error can hurt you badly. He became a perfectionist with a pathological fear of failure and embarrassment, which helped propel his career, but only so far. In this new, high-level position, his fear of failure only guaranteed that he would fail. He could not learn how to delegate responsibility to his employees and he suffered a humiliating demotion as a result. In psychological terms, the executive's emotional "low adjustment," which had nothing to do with his intelligence or competence, made it impossible for him to be an effective leader.

Any time you delegate a task to an employee, a contractor, or a freelancer, it takes a certain level of emotional maturity to accept that they will make mistakes, including some dumb mistakes that you feel certain you never would have made yourself. Brodsky points out that if you really want your employees to learn and grow, you have to let them try things that you *know* will fail. Brodsky recalls approving a promotional program that offered free introductory rates, "even though I know that giving away stuff for free never works." Unless an idea threatens to do real damage to the company, Brodsky is willing to let his employees try it, regardless of what he thinks. The alternatives, he says, are to try to do every job by yourself, or lay down a lot of rules about how things are done. Either way, you will put a stifling, self-defeating limit on your company's ability to grow.

Inevitably, though, one or another employee will abuse the freedom you give them. They will betray your trust. You need to keep your eyes open, Brodsky says, but you can't respond to one person's betrayal by tightening the reins on everyone. He says, "When somebody is stealing from your company—and it happens to all of us—if you develop mistrust and decide to trust nobody as a result, that's the death knell for growth." And if you're not growing, then you're not really in business. Once you choose to put growth and opportunity in the backseat behind security and control, you're just following your worst, most fearful instincts—instead of following the money.

➤ The Retirement Trick

Norm Brodsky didn't spend much time at home once he launched Perfect Courier in 1979. When the company was young and understaffed, Brodsky really did try to do everything himself. He wore a beeper that went off at all hours of the night and sometimes he even filled in for absent delivery drivers. Later, as the company grew and staffed up, Brodsky got even busier bringing in new clients and acquiring other companies. Then came the long hours of wrangling with creditors through the bankruptcy, followed by building Perfect Courier from the ground up all over again. He never complained about the hours he put in. "I don't consider what I'm doing to be work," he'd say. "Mowing the lawn—that's work." But Brodsky's absence was a big problem for his family. In 1988, his wife, Elaine, wrote a magazine article called "Confessions of a Woman Married to a Man Married to His Business."

Self-made millionaires work much longer hours than the middle class. This is true especially of millionaires in the $1 million to $10 million range of net worth. According to the Business Brilliant survey, this particular group averages 65 hours per week, compared with just 42 hours for the middle class. (The longest hours—70 per week—were reported by female millionaires in the $1 to $10 million group.) Their exact purpose for working so many hours, however, is not entirely clear. More than 8 out of 10 say that "the results I achieve are more important than the number of hours I work," but 7 out of 10 also say "the number of hours I work is a critical factor to becoming wealthy." So results are more important than hours worked, they say, but long hours are extremely important anyway.

The richest survey respondents polled in the Business Brilliant survey were a little more consistent in their thinking. These people, with net worths exceeding $30 million, work 57 hours per week on average, and yet only 3 out of 10 say that long hours are critical to becoming wealthy. They work 12 more hours per week than the middle class not because they need to. They want to.

These figures point to something Harvard business professor Thomas J. DeLong has called "The Paradox of Excellence." High-performing businesspeople have a tendency to lock themselves into routines on their path to success. They are so driven and motivated that, as their responsibilities expand, they keep taking on more tasks related to whatever made them successful in the first place. An article DeLong co-authored with his daughter, a psychotherapist, states that "When [executives] find themselves in over their head they're often unwilling to admit it, even to themselves, and refuse to ask for the help they need." They are often guilt ridden and fear failure, so they seek satisfaction doing what they know. They keep the pace even when their activities aren't the best use of their time, even when their activities exhaust and overwhelm them.

So the hours pile up. You start out following the money as a sole proprietor or with a small business on the side and you grow accustomed to the long workdays because that's what it takes in the early phase of any business. Then, as you add employees to help deal with growth, you continue doing all the things that attracted you to the business in the first place. If you do things right, or if you're lucky, you soon find you've got too much to deal with. That's the inevitable price of success. Recall the story of guitar teacher Paul Green, in chapter 5, complaining to his dentist how he was running himself ragged, trying to operate two School of Rock locations at once. Green had reached something business coach Dan Sullivan calls a "ceiling of complexity." Once you hit that ceiling, no amount of additional hours or diligence will produce better results. You need to spread the workload. Otherwise, you either run in place forever or you burn out and fail.

Self-made millionaires allow their long work hours to spill over into evenings and weekends, and most say they prefer it that way. More than 8 out of 10 said "I would rather have control over my time (able to participate in personal matters during the day) even if it means I have to work longer hours and work nights and weekends." The middle class, by contrast, would rather punch the weekday time clock. About 2 out of 3 said "I would rather work only during business hours even if it means I don't have any control over my time during those hours."

Taken at face value, these results suggest that most of the middle class don't care to put in the long hours necessary for financial success. But Dan Sullivan says that long hours are a symptom of wealth, not the cause of it. Sullivan's company, Strategic Coach, is one of the world's premier small-business training programs. It promotes the idea that business owners hurt themselves and put their companies at risk by working long, exhausting hours. The one constant in business these days is change, Sullivan points out. The businesspeople who most often fail to adapt to changes in their markets are the ones who tie themselves down to a punishing daily work schedule. To use a sturdy cliché, they can't see the forest for the trees.

Coaches at Sullivan's company encourage business owners to delegate everything involving day-to-day operations so they can free themselves to set strategy and deal with tasks that have a longer-term impact. Sullivan actually advocates that owners set aside 150 days a year for "free time" away from the office, which prompted one business magazine to call him "the nation's most successful *demotivational* speaker." But Sullivan drinks his own Kool-Aid. He is absent from work and unreachable by phone or e-mail for the equivalent of five months of the year. By doing that, he has built Strategic Coach into a $20 million company with offices in Chicago, Toronto, and London.

Executive coaching has become a billion-dollar industry in the past decade, precisely due to the issues raised by DeLong and his "Paradox of Excellence." It's not a coincidence that the field is exploding just as smartphones and other technologies make the drift into work addiction more seductive than ever. Most new clients of Strategic Coach say they are incapable of spending even a single day without phoning, texting, or e-mailing the office.

Evidence of that level of work addiction is apparent in the Business Brilliant survey. Even the members of the over–$30 million group—people who presumably have vast abilities to delegate responsibilities—are hooked on work. Only 2 out of 10 say "I know how to detach from work and rest or relax." And although 9 out of 10 say "I am interested and excited by what I do at work," 8 out of 10 also agree that "I find work stressful and not enjoyable." Why do they continue to do stressful and unenjoyable work? Partly because 8 out of 10 also believe their work habits are responsible for making them successful. They expressed a stronger faith in the importance of their work habits than any other group we surveyed. Even among the millionaire strivers, the $1 to $10 million group, less than half said their work habits are responsible for their success.

Obsessive work habits might not be such a big problem if working hours were devoted to strategy and taking in the bigger picture. But among all self-made millionaires, 8 out of 10 say they spend "a lot of time putting out 'fires.'" Among those with wealth exceeding $30 million, it's almost 9 out of 10. Think about that for a moment. The people with the greatest resources, who are best able to hand over emergency-response duties to others, are also the ones most likely to be dealing with emergencies themselves.

In executives, this "putting out fires" approach to work is often accompanied by an anxious, distracted leadership style, something psychiatrist Edward Hallowell has dubbed "Attention Deficit Trait." Hallowell discovered ADT while treating executives who came to him complaining that they might have attention deficit *disorder*. Hallowell noticed that these executives showed typical symptoms of ADD in their inability to focus their thoughts, but that the symptoms disappeared during their vacations, which would not be the case if they truly suffered from attention deficit disorder. Hallowell, writing in the *Harvard Business Review*, says that ADT leads to impatient, underperforming executives who have difficulty staying organized, setting priorities, and managing their time. "Executives with ADT do whatever they can to handle a load they simply cannot manage as well as they'd like," he writes. "[They feel] a constant low level of panic and guilt. Facing a tidal wave of tasks, the executive becomes increasingly hurried, curt, peremptory, and unfocused, while pretending that everything is fine." Some suggest that the housing bubble and the world financial crisis were exacerbated by, or even precipitated by, thousands of high-level executives functioning in this frenzied, survival mode of thinking.

A dozen years ago, Stan Doobin was one of those executives. By dint of hard work and long hours, he had grown his office-cleaning company, Harvard Maintenance, from a tiny outfit in Midtown Manhattan to a $90-million-a-year business with operations in three states. Just like Norm Brodsky, Doobin had started out as the smartest and best-educated person in his company. He was an accountant with an MBA, so he felt he needed to stay on top of all of the company's day-to-day operations. He proudly gave clients 24-hour access to his phone number, and since office cleaning takes place at night, Doobin was regularly awakened by emergencies. He was working 14-hour days, seven days a week, when a colleague recommended that he sign up with Strategic Coach. As Doobin recalls, "He noticed I was a workaholic and that something had to change."

It didn't take long for Doobin to realize where he'd gone wrong. "I was trying to do everything," he says. "I thought I could do every task better and that it was faster for me to do it myself than train and trust others to do it." He recognized also that his company was big enough that he could start cutting back his hours by delegating all the tasks he didn't enjoy. "I stink at the operational aspects of my business," Doobin says. "But there are tons of people who are passionate for it. They can do a much better job than me at a fraction of the time."

This chapter opened by discussing the commonsense idea of delegating tasks that you're not good at. But Doobin's workdays really opened up when he let go of tasks that, although he *could* do them very well, he recognized that he shouldn't be doing them at all. "There are activities that you have no passion for and are excellent at, that you are just wasting your time on," he says. For Doobin the accountant, this describes his oversight of the company's nitty-gritty financial details. He has learned over time to pull farther and farther back, and now, he says, "I couldn't even begin to tell you about the functions of the computer system. I have no clue."

As much as he can, Doobin tries to limit his involvement in Harvard Maintenance to the few things he has a passion for, because those are the things that give him energy, make him most productive, and also yield the best results for the company. He estimates he spends up to half his time recruiting new executives, wining and dining clients, and looking for new prospective clients. He went on an African safari with his son and had no contact with his office for two solid weeks. "Your staff is happier when you're not there," he says. "They actually do a better job if you're not meddling in functions you have no passion for." In the 12 years since Doobin started working fewer hours and moved away from day-to-day operations, Harvard Maintenance has expanded to 35 states and tripled its revenue, to $270 million.

Most self-made millionaires tell us that early retirement is not one of their goals. Only about 2 in 10 see retirement as their reason for becoming wealthy (compared with about two-thirds of the middle class). At Strategic Coach, they know this about their clients, so they schedule an exercise called the Retirement Trick. Business owners are asked to try to envision what retirement for them might look like, if they were able to perform only those tasks in their companies that they absolutely enjoyed the most. The exercise pries their minds away from any assumptions they have about onerous daily responsibilities. It prompts them instead to identify their absolutely rarest and most valuable abilities. Many realize they wouldn't go to staff meetings anymore, or would hardly ever show up at the office. One insurance executive was so inspired by the exercise that he started up an outdoor excursion company, just so he could spend more time hunting and fishing. For high-achieving people, the ultimate reward for great success is not the idleness of retirement. The reward is doing more of the productive things that they love the most, which, as with Doobin, often turns out to make the most financial sense anyway.

By now this book has come full circle. It started with "Do what you love but follow the money," and now it becomes clear that the grand prize for following the money extremely well is the rarefied privilege of doing only what you love. All the synergies of following the money that were outlined in chapter 1—looking for equity, maximizing your earnings, copying what works, making friends, making deals, and getting help— can add up to an incredible level of personal and creative freedom, but only if you take up this last, crucial step of sharing the workload. Otherwise, the achievement of wealth can amount to a life sentence of work addiction, a treadmill for stamping out fires.

There may only be one big question remaining. Often, although you may think you've done all the right things to follow the money, the payoff isn't there. Synergistic systems are like that. By definition they produce unpredictable results of *all* kinds. This means that sometimes they won't give you what you're looking for. Sometimes they give you something even worse. Sometimes they fail.

What then?

8

Nothing Succeeds Like Failure

ABOUT 7 IN 10 SELF-MADE MILLIONAIRES SAID THAT "SETBACKS AND FAILURES HAVE TAUGHT ME WHAT I'M GOOD AT."

FEWER THAN 2 OUT OF 10 IN THE MIDDLE CLASS AGREED.

➤ The Valentine's Day Massacre

An enormous snowstorm was making its way toward the East Coast on Valentine's Day 2007 when David Neeleman, the founder and CEO of JetBlue Airlines, made a series of decisions that would eventually cost him his job.

Dozens of JetBlue flights were scheduled to leave that day from JFK airport in New York. Other airlines operating out of JFK responded to predictions of heavy snow and freezing rain by canceling all their morning flights. Neeleman and his colleagues, on the other hand, chose to count on a forecast that temperatures might rise and turn the snow to rain by the time the storm hit New York. They kept JetBlue's planes on schedule.

In the early morning hours of Wednesday, February 14, nine fully loaded JetBlue flights taxied away from the terminals, headed for sunny destinations like Cancun and Aruba. But as the giant storm settled over New York, the precipitation turned to sleet instead of rain. Federal rules forbid takeoffs in freezing-rain conditions, so the planes had to sit and wait for the storm to let up. "We were just minutes away from taking off and the ice pellets started," Neeleman would later tell CNBC. "We waited and expected it to clear up, and waited. And then things kind of spiraled out of control."

As the nine planes awaited takeoff, other JetBlue flights continued to arrive at JFK, filling all the gates at JetBlue's terminal. Hours later, when JetBlue officials finally determined that the delayed flights had to be canceled and called back, there were no empty spaces at the terminal so the passengers could disembark. The entire JetBlue operation became gridlocked. Finally, at 3 p.m., shuttle buses were sent out to retrieve the passengers from the nine stranded aircraft.

Some travelers were trapped inside JetBlue's planes for as long as nine hours that day. Back at the terminal, they plied the media with tales of testy flight crews, overheated cabins, stinking toilets, and rationed food and water. One passenger had to tear up a T-shirt to make an improvised diaper for her baby. Another told the *New York Post*, "It was like—what's the name of that prison in Vietnam where they held [Senator John] McCain? The Hanoi Hilton." A *Post* headline trumpeted "Air Refugees in New JFKaos; Hordes Camp Overnight before JetBlue Says, 'Tough Luck, No Flights.'"

Neeleman had founded JetBlue in 1999 with the bold declaration that he would "bring humanity back to air travel" and for years the company had been ranked at the top in the industry for consumer satisfaction. Now JetBlue was being accused of creating conditions that one passenger complained were "right on the edge of human rights violations." Neeleman humbled himself by posting a video apology on YouTube in which he appeared to choke up. "We love our customers and we're horrified by this," he told an interviewer. Neeleman tried to reassure travelers that JetBlue flights would all be back on schedule before the weekend, but he was promising more than his company could deliver.

For the next six days, JetBlue had to cancel 1,200 flights all over the country. At first, the problem was that too many of JetBlue's planes were grounded in New York. But then the airline's operation faced new complications. The first round of cancellations had put many of JetBlue's flight crews out of position. The airline had too many planes at some airports, like JFK, and not enough crews to fly them. In other places, crews were sitting in hotel rooms awaiting instructions for when they'd get a plane to fly.

JetBlue had managed to make profits on its low fares through a philosophy of operating cheaply in ways that didn't show. Customers enjoyed the experience of bargain-priced luxury with leather seats, ample legroom, satellite radio, and satellite television screens in each seatback. But the carrier had neglected to upgrade many of its vital internal systems as it grew from 1 million passengers in 2000 to 18 million in 2006. JetBlue was still something of a shoestring operation when, on Valentine's Day 2007, the shoestring snapped.

For instance, the airline had no system in place to call ticket holders and tell them their flights had been canceled, so thousands of travelers showed up at JFK on the day of the big storm with no place to go. JetBlue's underpowered phone system was quickly overwhelmed by the volume of calls, and since the airline also had no computer software to track its 11,000 pilots and crew members, out-of-position employees calling in for instructions were subjected to the same hours-long busy signals as JetBlue ticket holders. Luggage handling wasn't computerized either, and bags from all the canceled and arriving flights at JFK piled up to the ceilings while being sorted slowly by hand. The entire debacle cost JetBlue $44 million and became known inside the company as the "Valentine's Day Massacre."

In the days following the storm, Neeleman responded by announcing a hastily drawn up program called JetBlue's Customer Bill of Rights. All JetBlue passengers now delayed for more than 30 minutes would get credits starting at $25 and those delayed longer than two hours would get free tickets for future flights. As a public relations gesture, it worked beautifully, and JetBlue's loyal customers were again filling its planes within the following week. But Wall Street was dubious about the potential cost of compensating passengers for future delays beyond the airline's control. The Bill of Rights seemed like an ill-considered plan that reflected the same seat-of-the-pants style that got Neeleman into trouble in the first place. JetBlue's stock price took a big hit that week and has never recovered. One day in May 2007, two of Neeleman's most trusted board members walked into his office and told him the board had decided to transfer his duties to JetBlue's chief operating officer.

The firing marked the third time Neeleman had been booted from a job in the travel industry. The first business he launched, at age twenty-three, was a travel agency that was forced to shut down in 1983 when one of its main customers declared bankruptcy. In 1994, after he'd helped found a small airline that was sold to Southwest Airlines, Neeleman took a job as a Southwest vice president, only to be fired five months later. Neeleman had to wait five years for the no-compete clause in his Southwest contract to expire before starting up JetBlue in 1999, where he held the CEO position until his firing in 2007.

So, after three crash landings in the air travel business, where is Neeleman today at age fifty-three? He's the founder and CEO of yet another new airline, a Brazilian domestic carrier called Azul.

In Brazil, Neeleman has pointed out, it doesn't snow.

➤ The Fruits of Failure

All the people profiled in this book have faced serious disappointments and setbacks in their careers, but the experience of failure is a key ingredient to developing Business Brilliance. David Neeleman is a self-made multimillionaire, but in the course of making those millions he also became an expert on how failure can provide the seeds for your next success. Neeleman points out that JetBlue, the nation's eighth-largest domestic airline, wouldn't even exist today if he hadn't failed so badly as a Southwest vice president. Failure is not really about what happens to you, he once said. "It's how you deal with it, and what you make of it."

Neeleman is hardly unique in the way he's partly paved his road to wealth with some shattering failures. The Business Brilliant surveys show that most self-made millionaires have had at least three serious setbacks or business failures in their careers. About one-fifth had four or more and one respondent reported having six. The middle-class failure rate, by contrast, averages just under two, which means that for most middle-class people, failure is something they have experienced either never or just once.

It may sound strange, but if you want to learn something useful about failure, go talk to the most successful person you know.

Every survey Russ Prince has done over the past 15 years tells the same story. The people who are the most brilliant at business are also those who fail most often along the way. As Warren Buffett might say, they succeed by surviving because Business Brilliance is a game of perseverance. It is not a game of averages, like high school or college, where failing 6 out of 7 tests always earns you an F. It's not like competitive sports, where a 1 for 7 average at anything will get you benched or cut from the team. In business you can fall short 6 times out of 7 and still enjoy great financial success. Marketing guru Seth Godin, himself the father of multiple business failures, puts it this way: "If I fail more often than you, I win. The ones who lose are the ones who don't fail at all and get stuck, or the ones who fail so big that they don't get to play again."

In my previous book, *The Influence of Affluence*, Russ Prince and I told the story of a self-made millionaire named Steve Dering who today is among the world's top experts in high-end vacation real estate. In the early 1990s, Dering left a career in marketing to pioneer the concept of "fractional" condominium ownership at a ski resort in Park City, Utah. By selling one-sixth shares of $750,000 condominium units for $130,000 each, he hoped to attract new, less-affluent populations of buyers and also net more money for condo developers. Fractional ownership of private jets had long been a profitable practice in aviation, so Dering was part imitator and part innovator in trying to apply the same concept to resort real estate.

Dering put together a development team, secured financing, and had sold $10 million worth of reservations for his first project when his Japanese funder bowed out due to a financial crisis in Asia. Even though the project went bust and Dering had to return all the deposits to disappointed buyers, his sales record encouraged him that he was onto something. So he tried again and partnered with another development team that already had a ski resort condominium under construction.

As Dering racked up sales for the new project, his partners realized they had him in a vulnerable spot. They kept renegotiating Dering's cut of the proceeds, and Dering kept giving in because he was desperate to prove the profitability of selling vacation real estate by the fraction. He sold all the units for a total of $22 million, which was $9 million more than the developers would have gotten if they had sold to individual owners. But Dering was left with little of the profit he had produced because his partners, as the party of least interest, had squeezed him until his equity was either gone or eaten up by expenses.

"They weren't purposely testing the courage of my convictions," Dering told us, "but that's how it turned out." The project left Dering nearly broke. His only way out was to find new partners and try again, and then again. By the end of the decade, his company DCP International was involved in dozens of fractional-ownership projects, some worth $100 million, all over North America and Europe.

Dering might not have pushed through all the frustration and disappointment he faced during his first years in real estate if he hadn't held fast to his convictions that setbacks are inevitable and that it pays to persevere. We've found that self-made millionaires hold absolutely consistent beliefs in this respect. About 9 out of 10 say that perseverance is very important to financial success and about 8 out of 10 agree that "failure is important to becoming wealthy." The middle class, however, is strangely divided on these two points. Their survey responses show that while 7 in 10 agree about the importance of perseverance, fewer than 2 in 10 believe in the importance of failure. The trouble with that line of thinking is that perseverance can't exist without failure. Who perseveres in the face of success?

The middle-class respondents said they lack faith in the value of failure and it shows up clearly in their actions. The survey results reveal that members of the middle class almost always respond to failure by quitting. More than half say they commonly react to a serious setback or failure "by giving up and focusing on other projects." Another 3 out of 10 say that they "try again, but in a different field," which, as we'll see later, is really the same thing as quitting. Self-made millionaires, on the other hand, react to failure just like Neeleman and Dering: They pick themselves up and take another run at whatever knocked them down. More than 8 out of 10 self-made millionaires said that their most common response to a serious setback or failure is to try once again in the exact same field. Just 1 out of 10 in the middle class says they share this same persistent "try, try again" response to failure.

We told Dering about these results and he was astonished by the middle-class response. If you don't go back and try the same thing after two or three failures, he explained, "then you don't get any of the benefits of learning from what went wrong." Dering certainly didn't count on his first real estate effort to go bust, but he always knew it was a possibility. By the time he'd gone through the painful experience of returning $10 million worth of deposits, though, he consoled himself with the hundreds of things he'd learned to do right through trial and error. He'd discovered the best ways to dig up prospects, he'd refined his sales pitch, and he'd figured out which amenities were most important to his buyers. By the end of his second project, Dering had also learned some new and painful lessons about partnership. But he'd reached his goal of bringing a fractional-ownership project to completion. He survived, if only barely, and then succeeded on his third and fourth tries.

Dering's story helps illustrate why self-made millionaires are so certain that failure is important and sometimes inevitable. You need to try things that are risk-prone and difficult because that's where the money is. Dering's series of stumbles was actually a testament to the untapped potential of fractional ownership. If it were risk free and easy to overcome buyer skepticism about the concept, other real estate agents would have jumped on fractional ownership years earlier. If securing financing for such an unusual project were a simple task, Dering wouldn't have needed to rely on his shaky funding from Japan. Selling one-sixth shares of condominium units is hard work because you need to dig up six times as many prospects, close six sales on each unit, and suffer through six times as many rejections and agonizing near-misses. The risks, the unknowns, and the difficulties were daunting enough to keep all other real estate people away, which is exactly why fractional ownership marked an opening and an opportunity for Dering.

Whatever line of work you're in, if you seek to follow the path of Business Brilliance you will suffer some setbacks and failures. That's because that path will present you with challenges that scare off most others in your field. Going where others fear to tread is what sets you apart. It confirms your unique value and ultimately can make you rich. Think of the frustrations that Guy Laliberté faced and the sacrifices he made while starting up his circus. Remember how Warren Buffett had to overcome his shyness and endure criticism and rejection in order to raise money for his first several partnerships. When Bill Gates met IBM's strict delivery date for MS-DOS after months of work, the software was so buggy that it had to be completely rewritten. How many maddening bug fixes did Gates and his team have to undertake before they handed over what they knew was a shoddy piece of work?

These periods of struggle, frustration, and failure amount to what Seth Godin calls "the Dip." He defines it as "the long slog between starting and mastery . . . the long stretch between beginner's luck and real accomplishment." It is the winnowing process that prevents all but the most tenacious from getting to the top of any field, which is where all the money is. "Successful people don't just ride out the Dip," Godin writes in *The Dip*. "They lean into it. They push harder, changing the rules as they go."

If you fail to appreciate this relationship between failure and success, you're likely to keep switching projects every time the going gets tough. A lot of hardworking and talented people make this mistake because it's only natural to feel like quitting when it starts to hurt. Again, in Godin's words, "Countless entrepreneurs have perfected the starting part but give up before paying their dues." Success, he says, belongs to the rare people who focus, who overcome the pain of failure and push through. "The Dip causes scarcity," he writes. "And scarcity creates value."

Chapter 4 touched on the way the media play up stories about companies with innovative "big ideas," even though the vast majority of highly successful businesses are imitators that execute on ordinary ideas. In a similar way, although the media love a good comeback story, most business stories focus on glowing successes that avoid the gritty details of setbacks and failures that have shadowed the growth of every successful enterprise. If the middle class doesn't believe that failure is important to success, part of the reason might be that the media rarely care to tell that story.

Successful companies aren't very keen to remind the public of their past failures, either. For instance, Pixar Animation currently reigns as the most successful movie studio in the entire history of motion pictures. Since the 1995 premiere of *Toy Story*, it has never had a box office flop. Every one of its dozen movies has earned a massive profit, and *Toy Story 3* grossed $1 billion worldwide. On the Pixar company website, the history of its dramatic rise is tracked on an interactive timeline. The release date and awards listings for every one of the company's movies are cataloged year by year, including a handful of very short computer-animated films made in the 1980s, some of which were only two minutes long.

What is missing from this timeline is the fact that when Pixar was founded, it was never meant to be a movie studio. Until 1991, Pixar was a computer hardware company that built huge, expensive 3-D imaging machines and marketed them with their special software to government, big business, and the healthcare and education industries. Feature film production came to Pixar by accident. Prior to 1988, the sole reason the company even employed an animation staff was to produce short promotional films that would help sell more computers.

Steve Jobs, the legendary cofounder of Apple Computer, had just been fired from Apple's CEO job in 1984 when he bought Pixar for $5 million. Jobs hoped to develop the $125,000 Pixar Imaging Computer into the must-have machine for the defense industry, oil companies, hospitals, and university research scientists. As one Pixar executive later recalled, "Steve's vision was that we were going to populate the world with Image Computers." When the company introduced 3-D software called RenderMan, Jobs wrote that "Rendering is extremely important now as we expect it to be a standard part of all computers in the next 12 to 24 months." He thought that every household would soon be putting out photorealistic 3-D images on their desktop inkjet printers.

To say Jobs miscalculated is an understatement. Not only was there little demand for RenderMan, but sales of the Pixar Imaging Computer slowly dropped away to almost nothing. Industries weren't ready to jump into something so expensive, new, and unproven, and that was especially true for the medical industry. Jobs thought 3-D imaging might replace two-dimensional CAT scans in hospitals, but radiologists preferred to stick with what they knew. Pixar started running out of money.

Until 1988, Pixar's animation team had never earned a dime for the company. The unit had made a series of short, clever movies with the sole intent of showing off the 3-D capabilities of Pixar's products. But when a new CEO joined the company that year, he met with the animators and told them that with the company in a cash crisis, they needed to start pulling their own weight. Out of pure desperation, Pixar began making TV commercials for companies like Tropicana and Listerine. Meanwhile, the animation team found time to make a new short film to promote the latest version of RenderMan software. The four-minute movie, called *Tin Toy*, wound up winning the 1989 Academy Award for best animated short film.

In 1991, Pixar laid off almost all its employees and shut down manufacturing of the Pixar Image Computer. The company kept the animation team only because at that point commercials were bringing in $2 million a year in revenue. Later in 1991, officials at Disney were impressed enough with *Tin Toy* and Pixar's TV spots that they offered the company a $26 million deal for three feature-length movies. It took four grueling years to complete the first one, *Toy Story*. The movie was almost scrapped in midproduction because Disney and Pixar were fighting over the script.

When *Toy Story* was finally released in 1995, Steve Jobs said he hoped the film would gross $100 million, because then Pixar would finally make money after 11 years of struggle. *Toy Story* grossed $365 million and the next four Pixar movies did even better. Altogether, Pixar's first five animated films made more than $2.5 billion, giving the studio the highest per-film box office average in Hollywood history. In January 2006, Disney bought Pixar for $7.6 billion. Steve Jobs, with his 50.1 percent ownership of the company, became a billionaire a second time over, in an industry he never had any intention of entering.

That's a great story of patience, persistence, and tenacity, isn't it? It's got Business Brilliance all over it. "It shows how small things, done well, can lead to big things," wrote David A. Price in his remarkable book, *The Pixar Touch*. Price notes also that each of the main actors who followed this circuitous path to success, Jobs included, "was, by conventional standards, a failure at the time he came onto the scene." It's actually the kind of losers-become-winners-against-all-odds story that has become de rigueur for Pixar movies.

It is also a story that Steve Jobs avoided telling. Appearing on the *Charlie Rose* show in 1996, Jobs gave the following outlandishly self-aggrandizing version of how Pixar came about:

I first got involved . . . when I heard about this incredible group of computer graphic specialists that George Lucas had assembled at Lucasfilm that he wanted to sell. And so I saw what they were doing. And I met the leader of this group, Dr. Ed Catmull. And Ed told me about his dream, which was to make the first computer-animated feature film someday and showed me what this team was working on. And I was blown away . . . and so bought into that dream, both spiritually, if you will, and financially. And we bought the computer division from George and incorporated it as Pixar . . . it took us ten years to do it. We were pioneering every step of the way.

That's the Pixar story that Jobs peddled to the public in 1996, with all the time and money that Jobs wasted with his unwanted Pixar computers written out of the script. By the time author Walter Isaacson was interviewing Jobs for his authorized biography, however, the Apple founder was a little more humble about how Pixar studios was an accident that almost didn't happen. Isaacson wrote:

> Looking back, Jobs said that, had he known more, he would have focused on animation sooner and not worried about pushing the company's hardware or software applications. On the other hand, had he known the hardware and software would never be profitable, he would not have taken over Pixar. "Life kind of snookered me into doing that, and perhaps it was for the better."

➤ The Truth About Failure

Pixar started out with great employees and state-of-the-art technology. What it didn't have was a sure path to profitability. That's the piece of the puzzle it took 11 years of heart-wrenching trial and error to find. During those years, there was only one thing Steve Jobs did on a consistent basis to force the odds in Pixar's favor. He pushed through adversity. Pixar's ultimate success was not the result of product testing, market research, or technical breakthroughs. Pixar became one of the greatest movie studios in history by chasing opportunities, from one crushing failure to the next, until feature filmmaking proved to be the best and most profitable application of the company's cutting-edge technology.

Ellen Langer, a psychology professor at Harvard, is a leading advocate for the concept of "mindfulness" as a way to deal with setbacks and failures. From her studies of creativity and learning, Langer says that too often people get frustrated over the specific task they failed at, when the more productive approach is to think beyond one's original intent.

If you remain mindful that failure may have also resulted in some new unanticipated possibilities, you're more likely to regard failure with an open mind. Langer points out that the first snow machines installed on ski slopes were adaptations of a failed crop-sprayer design. Minoxidil was a high blood pressure medication that produced some unfortunate side effects. It took creative thinking and some hard work to turn one of those side effects—unwanted hair growth—into the baldness treatment known as Rogaine.

Success in both these cases required mindful consideration of some dismal results—frozen insecticide and unwanted hair—and some creative thinking about what options they presented. Pixar's stumbling entry into the movie production business followed the same general route. Imagine if those $125,000 Pixar Image Computers had been a hit. Pixar's animation team might have remained a part of the support staff at a computer company, instead of the Hollywood moguls they are today.

The trouble with Langer's prescription is that most people don't like to think about their failures at all. They especially resist thinking about failure long enough to do anything productive with it. Psychology literature shows that the experience of failure threatens feelings of self-confidence and self-esteem in most people. On the other hand, research shows that they feel much better if, having failed in a task, they're allowed to change the subject quickly. When 9 out 10 members of the middle class say they respond to failure by giving up and doing something else, I have to assume that this flight-from-failure instinct is partly what's motivating them. Fewer than 2 out of 10 middle-class people say that failure is important in telling them what they're good at (it was 7 out of 10 among self-made millionaires). When the psychology literature is combined with our survey results, I have to conclude that for most of the middle class, failure is so painful that they don't want to hang around it long enough to learn from it.

Whenever something fails, whether it's a business or a toaster, failure creates uncertainty about what to do next. You may wonder why it failed, whether it's worth fixing, or whether you can manage without it. Langer's studies show that in general, most people feel uncomfortable with even trivial levels of uncertainty. It gives them the unpleasant feeling that they lack control over their lives. But from the mindful perspective, Langer writes, "uncertainty creates the freedom to discover meaning." Success may make you money, but failure makes you think.

To most self-made millionaires, failure is a wellspring of opportunity because every failure produces such a wide variety of unexpected results—lessons, experiences, relationships—that it can be an appealing challenge to sift the ashes and see what can be made of them. To some, a career like that of David Neeleman may seem chaotic and filled with intolerable uncertainty. But Neeleman is a living example of how a mindful response to failure can reap enormous rewards and personal growth. Through soaring victories and terrible defeats, we can see how each of his triumphs was shaped in large part by the lessons he learned and the meaning he derived from all his previous flameouts.

Way back in 1983, Neeleman was living in Salt Lake City and running a travel agency that specialized in air-and-hotel packages to Hawaii. A recent college dropout, he had 20 employees, no debt, and $8 million in annual revenues when, in December of that year, Hawaii Express airline suddenly went bankrupt. Neeleman's agency relied on Hawaii Express flights for nearly all its travel packages, so when the airline stopped flying and the Hawaiian hotels refused to return Neeleman's advance payments, his travel company ran out of cash and folded.

Feeling discouraged is a natural response to failure and Neeleman was no different from most people. He was so demoralized by the sudden loss of his company that he considered moving to Arizona and joining his in-laws in the drapery business. But the head of Morris Travel, Utah's largest travel agency, took Neeleman in and gave him a chance to redeem himself. Neeleman soon realized that the only real mistake he made with his failed agency was that he had run it with too little capital. When Hawaii Express collapsed, Neeleman didn't have enough cash reserves to ride out the storm. That was a mistake he never made again.

From 1984 to 1993, Neeleman helped build Morris Travel into a full-fledged airline called Morris Air. He was running 23 jets serving the western states, when his chief concern about the growing carrier was its thinning cash reserves. He persuaded the Morris family to put more money into the company and then he courted investors and raised an extra $14 million, which the airline ended up never touching.

Times were tough in the airline industry in 1993. But Morris Air was one of only two U.S. carriers to turn a profit that year and Southwest Airlines responded by offering to buy the airline for $129 million. Neeleman idolized Southwest founder Herb Kelleher. He created Morris Air with Southwest in mind, and copied Kelleher's approach and practices whenever he was able. Now with the sale of Morris Air, Neeleman owned $25 million in Southwest stock and had a new job as executive vice president. At the time, Kelleher regarded Neeleman as a kindred spirit. According to Neeleman's biography, Kelleher told Neeleman, "We need a guy like you."

But the impetuous Neeleman proved to be a poor fit for Southwest's lumbering corporate culture. He had grand plans for upgrading Southwest's antiquated ticketing systems, only to find that Southwest's policy was to let competitors struggle with risky, unproven technologies. His other ideas were either shot down or ignored. Neeleman grew frustrated with the endless meetings on the executive steering committee and Southwest executives grew frustrated with Neeleman. Five months after Neeleman started, Kelleher took him to lunch and fired him. "You're a pain," his idol told him.

Saddled with a five-year agreement forbidding him from working for competing airlines, Neeleman took some of his millions and consoled himself by dabbling in venture capital. He lost money on a pretzel bakery, a skin-care product manufacturer, and a fitness company, among many others. The lesson he took was that he should stick with what he knew and loved. He entered two businesses in the airline industry that didn't compete with Southwest, cofounding an automated airline ticketing company and working with a carrier in Canada, where Southwest doesn't fly.

By 1999, when he was free to raise money for the start-up of JetBlue, Neeleman had drawn three hard-earned lessons from his previous failures: Overcapitalize, do what you love, and be your own boss. JetBlue launched in 2000 with $130 million in investment capital, the largest initial capitalization in airline history. Then the airline released a stock offering in near-record time, earning CEO Neeleman a $118 million payday. By 2007, Jet Blue was the eighth largest carrier in the United States and its stock was trading at nearly 40 times earnings—until the day that freezing rain put Neeleman's job on ice.

Although Neeleman told the media in 2008 that he had no intention of starting another airline, his fourth lesson from failure was that if he ever did take another CEO role, he would retain voting control over the board. In 2009, an investor group approached him with an offer to start a new carrier in Brazil and they agreed to Neeleman's terms. He would put in $15 million of his own money, they would put in $135 million, but he was to have 80 percent voting rights on the board. He told *Fortune*, "I've set it up so I can't get sucker punched again."

There is another way to view Neeleman's succession of failures. You could conclude that Neeleman is kind of a mess. Shouldn't he have known he needed more cash on hand before his first business failed? Wasn't it obvious that as an entrepreneur he'd hate working for corporate Southwest? And didn't he know that a CEO is supposed to be responsive to the board of directors?

The answer to all of these questions is yes, Neeleman is kind of a mess. He is impulsive and obsessional. It wasn't until he turned thirty-three that he was diagnosed with attention deficit disorder. But none of these traits explains why he was undercapitalized, decided to work at Southwest, or left his JetBlue board out of the loop.

On each of Neeleman's rebounds, it was never a simple matter of going back to do what he had failed to do in the last attempt. Each time he returned from failure, he had a different outlook and a different approach. He was a different person. In order to learn from bad business decisions, 7 out of 10 self-made millionaires say that the most important change they make is within themselves. Less than 2 percent say they try to change their partners' behavior.

They keep the focus on themselves.

Changing your behavior is not done casually. So while it might seem easy in retrospect to say that Neeleman should have known that his first business needed more cash reserves, few small business owners are inclined to raise money that they intend to sock away for a rainy day. And nothing could have prepared Neeleman for his brief unhappy stay at Southwest. If he had passed up the opportunity to work with his idol Kelleher (and possibly succeed him as CEO) he would have always regretted it. With JetBlue and its board, Neeleman no doubt felt that JetBlue was his baby and no one would ever dare take it away from him.

The thing about failure that makes it so painful is the thing that makes it so instructive. The pain of failure yields a premium if you hold it correctly. Randy Komisar, a Silicon Valley veteran of the tech boom and bust years, puts it this way: "You got to feel it if you're going to learn it. . . . Ultimately, the only way to really, really, to get your money's worth out of failure, *it better be your own.* And that's largely because of that hollowness in your stomach, the disappointment of 250 people whose lives and families depend on you, the chagrin of your board members. You got to feel it." Komisar is a partner today with one of the Valley's private equity firms. In a lecture series he videotaped with Stanford University's business school, Komisar advised students to look at "constructive failure" as a way to deal with setbacks, try again, and then "take your experience and cash in on it as an asset."

In certain industries, like technology and pharmaceuticals, this process of constructive failure is a necessity. But in the rest of the corporate world, failure has very few friends. Amy Edmondson, a professor at Harvard Business School and an authority on failure inside organizations, writes, "The idea that people and the organizations in which they work should learn from failure has considerable popular support—and even seems obvious—yet organizations that systematically learn from failure are rare." Another Harvard professor, Stefan H. Thomke, says that when he speaks before business groups, "I try to be provocative and say: 'Failure is not a bad thing.' I always have lots of people staring at me, [thinking] 'Have you lost your mind?'"

Public companies interested in attracting investors and protecting their stock prices prefer to keep their failures private if they can. Even Pixar, a wildly successful studio with a golden reputation, has basically rewritten its history and wiped out all but a few incidental references to the failed Pixar Image Computer, from which the company got its name. One-third of the CEOs in *Inc.* magazine's list of fastest-growing companies said they started their companies after being fired from their previous employers, and iconic business founders like W. H. Macy, Henry J. Heinz, and Colonel Harland Sanders were legendary for their perseverance and determination to overcome failures. But it is unlikely that any of these companies carry on their founders' legacies and declare themselves as places where failure is the path to success.

The most disturbing findings in Edmondson's work on organizational failure have been the result of her research on hospitals. While studying a particularly well run nursing unit she found that the reported rates of errors were unexpectedly high. It made no sense to her, until she dug deeper and discovered that the poorly run nursing units were making far more mistakes, but chose not to report most of them. Despite all the public claims by hospital officials about safety programs and quality-assurance regimes, the hospitals Edmondson studied were not learning from the errors encountered by their workers. She found that more than 90 percent of errors, when they were discovered, were remediated by quick workarounds so that neither the hospital nor the coworkers were able to learn why, within the hospital system, any of those errors had originated.

These results are reminiscent of the story in chapter 1 regarding Dr. Richard Shannon and his drive to bring the quality record of Toyota manufacturing to his hospital's intensive care unit. He found that even though several dozen patients were dying in the unit every year from infections, there had never been an effort to identify what was happening. Shannon's staff discovered that most deaths involved blood catheters inserted in patients' groin areas. In a concerted effort to prevent infection, Shannon had all catheters moved to the patients' shoulders, and the infection deaths dropped to zero.

To this day, few hospitals have ever even attempted to imitate Richard Shannon's great success in controlling infection. Medicine remains a field that resists learning from failure because, first and foremost, it resists even acknowledging failure.

➤ The Failure Faith

The belief that failure is necessary for success, a belief shared among self-made millionaires but not among the middle class, could be the most important finding our survey has uncovered. To believe that failure can be good, that failure can work, is essential to developing your Business Brilliance.

I call it the Failure Faith. It's the conviction that failure may result whenever you try to stretch and achieve something special, that failure yields unforeseen lessons and benefits, and that failure sets a bar that your competitors will likely trip over.

Think for a moment about just two or three of the self-made millionaire habits, traits, and attitudes that have inspired you the most. Now consider what the Failure Faith adds to the mix. Every special talent found among self-made millionaires as thinkers, strategists, negotiators, networkers, and delegators becomes more potent when it is tied into the simple belief that failure is necessary for success.

When you have the Failure Faith, when you're comfortable with the idea of failing, it makes sense to risk failure *whenever the cost of failure is little or nothing.* The Failure Faith puts into perspective any fear you may have of personal rejection, because rejection is a form of failure that has no downside. When you don't get the job, can't land the account, or fail to make the winning bid, consider it a practice run for the next attempt. You've honed your approach, learned something new, and perhaps made a new connection or two. Rejection is a zero-cost failure. And since the risk of rejection offers only upside, you might as well go out and risk as much rejection as you can.

The Failure Faith tells you to ask more than once for an equity share in your work because there's no downside risk in asking. It tells you to ask for a raise and to leverage the request by getting job offers elsewhere. You invite other people to invest with you because it protects you if your business fails. You negotiate hard to make sure a deal is just right because you need to maximize your upside and protect your downside because every deal carries a risk of failure. You delegate everything you can and focus on what creates the most value. And, finally, if you believe that failure is necessary to achieve success, then you will look at every hiccup in your operation, every missed call, and every screwup a little more carefully, with an appraising eye of "What can we do with this?" In the words of Ellen Langer, the Failure Faith lets you "discover meaning" in situations where others may experience only pain, loss, and disappointment.

And if you lack the Failure Faith? If you *don't* believe that failure is necessary? Everything runs in the opposite direction. Without accepting the point or purpose in rejection and failure, you will always tend to hang back and keep a lookout for low-risk pain-free opportunities. You won't ask for equity or even a raise at work unless you feel sure the answer will be yes. You dream of a big idea that will be your can't-miss score, instead of trying to grind out your success in a field that you already know well. You invest only your own money because asking someone else to risk their money with you bears too much risk of rejection. You try to settle negotiations on a win-win basis because it matters what the other side thinks of you. You don't like delegating any of your work because you fear giving up control. And finally, you quit whenever you've failed at something because you think that's the reasonable and logical response. The fact you failed is evidence enough that the project was a poor fit for you or wasn't worth the trouble. No need to look deeper. No need to cry over spilled milk. Just try to forget that it happened.

I've noted before that when it comes to money, self-made millionaires and the middle class seem to live in separate worlds. When it comes to failure, they live by separate codes. The self-made millionaire believes "Anything worth trying is worth trying over and over and over again." The middle class believes "Nothing that fails on the first attempt is ever worth trying a second time." The middle-class attitude seems intent on suffering all the pain and hard work of failing while enjoying none of the benefits of true persistence. It's like the old joke about the boy who swam halfway across a river, decided he couldn't make it, so he swam back.

If you look through the previous chapters of this book, starting with Dr. Shannon's ideas about using factory-floor methods to save lives in his hospital, you will see that perseverance and faith in the productive value of failure were a crucial factor in every success story I tell. It's Guy Laliberté's circus failing in its first Canadian tour, Paul Green waiting tables to support his school of rock and roll, and Warren Buffett losing a fifth of his life savings in a shuttered gas station. Painful, humbling failure has, at times, been a fact of life for every self-made millionaire and billionaire.

All failure is painful, but the difference is that for the self-made millionaire the pain of failure is like a trip to the dentist. You know it happens occasionally, you don't look forward to it, but you're better off having gone through it. For the middle class, failure is more like a punch in the mouth. It's something that should never happen, it takes you by surprise, it's humiliating and painful, and you'd like to forget it ever happened.

Here's one wrinkle in the Business Brilliant survey that I've saved for the end of this chapter. Almost everybody in our survey reported at least one setback or failure, including 70 percent of the middle class and 80 percent of self-made millionaires. About 80 percent of self-made millionaires also say that have associates who have had failures and setbacks, which only stands to reason. But here's the wrinkle. Among the middle-class respondents, just 20 percent say they have associates who have experienced at least one setback or failure.

Think about that for a moment. About 70 percent of the middle class has experienced failure, but only 20 percent say they know colleagues who have failed. The discrepancy in these two numbers suggests that when middle-class people fail, most try not to tell anyone they know. Whether they are part of the corporate culture that frowns on failure, I don't know. But I do know from personal experience that if you're going to experience failure, it's better to do so with colleagues who have been there, who share the Failure Faith and that it's all for the best, even if it doesn't always feel that way.

For one thing, discussions about failure are almost always more productive than discussions about successes. Don't take my word for it. Amy Edmondson, Harvard's resident expert on failure, puts it this way: "When facing an uncertain path forward, trying something that fails, then figuring out what works instead is the very essence of good performance. Great performance, however, is trying something that fails, figuring out what works instead, and telling your colleagues about it—about both the success and the failure." The result, Edmondson says, is what she calls "execution-as-learning." Discussing failure along the way is how to get work done while also considering how to do it better.

Chapter 6 discussed the social research on how the desire to conform to group norms of behavior can affect people's weight, their smoking habits and, of course, their income. I wonder if social conformity is the main reason why the middle class behaves in ways so deeply at odds with the behaviors of self-made millionaires. If you are the only one on your block or in your circle of friends who suffers repeated business failures, you're not likely to get much sympathy from your friends. They're likely to wonder why you don't just give up after the first failure—like everyone else they know. You certainly won't get any informed advice about what to do next and you definitely won't raise any investment capital.

With self-made millionaires, the fact that 80 percent have colleagues who have failed suggests to us that they are surrounded by people who appreciate failure. They don't have problems admitting setbacks and failure to each other because they share the Failure Faith. Failure is painful for everyone, but the middle-class person who fails is more likely to suffer the additional agony of loneliness and social isolation.

A business culture that accepts failure, that has faith in its power to educate and create new opportunities, can serve as an important piece of that synergistic system of success we described in chapter 1. "We already live in a world where taking risks is an essential element of everyday life," says Russ Prince. "I don't think there's anything particularly redeeming about trying to avoid failure at every juncture. If you're lucky, I suppose you might be able to beat your chest and tell others that you never fell down, but you probably have very little to show for it."

Or as Norm Brodsky says, "If I had to choose, I'd rather be wise than smart."

Brilliant.

9

Mastering the Mundane

Can Business Brilliance be learned? Is it a talent that some are born with or does it rely mainly on a set of habits, practices, and techniques that motivated individuals can adopt as their own?

Academic researchers studying entrepreneurship—the highest form of Business Brilliance—have long struggled with this question.

Russ Prince himself is not so sure. As a coach to some of the world's wealthiest families, he knows that having a knack for Business Brilliance is essential. But he also knows from his own coaching that many of the skills for Business Brilliance can be learned, or at least enhanced, through study and practice.

Part of the confusion stems from the fact that so many successful entrepreneurs have demonstrated Business Brilliance many times over without ever having gone to business school. It might stand to reason that the people most likely to be Business Brilliant are those who have benefited from years of training in the ways of money. But when a pair of professors at the University of Pennsylvania's prestigious Wharton School of Business tested this theory some years ago, they were shocked by the result. Their random survey of Penn alumni showed that graduates from the arts and sciences college—with majors in fields such as history, biology, and math—were two or three times more likely to be entrepreneurs than graduates of Wharton.

Other studies have shown similarly surprising patterns among the self-employed. For instance, people who change jobs frequently in their careers are much more likely to end up going into business for themselves, suggesting that Business Brilliance has something to do with having an innately restless nature. Another study showed that teenagers who deal drugs are more likely than most people to become entrepreneurs when they approach middle age.

Findings like these, along with the familiar observation that so many entrepreneurs are immigrants with limited formal education of any kind, lend credence to the notion that Business Brilliance is a gift. Like good looks, charisma, or natural rhythm, some have got it and some don't.

This same sort of assumption is made often about the very best school teachers. The great ones are great, the thinking goes, because of their profound level of personal commitment, their natural talent for connecting with students, and their creative ways of inspiring students to learn. With movies like *Dangerous Minds* and *Stand and Deliver*, Hollywood has helped perpetuate the idea that there can be no playbook for fixing broken schools. To make a difference with children it takes heroic individuals who disregard whatever training they've had and rely instead on their passion and unique personal instincts.

An educator named Doug Lemov was frustrated by this thinking and a little offended by it, too. For years, Lemov has worked for a charter school company that specializes in serving low-income inner-city neighborhoods. He knew from the research that no single factor accounts more for student success than a quality teacher. He also knew that research had failed to identify any teacher-training methodology that reliably produces good teachers. So he set out on a quest to find out what the best teachers in America were doing in order to be successful.

Identifying outstanding teachers is not that difficult to do. Student test results in primary and secondary schools correlate very closely with family income. This means that schools in which 90 percent of students come from very low-income families almost always produce low average scores on standardized tests, while schools in which 90 percent of the students come from high-income families produce high average test scores. To find exceptional teachers, all you have to do is identify schools with test scores significantly higher than what their student poverty rates would predict.

Lemov is a self-confessed data geek. He studied countless scatter graphs, and picked the outliers, those unusual public schools with high poverty rates *and* high test scores. Then he started visiting the schools. He ended up sitting in the back of hundreds of classrooms where high test scores had been achieved against all the odds. Lemov took notes and brought a video camera that generated thousands of hours of tape.

"He did not find magicians mixing secret alchemical teaching potions or derive the elusive DNA for charisma," writes Lemov's friend and mentor Norman Atkins. "His big 'aha' was to identify the tools that master teachers used to make their classrooms into cathedrals of learning."

It took him a dozen years, but Lemov compiled a list of effective teaching techniques shared by many of these "master teachers." The list has gone through 25 revisions, and today it totals 49 classroom techniques that include the very best practices for planning classwork, delivering lessons, and maintaining discipline. Lemov presents each of the 49 in a way that is "specific, concrete and actionable." In other words, they can be replicated. They can be learned. In 2007, Atkins founded Teacher U, a revolutionary teacher-training program that is built around the 49 points. Atkins declares that what Lemov has discovered "is surprising for its simplicity and portends good news for the teaching profession."

I see in Lemov's research some interesting parallels with my own work. I've also been at this for a dozen years—Prince has been at it twice as long—and just as Lemov searched for excellence from among resource-constrained public school teachers, I've limited my studies of financially successful people only to those who grew up in typical middle-class households. Sifting for signs of the extraordinary from among the ordinary is a very sound method of isolating the precise factors that account for high performance and success.

And my results are also surprising in their simplicity. My research tells me that there are four broad areas of daily activity that successful self-made entrepreneurs undertake more effectively and consistently than most people. I call the four Learning, Earning, Assistance, and Persistence.

Together these four words spell out LEAP.

LEARNING means that self-made millionaires expend more time and effort discovering what they do best and pursuing opportunities related to what they do best.

EARNING means they take on projects and make deals that maximize the dollar potential of those opportunities while limiting their downside risks.

ASSISTANCE means that they actively cultivate networks of friends, associates, and partners so they can get help and advice on all the tasks beyond the bounds of what they do best.

PERSISTENCE means they take an authentic interest in their setbacks as an important *and* necessary aspect of the success process.

Inspired by Lemov's taxonomy of 49 teaching techniques, I've broken out these four categories into my own list of 17 Essentials of Business Brilliance, following closely Prince's own methodology for coaching his Business Brilliant clients. For each of the 17 Essentials I offer a general strategy, followed by a specific technique that, like each of Lemov's techniques, is specific, concrete, and actionable. Each offers a simple and clear set of actions that help position you to fall into money. Most of these techniques involve ten-minute decision-making exercises. None of them takes more than an hour.

I believe that if you do your best at executing these 17 techniques on a regular basis, you will find yourself on the path to Business Brilliance and a quantum LEAP in your income. If you set some financial targets for yourself (Essential 1: Write down your goals), prepare a project with those goals in mind (Essential 6: Protect your bottom line), rely on the people around you (Essential 10: Manage your network upward), and engage your natural fear of disappointment (Essential 13: Make friends with failure), your relationship with making money will be fundamentally transformed.

You will likely experience this transformation in ways that you would least expect. That's because the 17 Essentials constitute a complete, synergistic system for becoming Business Brilliant yourself. As you may recall from chapter 1, synergy by its very nature produces results that are unexpected and novel—results that may shock and amaze you.

I've done my best to design these techniques so they are straightforward, easy to understand, and, above all, mundane. Remember, mundane is good. As we saw most vividly in chapter 1, Allegheny General Hospital all but eradicated infections in its intensive-care units by demanding that all medical personnel faithfully adhere to the most mundane procedures and protocols. Mastering the mundane saved dozens of lives each year at Allegheny General, lives that had been lost in previous years despite its highly trained and well-educated staff and all their world-class medical technology.

One of Lemov's 49 techniques is something he calls Tight Transitions. A major source of disruption and wasted time in grade school classrooms is the simple act of passing out and handing in papers, which happens about 20 times a day and consumes one or two minutes each time. Lemov shows a video of a Connecticut teacher who has taught his students how to pass out papers through the entire classroom in 8 to 10 seconds. Executing that simple procedure so quickly ensures that the class is not distracted, while the teacher recovers a total of 30 minutes of instruction time every day. Thanks to the way they handle papers, the children in that classroom will benefit over the course of the year from about eight more *days* of instruction than the children in the next classroom, which is one reason why the Connecticut teacher's students outperform on their standardized tests. Time and focus—the two most precious commodities in any kind of mental work—are preserved by mastering this most mundane of tasks.

Thousands of students graduate with degrees in teaching every year and not one of them has gotten instruction in how to pass out papers. For all their value, techniques such as these are beneath the notice of the educational establishment. In a similar way, you won't find these 17 Essentials included in any college or graduate school course on business or entrepreneurship. They're too mundane. But they're also extremely valuable, because they are designed to protect your precious time and focus.

If you want to go deeper into any of these 17 Essentials, I've provided a bibliography of resources in the back of the book. But don't get bogged down in the paralysis of analysis before you begin. It's best to start out with the simple and mundane. The reason can be found in Essential 16: Don't Procrastinate. Most of our middle-class survey respondents struggle with procrastination, a problem shared by very few of the self-made millionaires. It's important to dive in and get moving. That's the true meaning of Persistence. And if you can't get moving, get help (Essential 12: Get a coach). That's what Assistance is all about.

If you need a short action list to set you on your way, just try and make sure you're always doing at least one of the following every day:

Learning what you do best.
Earning some dollars at it.
Getting Assistance with what you don't do best.
Using Persistence to overcome self-doubt.

Learning. Earning. Assistance. Persistence. LEAP. The sooner you put them into action, the sooner you'll be doing more than just following the money, you'll be LEAPing into it.

➤ Learning

Becoming Business Brilliant first requires learning—learning about yourself, your goals, and the best ways of reaching them.

ESSENTIAL 1: WRITE DOWN YOUR GOALS

Having a long-term goal, expressed in monetary terms, gives you a point of focus for all your efforts toward Business Brilliance. Dollar goals are valuable because they are easy to measure, and what can be measured can be managed. Goals make becoming Business Brilliant a manageable task.

Ideally, all your daily priorities should be informed by the amount of wealth you'd like to achieve 10 years from now. If you set a goal of having a net worth of $10 million or more in 10 years, you probably need to aim for an equity share in one or more salable businesses. Your choices of prospects, partners, and projects need to be defined by that objective, driven by your 10-year goal. What *kind* of businesses? Save that for later. The goal is what matters. It gives you the decision-making power to respond to those and all the other questions you'll face down the road.

Once you've chosen a 10-year goal, you'll need incremental goals to guide you on the way. Let's say your 10-year goal is to have $2 million in investable assets. How much money would you have to have over each of the next five years to position you for reaching that goal? How much would you need to make per month in the coming year? If you are a professional who charges by the hour, what does your target hourly rate need to be?

Incremental goals clarify and simplify what you need to do. Hitting them helps preserve your sense of purpose and forward progress. But sometimes these incremental goals do the most good when you fall short of them. Failing on your monthly income targets will expose your need to make some adjustments more quickly. On the other hand, it's just as likely that you'll reach some of the short-term goals faster than you thought possible. Then you might need a new long-term goal, because your capabilities are greater than you had thought.

THE TECHNIQUE: Take 20 minutes. Choose a goal for your net worth and write it down as Year 10 on the right-hand side of a sheet of paper. Then, moving from right to left, write down your average monthly income goals for Year 5, 4, 3, and 2. Finally, write down your monthly income goals for each month of the coming year, starting with next month. Post the sheet in a place where you can see it every day from your desk. Repeat this process every time you complete a deal or have a windfall.

ESSENTIAL 2: COMMIT TO WHAT YOU DO BEST

Focusing your energies on what you do best is the path taken by the world's most extraordinarily successful people—everyone from Bill Gates to the Beatles. It's the path taken by *ordinary* successful people, too, like the millions of self-made millionaires out there. Through trial and error, most of them have found the handful of things they do best, cut back on distractions and diversions, and executed on their special talents in ways that allowed them to hone their Business Brilliance.

This idea goes by a lot of names—identifying your strengths, discovering your core competencies, or distinguishing your special abilities. I like to call it "finding your Center" or just plain "Centering" because it's a visual term that's easy to remember.

Most people aren't Centered at all. Polling by Gallup shows that only 1 out of 3 employees is able to say that "at work, I have the opportunity to do what I do best every day." This is a big reason why average wages for college-educated workers have barely grown in the past 15 years. They have no leverage to bid up the price of their labor since they are only adequately suited for the work they do. If you're not engaged with what you do best every day, you're poorly positioned to become Business Brilliant. And in an age when millions of routinized white-collar jobs are being sent overseas, Centering might be your most vital economic survival skill.

Centering should be something that is *central* to your daily life. One of the best things about it is that it lends value and meaning to even your worst setbacks and disappointments. When you work at what you do best, even a crushing defeat can be an important source of self-knowledge and progress toward your Center. Most self-made millionaires say they *count* on setbacks to help them redefine what they do exceptionally well. They use trial and error to get more Centered. That way, even when their best efforts go unrewarded, they are still refining their expertise.

THE TECHNIQUE: Take 10 minutes. Write down as many examples as you can of tasks you believe you do exceptionally well. Try to choose skills and capabilities you think you could convincingly explain to a stranger who has some knowledge of your field of expertise. Repeat the process for 10 minutes the next day. Then start editing the list until you only have three items. Next to each of these three items, write down three clear statements that provide evidence these items are true.

ESSENTIAL 3: FOLLOW THE MONEY

Look at the top people in any field and you will see who has gotten there by following the money in that field. They are working at their Centers and sharing in the rewards that come from creating things of great value for others.

The chefs who fall into money run restaurant partnerships, write cookbooks, and star in their own cable shows. The carpenters who fall into money own their workshops, do high-end custom work or partner in real estate–development deals. Top managers in the corporate world either earn bonuses for producing strong financial results or gain equity stakes in their companies.

All of these people are positioned in "the Line of Money." Whenever they help create value and money changes hands, they are *in line* to collect a share of the rewards. Business Brilliance only happens to people who put themselves in the Line of Money first.

The greatest rewards in any profession or occupation are reserved for whoever is most Centered *and* most directly in the Line of Money.

I've studied this in the medical profession. On average, doctors are the most highly paid professionals in our economy. But the doctors who rank in the top 10 percent of income among doctors are not necessarily the smartest, the most proficient, or even the most popular doctors. The wealthiest doctors are those who first chose the specialty that best suits their skills very well and then took an ownership stake in a practice that specializes in that type of medicine. They are Centered and in the Line of Money.

The same goes for lawyers, engineers, and even academics. The charter school movement has allowed large numbers of educators to start working for shared rewards instead of salaried compensation. If you consider the proliferation of Bible Belt megachurches, you will see that even some *clergy-people* are Centered and in the Line of Money.

Following the money generally means your main source of income comes from being in the Line of Money. It's not necessary to quit your job if you want to get into the Line of Money, but our surveys tell us that only 1 in 10 self-made millionaires became wealthy by working for someone else. Most of them worked at salaried jobs where they honed their skills and found their Centers, and then transitioned into self-employment or a partnership.

THE TECHNIQUE: Take 20 minutes. Go over your list of three things you do extremely well from the Centering exercise and write down the occupations that, to your knowledge, most often use those skills to make the most money. This might seem a pedestrian exercise, but it's not. With a little bit of thought, you should have two or three things you've never considered before.

ESSENTIAL 4: CLIMB THE LINE-OF-MONEY LADDER

Wherever you find your Center, you should be able to see countless ways to use it to get in the Line of Money. Some of these ways are more rewarding than others, though, so it's important to sort them all out. When you can picture all the different ways you might follow the money, then you're ready to take a harder look at the Line of Money as though it were a ladder. Each rung on the Line of Money Ladder is defined by the type of *price* you put on your participation. Each step up yields higher rewards, with equity at the very top.

PREMIUM PRICING is the bottom rung on the Line of Money Ladder. It is occupied by self-employed consultants and other independent contractors who price their efforts at hourly rates. Because time is finite, this is the most difficult way toward Business Brilliance, although top-tier trainers, tutors, psychoanalysts, and other personal-service professionals are good examples. They demonstrate their own brand of Business Brilliance by cultivating such high demand for their time that they bid up their hourly rates.

PROJECT PRICING is the next rung up the ladder. When you work on a project basis, you enjoy the advantage of being rewarded for achieving a result, regardless of your time commitment. Your brilliance comes by charging as much as you can, and then handing off portions of the work to other professionals to get the job done more quickly.

PERCENTAGE PRICING is another rung higher, because a percentage means you're getting a discrete cut of the rewards for success. This is commonly the lucrative add-on in an agreement to project pricing. Many deals closed with project pricing have a component of percentage pricing worked in, offering additional shared rewards for delivering on a winning effort.

PROPRIETOR PRICING is another name for equity participation. It's the top rung in the Line of Money Ladder. When you're in the proprietor role of a business, you're not just playing in the game—you also own the team. Each successful project and each profitable quarter builds more value into the business you own either fully or in partnership. Most of the personal wealth in the world has been gained through equity. It is the highest achievement in Business Brilliance and it should be the ultimate objective in your negotiations. You want an ownership stake, even if it's just a small share, of anything that might be destined to be sold later at many multiples of its current value.

THE TECHNIQUE: Take 30 minutes. Draw a four-rung ladder on a sheet of paper, with "Proprietor" at the top, then "Percentage," "Project," and "Premium" on the next three rungs. Leave about five lines of empty space under each heading. When you're done, you'll have ideas for 12 projects, arrayed from lowest value to highest value, each one building on those below it. You've mapped your path for Business Brilliance. Redo it every time you land a new project.

➤ Earning

Once you're ready to take on a specific project, your focus needs to shift from learning to earning. Earning is how ideas turn into opportunities.

ESSENTIAL 5: RUN THE NUMBERS

There are five critical dimensions to every prospective project, regardless of size. Each dimension requires a good hard look before you spend too much time or money on the project:

1. WHAT WILL IT COST TO PLAY? What will you have to spend in order to get started? Add up everything you need to buy, all the services you need to employ, and all the work you and your partners will probably need to put in before you earn your first dollar.

2. WHAT WILL IT COST TO STAY? How much will it cost to operate your project once it's running? Add up all the anticipated monthly bills and labor costs. Add the dollar value of your hours, too.

3. HOW HIGH IS THE CEILING? Estimate the *potential income*. This is a reasonable high-end number of dollars the project would generate if everything ran perfectly. Most projects face certain capacity limits and you need to know what they are. A restaurant's revenue, for instance, is limited mainly by its entrée prices and the number of tables.

4. HOW HARD IS THE FLOOR? What's the worst possible result? You will earn some revenue. But what is the absolute lowest monthly revenue your project will likely earn? How hard will it be for you to take a total loss? Prepare for the worst, and see what it might look like.

5. HOW BIG IS THE CHERRY ON TOP? If you're working at your Center, every project offers some "soft rewards" that will benefit you in the long run even if the project itself isn't a ringing success. List those benefits: a respectable track record, a set of new connections, a higher public profile, and so on. But a pro forma requires a dollar estimate. It turns out it's easy to attach a dollar value to the Cherry on Top. If someone were willing to buy out your share of the project before it even starts, what is the lowest dollar amount you would accept to walk away? That, minus any cash you put into the project, is the exact value of the Cherry on Top.

The first job of the pro forma is to keep you out of trouble. It gives you the chance to stare at all the most important numbers and rethink the project or abandon it altogether. The rock-bottom expense of playing and staying might come too close to your ceiling on earnings. You need to ask yourself why you'd go into something with such a limited upside potential. Maybe the Cherry on Top is the answer. Maybe not.

Play. Stay. Ceiling. Floor. Cherry on Top. Whether you plan on flipping burgers or flipping real estate, these five numbers will help you determine the look and shape of what you want to do, and whether it's worth trying.

THE TECHNIQUE: Take 30 minutes to draw up a pro forma. Leave lots of room for what you don't know and what you still need to find out. The numbers you use will always be gross approximations, but the exercise will force you to come to grips with what it will take to succeed.

ESSENTIAL 6: PROTECT YOUR BOTTOM LINE

Once you've run the numbers and decided to go forward, the pro forma should have helped you arrive at your bottom line. Not the project's bottom line. Your own personal bottom line. This is the minimum reward—and maximum risk—you must have in order to participate. Until you decide on these numbers, you're not ready to negotiate a deal with anyone.

If you put too high a premium on achieving a win-win solution, it might very well end up win-lose, with you holding the bag. Remember the Stephen Covey story about the landlord who was locked into a bad long-term lease because he felt he needed to close a "win-win" deal with a tenant? If the landlord had entered those negotiations with a clear idea of his personal bottom line, he would have known exactly when the tenant was asking too much. He could have walked away with a clear conscience.

I've shown how self-made millionaires are much better than most people when it comes to walking away from a deal that isn't quite right. For some this ability may reflect their sizable egos, but that's not the whole story. People who appear most comfortable putting their personal interests first are actually just executing on a predetermined plan. They come to the table knowing in advance exactly what they must have. It's not about ego. It's about respecting your own goals.

Linda Babcock in her college negotiating courses advocates the same approach to salary offers. You must draw a line below which you won't compromise. It's an essential part of negotiating, but most people never do it.

In a business deal, a bottom line of this kind should also involve putting limits on how much you put at risk. You want to shrink your downside risk wherever possible and walk away if it appears too high. Many business beginners make the fatal mistake of investing so much of their own capital in a business deal—maybe a franchise or an investment property—that if the deal fails they won't ever have the resources to give themselves a second or third chance to succeed.

THE TECHNIQUE: Take 20 minutes. Consider your short-term goals and how much money you need from this deal to contribute to those goals. Compromising your goals just to get a deal done is the fastest way out of Business Brilliance. Putting too much at stake in the deal can keep you outside of the line of money for years to come. Don't ever take on so much risk that if a project fails, you will lack the resources to try again (Essential 15).

ESSENTIAL 7: PRESS YOUR ADVANTAGE

Once all your goals are clear, the basic negotiating formula for Business Brilliance is this: You bring people to the table according to their strengths. You negotiate with them according to their weaknesses.

That may seem a little cold-blooded, but you have to accept that in almost all business transactions, you are being sized up in the exact same way. In chapter 3 we saw how just about every boss who's ever hired you with a smile and a handshake was also eager to exploit your vulnerabilities by offering you the absolute minimum salary he or she could get away with.

So if you want a negotiation to work for you and your goals, it's not enough to go in knowing all about your own bottom line. You also need a strong sense of what the other side's bottom line looks like, too. Before you sit down to make any agreement, you should know what motives, beyond money, might be driving the other side's participation.

Let's say you have partners who lack expertise but have access to cash. You lack cash but have expertise. Your partners will want to bring you and your expertise into the deal for as little money as possible, in order to preserve their return on investment. They will squeeze you and try to give you as little as possible in terms of project pricing, percentage pricing, and equity.

What ability do you have to squeeze them back? This is largely determined by what you know about them. How badly do they need you for this project? How easily could you be replaced? Are they in love with the project? That's important because love can be blind. Even the most successful businesspeople give away concessions without thinking if they want a project to happen right away. The more you know about their vulnerabilities, the better able you are to press your advantage.

Here's a story that illustrates the point. Marlon Brando was shooting a movie in which he had a small equity stake, known as points. But he also had tax problems and owed the federal government $100,000. Brando's manager called the movie producer and explained Brando's problem. He asked for a cash advance during the shoot. The producer checked with the studio head, who was delighted. "Give it to him," he said. "But get back his points." So Brando agreed to give up his equity share in the movie for $100,000. The movie was *The Godfather*. Within a few years, that $100,000 check from Paramount had cost Brando about $11 million.

The studio head hired Brando because of Brando's strength as an actor. He negotiated with Brando, however, on the basis of Brando's weakness as a tax debtor. That's why Paramount fell into money on *The Godfather* and Brando did not.

THE TECHNIQUE: Take 20 minutes. Before you negotiate on price or equity, redo the deal's pro forma from your partner's point of view. If you're a landlord do it from the tenant's point of view. When you're done, circle all the areas where you have serious questions. What are the soft benefits for them? How have they limited their own downside risk? If you can't get them to answer these questions in casual conversation, ask around. Every clue you have about their motivations will help you press your advantage.

ESSENTIAL 8: PLAN THE DIVORCE IN ADVANCE

Just like a prenuptial agreement between mature adults, every good partnership should have the divorce terms built in from the wedding day. A deal that goes bad can be like an anchor around your leg. You should always have a way to cut the cord.

When you begin a new project, everyone is in love with each other, but then things change when the money starts to move. Expect the unexpected. Some partners suddenly realize they gave away too much in negotiations once the dollars aren't flowing in their favor. They start whining and beg to renegotiate. If you don't have divorce terms written out for all parties by mutual agreement, then there's no way to respond.

The divorce clause is the last line of defense for your bottom line. If a deal is souring in a way that obliges you to continue to fund and work it, even though you feel certain there is no prospect for success, you want a prior agreement to back you up so you can quit. You can't lose sight of what's called "opportunity costs." Every day you toil at a losing deal is one more day you are not out looking for a winner. You are one day farther from reaching your goals.

The most powerful thing about a divorce clause is that you don't have to leave the project for it to be useful. It can just be a point of leverage in renegotiating terms that protect your bottom line. You can say, "I can't afford to keep doing this unless I get more money." Then it's up to your partners to decide what your participation is worth to them. Either way, you've protected yourself, and your goals.

THE TECHNIQUE: Before any negotiation, use your pro forma to anticipate what might go wrong, and under what conditions you will want the divorce clause to either let you out with a minimum of loss or give you leverage to negotiate for more money. If you want the divorce clause to work best for you, then it's up to you to propose it and provide a draft of the terms.

➤ Assistance

It doesn't take money to make money, but it does take teamwork and support. You can't do it all and you shouldn't try, because then you're not doing what you do best.

ESSENTIAL 9: KEEP YOUR NETWORK SMALL AND FOCUSED

If you want to become Business Brilliant, your network is your most valuable asset. Not even the skills and capabilities at your Center are as important as the network you rely on for new business opportunities. Without opportunities, your skills and capabilities will go to waste.

On average, self-made millionaires tell us they maintain a circle of six people with whom they "closely network in order to source new business." The middle-class survey respondents claim an average of nine people for the same purpose.

Why would the millionaires have *smaller* networks? I suspect it's because the millionaires are actively managing what Russ Prince calls Nodal Networks. They're not randomly collecting business acquaintances. They're maintaining a deliberately compact set of capable people, each one of whom serves as a strategic point of contact, or a "node," for that business person's channel of trade.

Let's say you're running a bakery. Your Nodal Network should be made up of six people who are well positioned to send cake-buying business your way. It might include a wedding planner, a party planner, and four catering-hall managers. These are people who like your cakes, consider you reliable, and will gladly recommend you to their clients. You value these people and go out of your way to cultivate their friendship and stay in touch with them because your livelihood depends on them.

But why stop at six? Wouldn't it be better if the baker's network had 10 or 20 caterers and party planners?

The baker probably does know 10 or 20 other caterers and planners. But he *relies* on the six in his Nodal Network for perhaps 80 percent of his revenue. You can't really rely on more than six people for the simple reason that paying proper attention to those six takes a lot of work. Maintaining a Nodal Network well and faithfully demands more effort than you could ever devote to 10 or 20 people. You can't have 10 or 20 people in your Nodal Network any sooner than you can have 10 or 20 best friends. Someone who counts 10 or more people in his or her network probably has no useful network at all. True Nodal Networks work only when they're small and tight.

THE TECHNIQUE: Take 10 minutes. Make a list of the top *dozen* people you would go to tomorrow for advice on finding a new project in the work you do best. Rank the top six you are closest to or who are best positioned to help you. That's the beginning of your Nodal Network. If you work in a salaried job, make up similar lists of people you would go to regarding either a promotion or changing jobs. What could be more important?

ESSENTIAL 10: MANAGE YOUR NETWORK UPWARD

Nodal Networks are always in flux. People come and go, businesses change direction, your own priorities change.

The best way to deal with change is to take change into your own hands. If you accept the premise that your Nodal Network is your most valuable asset, then it makes sense to manage it just as you would any asset portfolio. You want to be on the lookout for new promising network members while withdrawing your connections with underperformers.

Let's go back to the bakery shop with its Nodal Network of one wedding planner, one party planner, and four caterers. Maybe wedding cakes are the highest-margin product and you want to get more of that kind of business. And maybe one of your four caterers, with lower-margin cakes, has dropped off in referrals. So you consciously start trying to identify a second wedding planner to add to your Nodal Network.

The act of networking has gotten a bad name. Its main pitfall is that it tends to be casual and random. Online "social networking" has made things worse. It's hard to keep a network small and tight when you've got old college buddies and former workmates linking in unannounced and adding you to their own networks.

If you're in the serious business of Nodal Networking, you collect information about your prospective network members, look for mutual connections, and reach out to them. You're not cold-calling, as a salesperson might. You're marketing your services in the hope of finding a good alliance, some shared values about the business that makes it advantageous for you to be in each other's networks.

And if you ever show up at an industry networking event, go there with an agenda in mind. You're going to meet three prospective members for your network and you're going to ask their advice about a problem or an issue you've been facing. Few people enjoy sales pitches, but almost everyone enjoys dispensing advice. This way you have a direction for each conversation you have at the event. And you can excuse yourself from spending more than a minute or so with anyone who can't help you. You just apologize politely and explain you've got to find someone who can help you. It's a networking strategy Prince calls "NEXT"—Never Extend eXtra Time.

THE TECHNIQUE: Put together seven file folders—paper folders or computer folders. Mark one folder with the name of each of the top six people you came up with in Essential 9. This is the Nodal Network your livelihood depends upon. Is there anything you shouldn't know about these six people? Fill each folder with items from their company websites, facts about the companies, their corporate board memberships, charity involvements, and the names of their spouses and names and ages of their children. Ultimately, you'll want to know as much as you can about their business aspirations. How much money do they earn? How much do they want to earn? What's their ultimate financial and professional goal? And so on. The seventh folder should be marked "Bench." This is where you toss information about all your potential network members. Check it once a week to reevaluate the status of your network.

ESSENTIAL 11: BUILD A TEAM

This is the inevitable corollary to Essential 2—Commit to What You Do Best. Falling into money requires you to spend as much of your time and focus as possible on your exceptional skills and talents. For everything else, you need a team.

Team building may be little more than taking a new, more direct business approach with people you already associate with. Once you've committed to what you do very well, you'll see that people with complementary skills are all around you. The ones you don't know are likely just one degree removed from you—through your Nodal Network.

Let's say you're an architect. You've determined that your true strength is project management and not design. You want to use this strength to go into real estate development and get an equity stake in a property. There's a lot you don't know. But you probably already know many of the people who can help: realtors to identify building sites, bankers to set up construction financing, investors to provide capital, and contractors to build your development.

Even the worst, most hermitlike architects know a few real estate brokers, contractors, and lawyers. They would make up your Nodal Network. They would be your first natural points of access to your other missing parts—investors and bankers. A Nodal Network by definition puts you just one degree of separation away from all the people in the respective networks of *each* of your network's members. Follow through and you will have a prospective team for the project before you know it. Following through and making it happen involves most of the other

Essentials. But even a rudimentary Nodal Network assures you that your project will not die from a lack of prospects.

It's easy to feel daunted by the idea that you need to manage a team of people. Think back to Essential 3, Follow the Money. You may love to cook, but the thought of running a restaurant makes you nauseous. You enjoy woodworking but can't stand the real estate game. And while you have a knack for managing people, the corporate ladder is a tough climb and running your own business may feel completely beyond you. The thought of these added responsibilities might give you an ache in the pit of your stomach.

Everyone who becomes Business Brilliant feels that same ache—of anxiety, of the unknown, of the suspicion that what you don't know or can't do yourself will sneak up and destroy you.

The difference is how they interpret that ache. Self-made millionaires take it as a signal that they need to go find some partners to take on these other tasks. For them, the ache is a valuable source of information. It tells them that there's something they don't know how to do, that they're not good at, that it's time to draw on their Nodal Networks and go outside their Centers for help.

Once again, your Nodal Network is your most valuable asset. Time and focus are your two most valuable resources. Business Brilliance requires you to rely on your most valuable asset to find help conserving your most valuable resources.

THE TECHNIQUE: Take 30 minutes. Do a quick pro forma on the one time-consuming task you either don't do well or know you shouldn't be doing yourself. Use the pro forma to calculate the minimum value you could create if someone else were taking the time to do that task. That number is your budget. Go through your Nodal Network, call around, and find someone who can do the task for that much and not one penny more. Even if the number is very low, get creative. It works.

ESSENTIAL 12: GET A COACH

By now it should be obvious that it doesn't take money to make money. It takes people. That should come as good news because accessing people is usually easier and more fun than accessing cold hard cash.

Here's the drawback: People are human. Your network members, your team members, your clients—each of them has a uniquely human set of wants, desires, quirks, and limitations that you need to understand and accommodate. These people hold the keys to your financial goals but, very naturally, they are committed to their own goals first. Every day you run the risk of neglecting your own purposes in the whirl of responding to other people's requests and concerns.

This is why you need a coach. You need someone who will keep you accountable to your own goals and avoid procrastinating on your projects. With the right kind of coach, you will have one person among all the people in your business life and your personal life who you can rely on to help you put your own objectives first. No matter how proficient and goal oriented you are, an effective coach can make you better.

Types of coaching services vary widely, but our studies of coaches in the financial services sector showed that fairly moderate and inexpensive coaching—consisting of weekly phone consultations—can raise revenues for their clients by 25 percent or more. If you think of a coach as a "boss you can fire," as someone you are accountable to but not working for, you can make sure there's always someone ready to help you avoid getting diverted and distracted from your goals.

THE TECHNIQUE: As with finding any personal-services professional, you should interview a few coaches before settling on one. If you're using this book as your guide for developing your Business Brilliance, you want to identify a coach willing to work with you on the 17 Essentials. There are countless online resources for finding coaches, but you shouldn't pass up this opportunity to source your Nodal Network for referrals first.

➤ Persistence

How do self-made millionaires manage to succeed when, on average, they *fail* more often than everyone else? It's simple. They fail more often because they try more often.

ESSENTIAL 13: MAKE FRIENDS WITH FAILURE

It's never fun when a project falls short. The only thing worse than failing, though, is failing to learn from failing. To develop your Business Brilliance, you need to embrace the setbacks that come your way. You need to examine each one carefully and use that analysis to make adjustments in a second effort. Why? Because anything worth trying is worth trying again.

It's *natural* to want to give up and run away from the pain of disappointment. A failed attempt of any kind will give you plenty of evidence that the project was fundamentally unsound, or that you're not cut out for it. That's the trap that failure sets for us, a trap most of our middle-class survey respondents say they fall into. I've learned through two separate surveys that their most common response to failure is to give up and do something else.

The vast majority of self-made millionaires are different. They go right back at whatever failed because they know that it often takes more than one attempt to gain the insights and knowledge necessary for succeeding at anything. Each time they miss the mark, they bring themselves that much closer to making it on the next try. They end up becoming Business Brilliant because it is this rare quality of persistence that ultimately sets them apart.

THE TECHNIQUE: Take 30 minutes. Look at the pro forma (Essential 5) on the project that failed. Take down a few notes on each assumption within the pro forma that fell short of expectations. Even if you feel it's obvious what went wrong, write it down for the same reason you commit your financial goals to paper—to make it real. A concrete set of failed expectations, clearly written out, gives you some firm points of reference and sets the stage for the second or third try.

ESSENTIAL 14: KEEP YOUR CHANGES TO YOURSELF

There is a difference between persistence and banging your head against a wall. Before you try a second time at something that didn't work, you need to consider what's worth trying to change and what's not.

Self-made millionaires are almost unanimous on one point: When rebounding from failure, don't try changing other people. Only 1 percent said they are most likely to "Try to change your partner's behavior or approach the next time." Instead they put the onus on themselves. About 7 in 10 said they were most likely to change their own behavior or approach, with the other 3 in 10 saying they would likely try to change circumstances on a second try.

It's a point that's pretty consistent with all the 17 Essentials. Whatever happens, you should assume it's 70 percent due to your own actions and 30 percent due to circumstances, because those are the only two factors you can control or change next time. When you take that next crack at anything that failed or fell short of expectations the first time, you will save yourself a lot of wasted effort if you keep this much in mind.

THE TECHNIQUE: Take 20 minutes. Go back over the notes you made in Essential 13. Rewrite each element of what went wrong in language that makes you accountable for making sure it goes right next time. Wherever it appears that one of your partners dropped the ball, scratch it out. You need to take the risk he's learned from the mistake. There's little or nothing you can do about it, short of getting a new partner.

ESSENTIAL 15: TRY, TRY, TRY, TRY AGAIN

Discovering your full Business Brilliance is an "iterative" process. The term comes from the Latin word *iterare*, "to repeat." Mathematicians who use iterative calculations start out with an initial guess at an answer. Then they run a series of ever finer approximations to get closer and closer to the correct result. The reason they use the iterative method is very instructive: Some equations would take longer than a lifetime to solve if they were computed by exact mathematical formulas.

The same is true with Business Brilliance. It can't be done perfectly and exactly. There aren't enough hours in a day or in your lifetime to find the precise method of getting it right on the first attempt. You're better off starting out today with iterative expectations. You draw up your pro forma, you make your deal, and you move forward, knowing that there's a lot you don't know.

Maybe you succeed. Maybe you succeed only modestly. But if you fail or merely disappoint yourself, consider that you've just taken the first step toward homing in on your target. Now you're better informed. You know where some of the pitfalls lie. The second go-round might reveal still more pitfalls, but because it's your second time, you'll be better prepared to deal with them, too.

Remember that anything worth trying is worth trying again. And again. And again.

THE TECHNIQUE: Take 30 minutes. Review your worksheets from Essentials 13 and 14. Then go back to Essential 5 and run the numbers all over again for a new pro forma.

ESSENTIAL 16: DON'T PROCRASTINATE

Procrastination is largely fed by fear of failure. If you can acclimate yourself to occasional setbacks and disappointments, it's easier to move ahead because you're starving procrastination of its fuel.

Procrastination is also about perfectionism. Lots of people put off pursuing their dreams because it can be more fun to imagine achieving something great than to endure the difficulties of achieving anything even reasonably good. Putting off making decisions and taking action are the two most certain ways to avoid bad decisions and poor results.

Business Brilliance requires that you take the opposite tack. You keep making decisions with imperfect information, because as long as you're doing more right things than wrong things, even a bad decision is usually better than no decision at all. That's the synergy effect of these 17 Essentials. When you set out with a strong set of goals and work at your Center, in the Line of Money, with a talented team and a strong network, the only real mistake you can make is the mistake of not trying.

THE TECHNIQUE: Go down the list of 17 Essentials. If you're procrastinating, find the one Essential that may have gotten you stuck. When in doubt, rely on your network. If you're really stuck, you may need a new coach.

ESSENTIAL 17: MAKE YOUR OWN LUCK

Self-made millionaires are lucky and they know it. In our survey, 7 out of 10 ascribed "luck" as important to their financial success. Only career choice and persistence ranked more highly. Education, creativity, and putting one's own capital at risk were all considered less important than luck when it came to financial success.

Researchers have studied people who consider themselves lucky. They find the same personal preferences and qualities among the lucky that I find among self-made millionaires. Lucky people nurture their goals and expect them to happen. They make the most of opportunities that come their way. They associate with other people who consider themselves lucky. They turn their misfortune into good luck by persevering and seeing the good side of even the worst circumstances.

Business Brilliance and making your own luck are really the same thing. They both draw upon the ordinary, mundane practices laid out by LEAP: Learning, Earning, Assistance, and Persistence.

LEAP, at long last, is just another way to spell LUCK.

THE TECHNIQUE: Double down on what you do best. Press your advantage whenever and wherever you have the advantage. Work your network. Try and try again. Above all: Ask. Ask for what you want. Ask even when it feels uncomfortable. Ask for more than what you need. Ask for what you're afraid to ask for, and ask for it more than once. Ask until the word "No" loses its sting. When you can laugh at "No" and look at each setback as a source of instruction, then you'll know you've become one of the lucky people destined to become Business Brilliant.

Notes

CHAPTER 1: "BUSINESS BRILLIANT"

3   His multiple Super Bowl wins and lifetime game-winning average of .683: Pro Football Hall of Fame (http://www.profootballhof.com/).

3   "arguably the greatest coach in the history of the league": From a personal interview with Charley Casserly on March 20, 2012.

4   "We specialized in vision, not just sight": From a personal interview with Dr. Harry Wachs on March 21, 2012.

4   Redskins scouts traveled the country carrying a Wachs-Berger toolkit: Ken Denlinger's roundup of advanced football training techniques in his article, "FOOTBALL SMARTS: Are Computers and Thick Playbooks Necessary When Team That Blocks and Tackles Best Usually Wins?" in the *Los Angeles Times*, January 10, 1988.

4   "football brilliant": a term Coach Gibbs uses often. I first heard him use it at a speech in Miami on June 5, 2011. He also uses it in his book *Racing to Win* to describe great football strategists.

6   For the past 25 years, Russ Prince has worked: I met Russ Prince in 2000. Even though we worked together for several years he wouldn't speak to me directly for the first year of our relationship. We worked through an intermediary. Eventually, we began working directly with each other and became friends, colleagues, and eventually coauthors and business partners. Most of what I know about wealthy people I've learned from Prince. Everything I know about Prince, I've learned from him firsthand because

no one has ever written about him. There's a pretty thorough, though out of date, bibliography of Russ's work at http://russalanprince.com/bibliography.html.

7   Prince and I go back a ways: A good place for chocolate milkshakes and reasonably priced food in New York is Burger Heaven at 20 East 49th Street.

7   In 2006, Prince and I: Russ Alan Prince and Lewis Schiff, *The Influence of Affluence: How the New Rich Are Changing America* (New York: Broadway Books, 2009).

9   or the way a poison gas: I am indebted to Harvard professor Amy C. Edmondson for this simple and memorable example of synergy. It appears on page 40 of her book, *A Fuller Explanation: The Synergetic Geometry of R. Buckminster Fuller* (Pueblo, CO: Emergentworld, 2009). On the same page, Edmondson quotes Fuller's elegant definition of the word: "Synergy means the behavior of whole systems unpredicted by the behavior of their parts taken separately."

11   In May 2003, Dr. Richard Shannon: The main source for this story is Naida Grunden, *The Pittsburgh Way to Efficient Healthcare: Improving Patient Care Using Toyota-based Methods* (New York: Healthcare Performance, 2008). See also Bernard Wysocki Jr., "Industrial Strength: To Fix Health Care, Hospitals Take Tips from Factory Floor," *Wall Street Journal*, April 9, 2004; Douglas McCarthy and David Blumenthal, "Case Study: Perfecting Patient Care at Allegheny General Hospital and the Pittsburgh Regional Healthcare Initiative" (Commonwealth Fund, 2006), http://www.commonwealthfund.org/Innovations/Case-Studies/2008/Sep/Case-Study—Perfecting-Patient-Care-at-Allegheny-General-Hospital-and-the-Pittsburgh-Regional-Health.aspx.

11   Tens of thousands of hospital patients: The 250 deaths per day figure was attributed to the Centers for Disease Control and quoted in a National Public Radio interview with Dr. Richard Shannon, "Q & A: How One Hospital Cut Infections," May 11, 2006.

14   In the past six years: According to the Federal Reserve, household net worth peaked at $67.5 trillion in the third quarter of 2007. Then it lost $16.2 trillion over the next 18 months, cratering at $51.3 trillion during the first quarter of 2009 (on March 6, 2009, the Dow Jones closed at

a 12-year low of 6,547.05). Three years later, during the first quarter of 2012, household net worth had climbed back to $62.9 trillion, which was still $4.6 trillion below the 2007 peak. *Flow of Funds Accounts of the United States* (Washington, DC: Board of Governors of the Federal Reserve System, June 7, 2012). See also *Federal Reserve Bulletin*, 2nd ed., vol. 98 (Washington, DC: Board of Governors of the Federal Reserve System, June 2012).

14   The Census Bureau estimates: Alfred Gottschalck and Marina Vornovytskyy, "Changes in Household Net Worth from 2005 to 2010," Random Samplings: The Official Blog of the U.S. Census, June 18, 2012, http://blogs.census.gov/2012/06/18/changes-in-household-net-worth-from-2005-to-2010/.

14   White-collar unemployment: Marios Michaelides and Peter R. Mueser, "Recent Trends in the Characteristics of Unemployment Insurance Recipients," *Monthly Labor Review* (Washington, DC: U.S. Bureau of Labor Statistics, July 2012). See also Lawrence Mishel, "White-Collar Unemployment Double Its Pre-recession Level for Almost 2.5 Years," Economic Policy Institute, Economic Snapshot, September 28, 2011, http://www.epi.org/publication/white-collar-unemployment-level/.

16   The vast majority of hospitals: Dr. Peter Pronovost of Johns Hopkins, a leader in the movement to reduce hospital infections, told ABC News in 2011, "Mistakes happen at every hospital. Our current response is to tell the doctors and nurses to be careful instead of making it impossible for mistakes to happen." Pronovost wants device makers and systems engineers to be hired to improve patient safety by implementing synergistic processes like the Toyota Way. "We need to invest in the science of health care delivery," Pronovost said. "The U.S. spends two pennies on the science of health care delivery for every dollar it spends on finding new genes." Katie Moisse, "Hospital Errors Common and Underreported," ABC News Medical Unit, April 7, 2011.

Pronovost blames arrogance among doctors and healthcare executives for producing a set of barriers to the development of "measurable, achievable and routine ways to prevent patient harm.... It's unconscionable that so many people are dying because of these arrogance barriers," Pronovost said in 2010. "You can't have arrogance in a model for accountability."

From "Bringing True Accountability to Health Care: Lessons from Efforts to Reduce Hospital-Acquired Infections," Johns Hopkins Medicine news release, July 13, 2010, http://www.hopkinsmedicine.org/news/media/releases/bringing_true_accountability_to_health_care_lessons_from_efforts_to_reduce_hospital_acquired_infections/.

17 It could be a question of motivation: From *Making Health Care Safer: A Critical Analysis of Patient Safety Practices* (Rockville, MD: Agency for Healthcare Research and Quality, 2001), 25. " [It] is undeniable that some industries, most notably commercial aviation, have safety records far superior to that of healthcare."

17 You've probably never heard: Haque's article, "The Economic Roots of Your Life Crisis," appeared in the March 16, 2012, entry of Haque's *Harvard Business Review* blog, http://blogs.hbr.org/haque/.

18 For the first time in U.S. history: In December 2001, 71 percent of Americans thought it was likely that children would go on to have better lives than their parents. By May 2011, that number had dropped to 44 percent, and was only 37 percent among households with annual incomes in excess of $75,000. Elizabeth Mendes, "In U.S., Optimism about Future for Youth Reaches All-Time Low: The Highest-Income Americans Are Among the Least Optimistic about the Future," *Gallup Politics*, May 2, 2011, http://www.gallup.com/poll/147350/Optimism-Future-Youth-Reaches-Time-Low.aspx.

19 And most people running hospitals: Richard Shannon used the phrase "theory of inevitability" in his May 11, 2006, interview with NPR and in the chapter he authored for *Infection Prevention and Control: Current Research and Practice* (Oakbrook Terrace, IL: Joint Commission Resources, 2007).

CHAPTER 2: DO WHAT YOU LOVE, BUT FOLLOW THE MONEY

23 If you had been one of Guy Laliberté's parents: Most of the facts and figures about Cirque du Soleil have been provided by the company. Details about Laliberté and Cirque's early history are drawn from the company's authorized history, Tony Babinski and Kristian Manchester, *Cirque*

du Soleil: 20 Years under the Sun—An Authorized History (New York: Harry N. Abrams, 2004).

24 Le Grand Tour had been conceived: Doug Fischer authored an excellent account of *Cirque*'s early years from a distinctly Canadian perspective in the *Ottawa Citizen*, October 4, 1988.

25 Thanks to his majority interest in Cirque's parent company: As of March 2012, *Forbes* put Laliberté's net worth at $2.6 billion, making his fortune the 11th largest in Canada and 464th in the world.

26 Marsha Sinetar said the idea came to her: From *Do What You Love, the Money Will Follow: Discovering Your Right Livelihood* (New York: Dell, 1989). Sinetar went on to publish more than twenty books, including one titled *To Build the Life You Want, Create the Work You Love: The Spiritual Dimension of Entrepreneuring* (New York: St. Martin's, 1995).

28 And that was the case with Guy Laliberté: For more on the story of Cirque du Soleil and its place in circus history, the best available book is Ernest J. Albrecht, *The New American Circus* (Gainesville: University Press of Florida, 1995).

30 Laliberté and Caron split on bitter terms: Caron's disparaging remarks about Laliberté appeared in Ian Halperin's unauthorized 2009 biography *Guy Laliberté: The Fabulous Life of the Creator of Cirque du Soleil* (Montreal: Transit, 2009). Halperin's book contained some salacious passages regarding sex and drugs at Cirque parties, and other allegations about Laliberté's personal life. Laliberté and Halperin took legal action against each other and then settled out of court in 2011. Halperin apologized to Laliberté without retracting any of the book's contents.

31 Hirst was born into even less auspicious circumstances: For Hirst's well-documented personal history, see Richard Lacayo, "Damien Hirst: Bad Boy Makes Good," *Time*, September 15, 2008, and Donald N. Thompson, *The $12 Million Stuffed Shark: The Curious Economics of Contemporary Art* (New York: Palgrave Macmillan, 2008).

32 By then Hirst's reputation had been solidified: *The $12 Million Stuffed Shark* includes a story on page 68 about a friend of Hirst's named A. A. Gill, who wanted to sell off a portrait of Joseph Stalin that he had bought for £200. Christie's auction house refused to handle the painting because

of its political nature, but Gill thought to ask, What if it were a Stalin portrait done by Hirst? Christie's replied they'd be happy to auction anything by Hirst. So Gill asked his friend to do him a little favor. Hirst painted a red clown nose on the Stalin portrait and signed it. Christie's estimated the portrait's top value at £12,000, but after 17 competing bids, it sold for £140,000. Writes Thompson, "It was, after all, a signed Hirst."

33   Around the time of that announcement: From "Dumping the Shark," *New York Times* editorial, July 20, 2007.

35   In the spring of 1969: From Deci's own account in his excellent book, co-authored with Richard Flaste, *Why We Do What We Do: The Dynamics of Personal Autonomy* (New York: G. P. Putnam's Sons, 1995).

36   "[This is] what millions of us": From Alfie Kohn's bestseller, *Punished by Rewards: The Trouble with Gold Stars, Incentive Plans, A's, Praise, and Other Bribes* (Boston: Houghton Mifflin, 1993).

41   O'Hurley appeared in just 20: Episode figures are from the Internet Movie Database, www.imdb.com.

41   Patrick Warburton, who played: Susan King, "A Life beyond Puddy," *Los Angeles Times*, March 15, 2001.

41   He popped up in TV commercials: Stuart Elliott, "Madison Avenue's Low Road; Deals, Not Enjoyable Campaigns, Were the Hallmark of 1998," *New York Times*, December 31, 1998.

41   He did radio station voiceovers: David Vinjamuri, *Accidental Branding: How Ordinary People Build Extraordinary Brands* (Hoboken, NJ: John Wiley & Sons, 2008).

41   An online video-tech: "The Peterman Principle," *Businessweek*, January 9, 2006.

42   O'Hurley made his Broadway debut: Ibid.

42   O'Hurley told one interviewer: Mabel Jong, "John O'Hurley, J. Peterman and Success: Yada, Yada, Yada," Bankrate.com, June 6, 2003.

CHAPTER 3: SAVE LESS, EARN MORE

47   When Suze Orman recalls her life: Susan Dominus, "Suze Orman Is Having a Moment," *New York Times Magazine*, May 14, 2009. The story offers

some interesting insights into Orman's perspective on her work. Although her books advise against the wastefulness of buying new cars, Orman appeared in General Motors ads touting a zero-percent-interest promotion. "I'm not in this for charity," she said in response to critics. "This is a business, and anybody who thinks that it's not a business is an idiot."

47   Orman's 1999 book: Suze Orman, *The Courage to Be Rich: Creating a Life of Material and Spiritual Abundance* (New York: Riverhead, 1999), 66–71.

48   *Newsweek* columnist Jane Bryant Quinn: Ed Slott, *Parlay Your IRA into a Family Fortune: 3 Easy Steps for Creating a Lifetime Supply of Tax-deferred, Even Tax-free, Wealth for You and Your Family* (New York: Viking, 2005).

49   Anyone who has taken a serious look: Randall Jones, *The Richest Man in Town* (New York: Business Plus, 2009).

49   Felix Dennis can be a fanatical skinflint: Felix Dennis, *How to Get Rich* (London: Ebury, 2006).

49   Despite all the evidence: Orman, *The Courage to Be Rich*, page 112.

50   Not to pick on Suze: "She's So Money: Questions for Suze Orman," interview by Deborah Solomon, *New York Times Magazine*, February 25, 2007. "My greatest pleasure is still flying private. I spend between $300,000 to $500,000, depending on my year, on flying private."

50   So when Orman claims that by scrimping and saving: Orman, *The Courage to Be Rich*, page 71.

51   The odds are that the sole reason: Robin L. Pinkley and Gregory B. Northcraft, *Get Paid What You're Worth: The Expert Negotiator's Guide to Salary and Compensation* (New York: St. Martin's, 2000).

51   In 1995, Linda Babcock: Linda Babcock and Sara Laschever, *Women Don't Ask: Negotiation and the Gender Divide* (Princeton, NJ: Princeton University Press, 2003).

53   Other studies have shown: Pinkley and Northcraft, *Get Paid What You're Worth*.

53   In the coming year, 50 million U.S. workers: There were 50.1 million new hires in the United States in 2011, representing 38.1 percent of total employment. From U.S. Department of Labor, Bureau of Labor Statistics,

"Annual Hires, Separations, Quits, Layoffs and Discharges, 2011," reported by TED: The Editor's Desk, March 14, 2012, http://www.bls.gov/opub/ted/2012/ted_20120314.htm.

55 Most hiring managers told Pinkley and Northcraft: Pinkley and Northcraft, *Get Paid What You're Worth.*

56 In the words of one popular negotiating guide: Jack Chapman, *Negotiating Your Salary: How to Make $1,000 a Minute* (Wilmette, IL: Jack Chapman, 2011).

56 After her first book came out: Linda Babcock and Sara Laschever, *Ask for It: How Women Can Use the Power of Negotiation to Get What They Really Want* (New York: Bantam Dell, 2008).

58 Babcock acknowledges that it is easiest: The story about the Bermuda hotel housekeeping manager appears in chapter 9 of *Ask for It.*

59 In her latest book: Suze Orman, *The Money Class: Learn to Create Your New American Dream* (New York: Spiegel and Grau, 2011).

59 It's true that the working world: Richard Vedder, "Why Did 17 Million Students Go to College?" *Chronicle of Higher Education* Innovations blog, October 20, 2010. Vedder is the director of the Center for College Affordability and Productivity. His analysis of Labor Department statistics also shows that "there are 5,057 janitors in the U.S. with Ph.D.'s, other doctorates, or professional degrees," http://chronicle.com/blogs/innovations/why-did-17-million-students-go-to-college/27634.

59 In 1979, about 28 percent of American workers: Analysis of Labor Department statistics by the New America Foundation; Sherle R. Schwenninger and Samuel Sherraden, "The American Middle Class under Stress," April 27, 2011, http://growth.newamerica.net/publications/policy/the_american_middle_class_under_stress.

60 The management consultant Umair Haque: In "The Economic Roots of Your Life Crisis" Haque writes fully in the spirit of Business Brilliance: "If we really want to smash through the straitjacket of life crisis, we must recognize the deeper dilemma and refuse to settle for anything less than breaking it. One tiny, trembling, but decisive step at a time, we can arc our own journeys towards a life searingly well lived. It's not easy. I know. It can feel paralyzing, debilitating, panic-inducing. But here's the secret inside the secret. Institutions fail. But life goes on."

62   On this subject, I'll give the final word to Linda Babcock: Babcock writes
      in the concluding chapter of *Ask for It*: "Always getting what you ask for
      in a negotiation—always hearing yes and never risking no—means that
      you never ask for enough. Excessive caution, rather than protecting you
      from rejection or losing face, can actually prevent you from getting all
      that you're worth, all you deserve, and all that's available."

CHAPTER 4: IMITATE, DON'T INNOVATE

65   Gary Kildall was a thirty-year-old Ph.D.: Three excellent books give some-
      what similar accounts of the Kildall-Gates rivalry: Robert X. Cringely,
      *Accidental Empires: How the Boys of Silicon Valley Make Their Millions,
      Battle Foreign Competition, and Still Can't Get a Date* (Reading, MA:
      Addison-Wesley, 1991); James Wallace and Jim Erickson, *Hard Drive: Bill
      Gates and the Making of the Microsoft Empire* (New York: Wiley, 1992);
      Stephen Manes and Paul Andrews, *Gates: How Microsoft's Mogul Rein-
      vented an Industry—and Made Himself the Richest Man in America* (New
      York: Doubleday, 1993). Additionally, one very thorough chapter devoted
      to Gary Kildall's story appears in Harold Evans, Gail Buckland, and David
      Lefer, *They Made America: From the Steam Engine to the Search Engine:
      Two Centuries of Innovators* (New York: Little, Brown, 2004).

67   By the mid-1980s: Gary Kildall's attempt to sell Digital Research to Bill
      Gates is recounted in Harold Evans et al., *They Made America*. The book
      provides the following entry from Kildall's unpublished memoir regard-
      ing Kildall's final meeting with Gates: "We parted friends for some rea-
      son I don't understand today. However, this rejection by Bill was one of
      his big business mistakes."

71   So in the late summer of 1980: In *Hard Drive*, James Wallace and Jim
      Erickson write: "In a series of meetings with Microsoft after the initial
      rebuff from Digital Research, Sams threw the operating systems problem
      in Gates's lap. 'This was the negotiating tactic we took with them,' said
      Sams. 'We wanted this to be their problem, to find us the right operating
      system, one that we could integrate successfully on our schedule.'"

73   Where did Kildall go wrong: The quote is from Gordon Eubanks, inter-
      viewed for the PBS documentary *Triumph of the Nerds*, Oregon Public

Broadcasting, 1996. Eubanks was a longtime friend and associate of Kildall who later went on to become president and CEO of Symantec, the antivirus software maker. Eubanks once told an interviewer that he learned from Kildall's example that "if you're going to run a company, you have to take the long view. You have to run it to succeed, and you have to run it for the people who work there. . . . Gary really didn't have the passion and the drive. He was a great person and we were very good friends. I really thought highly of Gary. He was a tremendous amount of fun, but running a business was not something that was high on his list. . . . Bill [Gates], for anything you want to say about him, Bill really wanted to build a business, and he was aggressive, maybe ruthless. But mostly he was just aggressive. Gary really had the upper hand. He just didn't play the cards right." Gordon Eubanks Oral History, Computerworld Honors Program International Archives, Cupertino, CA, 2000, http://www.cwheroes.org/archives/histories/Eubanks.pdf.

74　Thomas Edison did not: Kendall F. Haven, *100 Greatest Science Inventions of All Time* (Westport, CT: Libraries Unlimited, 2006).

74　And Henry Ford did not: Joseph W. Barnes, "Rochester and the Automobile Industry," *Rochester History* 43, nos. 2 and 3 (April and July 1981).

74　The names Swan, Selden: Dobrev's quotes are from Sarah E. Needleman, "In Race to Market, It Pays to Be a Latecomer," *Wall Street Journal*, January 20, 2011.

74　In *The Myths of Innovation*: Scott Berkun, *The Myths of Innovation* (Sebastopol, CA: O'Reilly, 2007).

74　Most inventors who: Thomas Astebro, "The Return to Independent Invention: Evidence of Risk Seeking, Extreme Optimism or Skewness-Loving?" *Economic Journal* 113, no. 484 (2003): 226–239. The study was also mentioned in an article about entrepreneurship, "Searching for the Invisible Man," *Economist*, March 11, 2006.

75　By Berkun's estimation: *Myths of Innovation*. The eight hurdles to innovation are: Finding an idea, developing a solution, sponsorship and funding, reproduction (manufacturing), reaching your prospective customer, beating your competitors, timing, and finally, keeping the lights on. Every invention requires the inventor to clear all eight hurdles, while tripping over any one of the eight spells failure for the entire effort. This is why, Berkun writes, there are more than 4,000 mousetrap patents, and yet only 20 have ever produced profits for their inventors.

75   The other side of the coin: The latest study by Paul D. Reynolds is *Entrepreneurship in the United States: The Future Is Now* (New York: Springer, 2010).

75   A survey of a far more elite group: Amar V. Bhide, *The Origin and Evolution of New Businesses* (New York: Oxford University Press, 2000).

76   The notion that you can get rich: Statistics from the International Shark Attack File say that there were no shark attack fatalities in the United States in 2011 and just 11 total between 2000 and 2011. Every year, however, there are about 50 insect sting fatalities, according to the American College of Allergy, Asthma, and Immunology. The National Weather Service counted 29 lightning strike fatalities in the United States in 2010. During the same year, the Bureau of Labor Statistics logged 129 fatal falls from ladders.

77   It wasn't until 2002: Adam Cohen, *The Perfect Store: Inside eBay* (Boston: Little, Brown, 2002).

77   Even without such corporate spin: Jeremy Seabrook, "E-mail from Bill," *New Yorker*, January 10, 1994.

77   If there is any harm done: Pino G. Audia and Christopher I. Rider, "A Garage and an Idea: What More Does an Entrepreneur Need?" *California Management Review* 48, no. 1 (Fall 2005).

78   As Dan and Chip Heath would write: Dan Heath and Chip Heath, "The Myth about Creation Myths," *Fast Company*, March 1, 2007.

78   Audia and Rider concluded: Audia and Rider, "A Garage and an Idea." Audia was interviewed for the radio program *This American Life*, episode 383, "Origin Story," June 19, 2009. He told host Ira Glass: "[If] you want to become an entrepreneur, the obvious thing to do is to first go get a job in an industry you're interested in and learn, and then eventually, later try to create a company."

78   Bhide came to a similar conclusion: The quote appears in *The Origin and Evolution of New Businesses*, 32–33.

78   Larry Ellison, the billionaire founder: Oracle Corporation CEO Larry Ellison quoted in Matthew Symonds and Larry Ellison. *Softwar: An*

Intimate Portrait of Larry Ellison and Oracle (New York: Simon and Schuster, 2003).

78   The passage of time: "[Gates's] genius has never consisted in seeing further than anyone else, but in seeing the near-future more clearly, and understanding much better than his competitors how to exploit it. Time and again, Microsoft has recognised the potential in someone else's idea and simply done it better, always in marketing and, less often, in design." "I Have a Dream," *Economist*, November 25, 1995.

79   Within six months: Gates's syndicated newspaper column at the time: "I revised *The Road Ahead* this year, and it's such a thorough overhaul that in many ways it is new. I rewrote several chapters and added about 20,000 new words.... It's unusual to revise a book completely just a year after it was published, but it was necessary because my near-term view of the future has changed so much in the past year. The rise of the Internet provoked me to reinvent my company, and the book needed the same re-evaluation." "Only Ever Wanted to Make Enough Money to Hire Friends," October 23, 1996.

79   "No matter how much Bill Gates": David L. Green, *IQuote: Brilliance and Banter from the Internet Age* (Guilford, CT: Lyons, 2007).

80   Steve Ballmer, now Microsoft's CEO: The Ballmer quotation is from an interview for the PBS documentary *Triumph of the Nerds*.

80   It was the summer of 2004: The quote about round numbers and other details is from the thoroughly researched and well written "The Accidental Hero," by Matthew Boyle, *Businessweek*, November 10, 2009; see also a Q&A interview with Frankel, "A Subway Hero," by Suzanne Zionts, FoxBusiness, November 18, 2009, http://smallbusiness.foxbusiness.com/entrepreneurs/2009/11/17/qa-subway-franchise-owner-dollar-foot-long/.

81   As ideas go: Robert M. Schindler, "The 99 Price Ending as a Signal of a Low-Price Appeal," *Journal of Retailing* 82, no. 1 (2006): 71–77.

82   The "irritatingly addictive" TV jingle: Boyle, "The Accidental Hero." "The idea was to use hand gestures and an irritatingly addictive jingle to convey both the price (five fingers) and the product (hands spread about a foot apart)." An executive with Subway's ad agency was quoted as saying, "We wanted to create the feeling that this was a movement taking hold."

82 One restaurant consultant told: "'Five dollars is the magic number now,' says restaurant consultant Malcolm Knapp. Boyle, "The Accidental Hero."

82 Paul Orfalea, the founder of Kinko's: The Kinko's 24-hour story is from Orfalea's brilliant autobiography, as told to Ann Marsh, *Copy This!: Lessons from a Hyperactive Dyslexic Who Turned a Bright Idea into One of America's Best Companies* (New York: Workman, 2005), 61–62.

83 A legend called: A version of "Columbus and the Egg" by Indiana-born children's author James Baldwin can be found at the Baldwin Project, www.mainlesson.com. A monument to Columbus on the Spanish island of Ibiza is in the shape of a large egg, commemorating the legend.

83 Damien Hirst, the conceptual artist: Sarah Lyall, "Is It Art or Just Dead Meat?" *New York Times*, November 12, 1995.

84 When Paul Orfalea sold: Six years after Orfalea and 125 Kinko's partners sold a 27.5 percent stake in Kinko's to a New York buyout firm, the firm paid Orfalea $116 million for his remaining stake. RiShawn Biddle, "Kinko's Cuts Ties to Founder," *Forbes*, January 13, 2003.

84 It's true that, even by Orfalea's own estimation: Orfalea and Marsh, *Copy This!*, 135.

84 Kinko's began as a one-man operation: Ibid., 7.

85 "The customer walks into a store": Ibid., 22.

85 Orfalea came to realize that: Ibid., 9.

85 Throughout *Copy This!*: Ibid., 61.

86 People should feel soothed: Ibid., 42.

86 He got angry when: Ibid., 45.

86 In the years before e-mail: Ibid., 55.

86 Once, Orfalea persuaded the local owner: Ibid., 43.

87 "In retail there are few secrets": Ibid., 202.

87 Losing out to Bill Gates: Evans et al., *They Made America*.

88 "I expected too much of educators": Kildall's friend and colleague, Tom Rolander, gave the eulogy at Kildall's memorial service and read aloud a four-paragraph excerpt from Kildall's unpublished memoir, of which this quote is a part. The eulogy and other documents related to Kildall and Digital Research can be found at www.digitalresearch.biz. On the site, Kildall's son writes an homage to his father: "Like other great inventors

before him, Gary was greatly disappointed when he discovered that innovation clashes with the business world. He learned the hard way that even in such a young industry, it is cutthroat business practices and not great products which guarantee success. It was simply not in Gary's nature to hoard knowledge, to buy out his competition, or to take credit for work that was not his."

88   Disappointed inventors: The movie *Flash of Genius* was based in part on a *New Yorker* article by John Seabrook, "The Flash of Genius," January 11, 1993. It was later included in Seabrook's book, *Flash of Genius: And Other True Stories of Invention* (New York: St. Martin's Griffin, 2008).

89   Kearns died: Matt Schudel, "Accomplished, Frustrated Inventor Dies," *Washington Post*, February 26, 2005: "In his final years, [Kearns] drove around in two aging vehicles: a 1978 Ford pickup and a 1965 Chrysler. Neither had intermittent wipers." See also Reed Johnson, "The Cantankerous Man behind the Wipers," *Los Angeles Times*, October 3, 2008: "Even so, the movie understates the real-life Kearns' volatility and vehemence. It also drastically underplays his family's resentment of Kearns' bullying, obsessive ways, which eventually shattered his 27-year marriage and caused his children to distance themselves physically from their father. As Tim, Kearns' second-eldest son, told me when I interviewed him: 'We all got to the point where it was him or us. And you always choose yourself.'"

90   In e-mails since made public: Evans et al., *They Made America*, 543.

90   The lawsuit dragged on: Ibid., 544.

CHAPTER 5: KNOW-HOW IS GOOD, "KNOW-WHO" IS BETTER

95   In 1951, a twenty-one-year-old stockbroker: The story of Warren Buffett's failed gas station appears in Buffett's authorized biography by Alice Schroeder, *The Snowball: Warren Buffett and the Business of Life* (New York: Bantam, 2008), 169.

97   Ed, if you hadn't: As of March 2012, *Forbes* ranked Buffett the third richest man in the world, with a net worth of $44 billion. Bill Gates's fortune ranks second with $61 billion, behind Mexican telecom magnate Carlos Slim's $69 billion.

98 Back in 1958: Buffett's history as a corporate raider is portrayed vividly in Schroeder, *The Snowball*, and in the unauthorized biography by Roger Lowenstein, *Buffett: The Making of an American Capitalist* (New York: Broadway Books, 2001).

101 During its first four seasons: Ian Halperin, *Guy Laliberté: The Fabulous Life of the Creator of Cirque du Soleil* (Montreal: Transit, 2009), 40–45.

101 In 1985, when a failed national tour: From Tony Babinski and Kristian Manchester, *Cirque du Soleil: 20 Years Under the Sun—An Authorized History* (New York: Harry N. Abrams, 2004), 78–81.

101 "Guy was a master networker": Ian Halperin, *Guy Laliberté*, 44.

103 About 750,000 new: Scott Shane, *The Illusions of Entrepreneurship: The Costly Myths That Entrepreneurs, Investors, and Policy Makers Live By* (New Haven, CT: Yale University Press, 2008).

103 Back in 1998, Green was: Sources about Paul Green and the School of Rock include official company communications and "History of the School of Rock" at www.sordc.com/history.shtml. See also James Iha, "Schoolhouse Rock," *Spin*, May 2002; "The Real School of Rock," *Guardian*, February 22, 2004; Lola Ogunnaike, "Class, Get in Touch with Your Inner Zappa," *New York Times*, November 3, 2003; David F. Tilman, "In Record Time, Rock On, Paul Green!" *Jewish Exponent*, February 5, 2004; Joel Topcik, "'School' Daze," *New York Times*, May 29, 2005; Wendy Tanaka, "Profits of Rock," *Philadelphia Inquirer*, May 26, 2005; Joey Sweeney, "Academy Fight Song," *Philadelphia Weekly*, January 2, 2002; Will Hodgkinson, "Rock School Saved My Life," *Guardian*, August 26, 2005; Becky Yerak, "School of Rock Rolls On with $5 Million Investment from Private Equity Group," *Chicago Tribune*, April 19, 2012; and "Paul Green Joins Woodstock Film Festival as Music Coordinator," Woodstock Film Festival news release, August 3, 2011.

105 Know-who got Green: "High uncertainty and low capital and opportunity costs create a 'heads I win, tails I don't lose much' proposition for entrepreneurs." Amar Bhide, *The Origin and Evolution of New Businesses* (New York: Oxford University Press, 2000), 361.

106 One study says that fewer than 4 in 10 businesses: Paul D. Reynolds and Sammis B. White, *The Entrepreneurial Process: Economic Growth, Men, Women, and Minorities* (Westport, CT: Quorum, 1997).

106 The most famous informal investor: "Body Shop Founders Sell Up in £625m Deal," *Times* (London), March 18, 2006. See also Sam Greenhill, "How a £4,000 Body Shop Loan Made £146m," www.thisismoney .co.uk, June 26, 2010.

106 By some estimates: Paul D. Reynolds, *Entrepreneurship in the United States: The Future Is Now* (New York: Springer, 2010).

107 Few people who have met Bill Gates: Walter Isaacson, "In Search of the Real Bill Gates," *Time*, January 13, 1997.

107 As one computer executive: The quote about Gates's knowledge of the computer industry is from a close friend of Gates, Eddie Curry, who was a cofounder of *PC* magazine. It appears in James Wallace and Jim Erickson, *Hard Drive: Bill Gates and the Making of the Microsoft Empire* (New York: Wiley, 1992). Curry's point was that someone like Gates, who knew everything about the industry and its players (someone with know-who, instead of mere technical know-how) was needed to bring order to the fragmented PC market. "You could not have relied on people like Gary Kildall," Curry said. "He didn't have the vision, the understanding of the problems," 213.

108 The word *entrepreneur*: The term "structural hole" comes from Ronald S. Burt, *Structural Holes: The Social Structure of Competition* (Cambridge, MA: Harvard University Press, 1992). Burt writes on page 2 of the Introduction, "Structural holes are entrepreneurial opportunities for information access, timing, referrals and control. . . . Competitive advantage is a matter of access to [structural holes in markets]."

109 Surveys continue to show: Nicholas A. Christakis and James H. Fowler, *Connected: The Surprising Power of Our Social Networks and How They Shape Our Lives* (New York: Little, Brown, 2009).

109 The majority of Americans have between: Christakis and Fowler credit sociologist Peter Marsden with coining the phrase "core discussion network."

111 Networking of this kind: A. Tversky and D. Griffin, *Strategy and Choice* (Cambridge, MA: Harvard University Press, 1991).

112 Christakis and Fowler wonder if this helps explain: Christakis and Fowler, *Connected*: "When it is easier to search and navigate social networks, the positive-feedback loop between social connections and success

could create a social magnifier that concentrates even more power and wealth in the hands of those who already had it," 167.

113 The authors of *Connected* admit: Ibid., 107.

CHAPTER 6: WIN-WIN IS A LOSER

117 Adam McKay had been the head writer: You can hear Adam McKay tell the full story of negotiating his *Saturday Night Live* employment terms on the WTF podcast with Marc Maron, episode 119, November 1, 2010.

120 In the fall of 1983 in Silicon Valley: Biographical facts about Philippe Kahn were sourced from Kahn's entry in Harry Henderson, *A to Z of Computer Scientists* (New York: Facts on File, 2003). The story of how Kahn got Borland computers into *Byte* magazine was told by Kahn to Robert A. Mamis in "Management by Necessity," *Inc.*, March 1, 1989.

123 Once you make it your priority: G. Richard Shell, *Bargaining for Advantage: Negotiation Strategies for Reasonable People* (New York: Viking, 1999): "We once had a negotiation speaker who said that the problem with many reasonable people is that they confuse 'win-win' with what he called a 'wimp-win' attitude. The 'wimp-win' negotiator focuses only on his bottom line; the 'win-win' negotiator has ambitious goals," 32.

123 In his book *Start with No*: Jim Camp, *Start with No: The Negotiating Tools That the Pros Don't Want You to Know* (New York: Crown Business, 2002). Camp heads the Camp Negotiation Institute, www.campnegotiationinstitute.com.

124 Covey tells the story: Stephen R. Covey, *The Seven Habits of Highly Effective People: Restoring the Character Ethic* (New York: Simon and Schuster, 1989), 212.

125 Negotiation guru Michael C. Donaldson: Michael C. Donaldson, *Fearless Negotiating: The Wish-Want-Walk Method to Reach Solutions That Work* (New York: McGraw-Hill, 2007). Donaldson is a Beverly Hills entertainment lawyer and also the coauthor, with Mimi Donaldson, of *Negotiating for Dummies* (Foster City, CA: IDG, 1996).

126 Dominick Misino, a former hostage negotiator: Dominick J. Misino and Jim DeFelice, *Negotiate and Win: Proven Strategies from the NYPD's Top Hostage Negotiator* (New York: McGraw-Hill, 2004).

126 Research shows that writing: Robert B. Cialdini, *Influence: How and Why People Agree to Things* (New York: Morrow, 1984). Cialdini writes in his sociology classic that "something special happens when people personally put their commitment on paper: They live up to what they have written down," 80.

127 A well-known study in Britain: The study is discussed in Shell, *Bargaining for Advantage*, 12. See also Neil Rackham and John Carlisle, "The Effective Negotiator—Part 1: The Behavior of Successful Negotiators," *Journal of European Industrial Training* 2, no. 6 (1978): 6–11, and "The Effective Negotiator—Part 2: Planning for Negotiations," *Journal of European Industrial Training* 2, no. 7 (1978): 2–5.

127 One famous illustration: Jeff Bailey, "Trash for Sand and Vice Versa; Oceanside and Arizona May Have a Perfect Trade," *Wall Street Journal*, March 6, 1997.

127 Misino, who often faced: Adam D. Galinsky, William W. Maddux, Debra Gilin, and Judith B. White, "Why It Pays to Get Inside the Head of Your Opponent: The Differential Effects of Perspective Taking and Empathy in Negotiations," *Psychological Science* 19, no. 4 (2008): 378–384. See also "Inside a Deal: It Pays to Get Inside Your Opponents' Heads Rather Than Their Hearts," *Economist*, May 1, 2008.

128 But what if you really do need the deal: Camp, *Start with No*, 32–34.

129 An apocryphal quote: A similar quote is attributed to Bill Gates, without citation, in Michel Villette and Catherine Vuillermot, *From Predators to Icons: Exposing the Myth of the Business Hero* (Ithaca, NY: ILR, 2009). A passage on page 79 bears repeating here because it reflects some of my points about Gates's Business Brilliance as the key to his success: "As for Bill Gates, he is, of course, a computer scientist, but he is also the son of a corporate lawyer and a banker. His slogan is a program in itself: 'In business, you don't get what you deserve, but only what you negotiate.' In short, even businessmen who focus on technology have two sets of skills. Concentration for a limited time on decisive technical problems is a manifestation of their sense of market placement and their skills as negotiators and strategists much more than of ignorance or incapacity to engage in market transactions." Gates focused on computer programming problems only if they provided a solution to a business problem,

like satisfying IBM. Programming was a means to an end for Gates, not a pleasurable end in itself, as it was for Kildall.

130 So with literally hundreds: Shell, *Bargaining for Advantage*, 32. Shell writes on page 33, "A certain amount of dissatisfaction is a good thing when you first start thinking seriously about improving how you negotiate. Dissatisfaction is a sign that you are setting your goals at a high enough level to encounter resistance from other parties and to take the risk that they may walk away."

132 However, according to Stephen Covey: Covey, *The Seven Habits*, 219.

133 Machiavellianism has been described: Anna Gunthorsdottir, Kevin McCabe, and Vernon Smith, "Using the Machiavellianism Instrument to Predict Trustworthiness in a Bargaining Game," *Journal of Economic Psychology* 23 (2002): 49–66. Descriptions of Machiavellianism noted in the Gunthorsdottir et al. study include "a general cool attitude, manifested as a detached, opportunistic stance toward values and social norms." See also P. E. Mudrack and S. E. Mason, "More on the Acceptability of Workplace Behaviors of a Dubious Ethical Nature," *Psychological Reports* 76, no. 2 (April 1995): 639–648. "Rational and often materialistic, [high scorers on Machiavellian tests] can calmly identify the optimal strategy in each situation [and] are more upset by inefficiency than by injustice," R. Christie and F. Geis, *Studies in Machiavellianism* (New York: Academic Press, 1970), 353.

134 In one clinical experiment: Gunthorsdottir et al., "Using the Machiavellianism Instrument."

135 One of the best stories: Michael Lewis, *The New New Thing: A Silicon Valley Story* (New York: W. W. Norton, 2000).

CHAPTER 7: SPREAD THE WORK, SPREAD THE WEALTH

141 For someone who had barely graduated: Jay Thiessens's story was drawn from the following sources: Sandra Chereb, "Nevada Entrepreneur Built Million-Dollar Firm before Learning to Read," Associated Press, *Chicago Tribune*, June 8, 1999; Michael Barrier, "Meeting Challenges the Blue Chip Way: Blue Chip Enterprise Initiative Program Winners," *Nation's Business*, June 1999; Karen Brailsford, "Reader's Block," *People*, August 9,

1999; Dade Hayes, "Toolmaker Jay Thiessens," *Investor's Daily*, September 9, 1999; Jean Dixon, "Sparks Man's Courage Featured on National TV," *Reno Gazette-Journal*, September 16, 2000; and Gail Liberman and Alan Lavine, *Rags to Riches: Motivating Stories of How Ordinary People Achieved Extraordinary Wealth* (Chicago: Dearborn, 2000).

143 A 2007 study concluded: Julie Logan, "Dyslexic Entrepreneurs: The Incidence, Their Coping Strategies, and Their Business Skills," Cass Business School, London, 2007.

143 "I know that sounds very strange": Julie Logan, interview with Steve Inskeep, National Public Radio, December 26, 2007.

143 As Logan explained: Brent Bowers, "Tracing Business Acumen to Dyslexia," *New York Times*, December 6, 2007.

143 The most successful dyslexic: As of March 2012, *Forbes* put Schwab's wealth at $3.5 billion.

144 When Schwab was applying to colleges: Richard Lee Colvin, "Word of Honor," *Los Angeles Times*, April 30, 1996.

144 "It was a very debilitating": Charles Schwab, video interview with Mark C. Thompson, "Transform Your Biggest Weaknesses into Your Greatest Strengths," Leadership Dialogues, www.LeadertoLeader.org.

144 Business school was somewhat easier: Betsy Morris, "Overcoming Dyslexia," *Fortune*, May 2002.

145 Orfalea's office at Kinko's: Paul Orfalea and Ann Marsh, *Copy This!: Lessons from a Hyperactive Dyslexic Who Turned a Bright Idea into One of America's Best Companies* (New York: Workman, 2005), xvii–xviii. Orfalea used to call himself Kinko's "Wanderer-in-Chief" due to his penchant for escaping the office and doing site visits of stores.

145 When assigned to a big group project: Ibid., 6–7.

145 Looking back, he says: Ibid., 2.

145 After selling his interest: Ibid., xvi.

146 Throughout his upbringing: Richard Branson, *Losing My Virginity: How I've Survived, Had Fun, and Made a Fortune Doing Business My Way* (New York: Three Rivers, 2004), 17.

146 In 1967, at age sixteen: Ibid., 30.

146 When Branson quit school: Ibid., 35.

146 Today Branson's wealth: As of March 2012, *Forbes* put Branson's net

worth at $4.2 billion, making his fortune the fourth largest in the United Kingdom and 255th in the world.

146 Once, at a board meeting: Branson told CNBC's Maria Bartiromo in 2002: "I am mildly dyslexic. It can be quite farcical . . . because although we have the biggest group of private companies, up until about a year ago, I still couldn't work out the difference between gross and net. And therefore, you know, in board meetings, we'd have discussions like, 'Is that good news or is that bad news?' But finally, somebody took me aside and said, 'Think of a fish net in the sea and the fish that are in the net. And what's left over . . . everything else is gross . . . That's the ones you ain't got.'" *After Hours with Maria Bartiromo*, CNBC, July 29, 2002.

147 Branson has explained: Branson, *Losing My Virginity*, 408.

147 Freed from poring over: Glenn Rifkin, "How Richard Branson Works Magic," *Strategy+Business*, issue 13, October 1, 1998.

147 According to one report: Ibid.

147 "I rely far more on gut instinct": Branson, *Losing My Virginity*, 177.

147 He once told *60 Minutes*: Branson, interview with Steve Kroft, "Richard the Lionhearted," *60 Minutes*, November 29, 1992.

148 Already you can zip through London's: www.virginlimobike.com and www.virgingalactic.com/booking. Actor Ashton Kutcher is the 500th "pioneer" to reserve a seat on the Virgin Galactic with a refundable $200,000 deposit.

148 Rock star Peter Gabriel once joked: Branson, *Losing My Virginity*, 411.

148 Charles Schwab has noted: Schwab, video interview with Thompson.

148 There is a great deal of common sense: Marcus Buckingham, *Go Put Your Strengths to Work: 6 Powerful Steps to Achieve Outstanding Performance* (New York: Free Press, 2007), 20. "Ask people point blank 'Is finding your weaknesses and fixing them the best way to achieve outstanding performance?' and in repeated polls, 87 percent either agree or strongly agree."

149 When asked to choose: Ibid., 40.

149 When Gallup asked parents: Marcus Buckingham and Donald O. Clifton, *Now, Discover Your Strengths* (New York: Free Press, 2001), 123.

150 Buckingham has a commonsense prescription: Buckingham, *Go Put Your Strengths to Work*, 201: "You're going to go up to your manager and

have a strong conversation with him. You're going to describe to this person what strengthens you and what weakens you, and you're going to have to do it in such a way that he winds up thinking not that you're trying to make life easy for yourself but, rather, that you are a responsible colleague looking for ways to contribute more—and at the same time make *his* life a little easier."

151 Norm Brodsky was pretty sure: Norm Brodsky and Bo Burlingham, *Street Smarts: An All-Purpose Tool Kit for Entrepreneurs* (New York: Portfolio, 2010). Quotations from Brodsky are from a personal interview on April 15, 2010. See also Robert A. Mamis, "Fatal Attraction," *Inc.*, March 1989.

154 The reluctance to delegate: Robert F. Hurley, *The Decision to Trust: How Leaders Create High-Trust Organizations* (San Francisco: Jossey-Bass, 2012), 41–48.

155 Brodsky points out: Personal interview with Norm Brodsky, April 15, 2010.

156 In 1988, his wife: Elaine Brodsky, "Confessions of a Woman Married to a Man Married to His Business," *Inc.*, September 1988.

157 These figures point to: Thomas J. DeLong and Sara DeLong, "Managing Yourself: The Paradox of Excellence," *Harvard Business Review*, June 2011.

157 Green had reached something: Roger S. Schulz, "Whose Job Is It?" *Journal of Financial Service Professionals*, September 2000.

158 Taken at face value: Tom Nawrocki, "Dan Sullivan on Tapping Your Entrepreneurial Strengths," *Journal of Financial Planning*, March 2011; "Here's One Way to Improve Profits in 2002—Give Up Your Office," Strategic Coach news release, *Business Wire*, January 16, 2002; Neil Young, "Small Business Owner, It's Time to Take a Vacation," *Kansas City Daily Record*, August 6, 2005; Dan Sullivan, "How Would You Employ Your Clone?" *Toronto Globe and Mail*, October 20, 2010.

158 Coaches at Sullivan's company: Gay Jervey, "Workaholics (Anonymous)," *Fortune Small Business*, March 2003: "Dan Sullivan is the latest business guru to capture throngs of fans and create a growing young company. His prescription for success: Take more days off. The nation's most successful *demotivational* speaker is building an empire."

159 In executives, this "putting out fires" approach: Edward Hallowell,

"Overloaded Circuits: Why Smart People Underperform," *Harvard Business Review*, January 2005.

160 A dozen years ago: Personal interview with Stan Doobin, January 12, 2012.

CHAPTER 8: NOTHING SUCCEEDS LIKE FAILURE

165 An enormous snowstorm: An award-winning case study of JetBlue's Valentine's Day Massacre, authored by University of North Carolina M.A. candidate Gregory G. Efthimiou, can be found at http://www.awpag esociety.com/images/uploads/08JetBlue_CaseStudy.pdf.

166 As the nine planes awaited takeoff: Jeff Bailey, "Long Delays Hurt Image of JetBlue," *New York Times*, February 17, 2007; Bailey, "JetBlue Cancels More Flights in Storm's Wake," *New York Times*, February 18, 2007; Bailey, "JetBlue's C.E.O. Is 'Mortified' after Fliers Are Stranded," *New York Times*, February 19, 2007.

166 Some travelers were trapped: John Doyle et al., "Air Refugees in New JFKaos," *New York Post*, February 16, 2007; Jennifer 8. Lee, "JetBlue Flight Snarls Continue," *New York Times*, February 16, 2007; "Trapped on an Airplane," *New York Times* editorial, February 23, 2007.

167 For instance, the airline: Mel Duvall, "What Really Happened at Jet-Blue," *CIO Insight*, April 5, 2007, http://www.cioinsight.com/c/a/Past-News/What-Really-Happened-At-JetBlue/.

167 In the days following the storm: Patricia Sellers, "Lessons of the Fall: Ex-CEOs from JetBlue, Starbucks, and Motorola Discuss What They Learned When They Lost Their Jobs," *Fortune*, May 29, 2008.

168 The firing marked the third time: James Wynbrandt, *Flying High: How JetBlue Founder and CEO David Neeleman Beats the Competition—Even in the World's Most Turbulent Industry* (Hoboken, NJ: Wiley, 2004).

169 Marketing guru Seth Godin: Godin, interview with Bryan Elliott, www .behindthebrand.tv.

169 In my previous book: For Steve Dering's story, see Russ Alan Prince and Lewis Schiff, *The Influence of Affluence: How the New Rich Are Changing America* (New York: Broadway Books, 2009), chapter 7.

172 These periods of struggle: Seth Godin, *The Dip: A Little Book that Teaches You When to Quit (and When to Stick)* (New York: Portfolio, 2007).

173 For instance, Pixar Animation: David A. Price, *The Pixar Touch: The Making of a Company* (New York: Alfred A. Knopf, 2008).

175 That's a great story: Ibid., 8.

175 It is also a story that Steve Jobs: "A Discussion with Steve Jobs and John Lasseter," *Charlie Rose*, October 30, 1996.

176 By the time author: Walter Isaacson, *Steve Jobs* (New York: Simon and Schuster, 2011).

176 Ellen Langer, a psychology professor: Ellen J. Langer, *The Power of Mindful Learning* (Reading, MA: Addison-Wesley, 1997).

177 Psychology literature shows that: Mark D. Cannon and Amy C. Edmondson, "Failing to Learn and Learning to Fail (Intelligently): How Great Organizations Put Failure to Work to Innovate and Improve," *Long Range Planning* 38 (2005): 299–319. Cannon and Edmondson cite two books in this regard: Daniel Goleman, *Vital Lies, Simple Truths: The Psychology of Self-Deception* (New York: Simon and Schuster, 1985), and Shelley E. Taylor, *Positive Illusions: Creative Self-Deception and the Healthy Mind* (New York: Basic Books, 1989).

178 Way back in 1983: This passage about Neeleman is sourced substantially from Wynbrandt, *Flying High*, as well as other sources listed above.

181 The thing about failure: Randy Komisar, "The Biggest Successes Are Often Bred from Failures," Stanford Technology Ventures Program Entrepreneurship Corner, School of Engineering, Stanford University, April 28, 2004.

181 But in the rest of the corporate world: Cannon and Edmondson, "Failing to Learn."

181 Another Harvard professor: The Thomke quote appears in "How Failure Breeds Success," *Bloomberg Businessweek*, July 9, 2006.

182 Even Pixar, a wildly successful studio: The "Pixar Timeline 1979 to Present" can be seen at http://www.pixar.com/about/Our-Story. The Pixar Image Computer is mentioned just once, incidentally, as a tool for creating the early film short *Red's Dream*. The company's struggles and near-failure have been written out of the timeline, so that Pixar's story appears to be a steady rise to success driven by the clear goal of making feature films.

182 One-third of the CEOs in *Inc.* magazine's: Amar Bhide, *The Origin and Evolution of New Businesses* (New York: Oxford University Press, 2000).

182 The most disturbing findings: A. C. Edmondson, "Learning from Failure in Health Care; Frequent Opportunities, Pervasive Barriers," *Quality and Safety in Health Care* 13, suppl. 2 (2004): ii3–ii9. Edmondson writes, "When small failures are neither identified widely, nor discussed and analysed, it is very difficult for larger failures to be prevented." This principle is at the heart of producing positive results through any synergistic system, including Business Brilliance.

182 Despite all the public claims: The original study Edmondson worked on, in which she discovered that the best nursing units had higher self-reported error rates, was L. L. Leape, D. W. Bates, D. J. Cullen et al., "Systems Analysis of Adverse Drug Events," ADE Prevention Study Group, *Journal of the American Medical Association* 274 (1995): 35–43.

186 For one thing, discussions about failure: Amy C. Edmondson, *Teaming: How Organizations Learn, Innovate, and Compete in the Knowledge Economy* (San Francisco: Jossey-Bass, 2012).

CHAPTER 9: MASTERING THE MUNDANE

191 But when a pair of professors: Richard J. Goossen, *Entrepreneurial Excellence: Profit from the Best Ideas of the Experts* (Franklin Lakes, NJ: Career, 2007), 189.

192 An educator named Doug Lemov: Lemov, *Teach Like a Champion: 49 Techniques That Put Students on the Path to College* (San Francisco: Jossey-Bass, 2010).

193 Atkins declares that what: Ibid., xi.

Bibliography

Albrecht, Ernest J. *The New American Circus*. Gainesville: University Press of Florida, 1995.

Babcock, Linda, and Sara Laschever. *Ask for It: How Women Can Use the Power of Negotiation to Get What They Really Want*. New York: Bantam Dell, 2008.

———. *Women Don't Ask: Negotiation and the Gender Divide*. Princeton, NJ: Princeton University Press, 2003.

Babinski, Tony, and Kristian Manchester. *Cirque du Soleil: 20 Years under the Sun—An Authorized History*. New York: Harry N. Abrams, 2004.

Berkun, Scott. *The Myths of Innovation*. Sebastopol, CA: O'Reilly Media, 2007.

Bhide, Amar V. *The Origin and Evolution of New Businesses*. New York: Oxford University Press, 2000.

Branson, Richard. *Losing My Virginity: How I've Survived, Had Fun, and Made a Fortune Doing Business My Way*. New York: Crown Business, 1998. Reprint, New York: Three Rivers Press, 2004.

Brodsky, Norm, and Bo Burlingham. *Street Smarts: An All-Purpose Tool Kit for Entrepreneurs*. New York: Portfolio Trade, 2010.

Buckingham, Marcus. *Go Put Your Strengths to Work: 6 Powerful Steps to Achieve Outstanding Performance*. New York: Free Press, 2007.

Buckingham, Marcus, and Donald O. Clifton. *Now, Discover Your Strengths*. New York: Free Press, 2001.

Burt, Ronald S. *Structural Holes: The Social Structure of Competition*. Cambridge, MA: Harvard University Press, 1992.

Camp, Jim. *Start with No: The Negotiating Tools That the Pros Don't Want You to Know*. New York: Crown Business, 2002.

Chapman, Jack. *Negotiating Your Salary: How to Make $1,000 a Minute*. Revised edition. Berkeley, CA: Ten Speed Press, 1996.

———. *Negotiating Your Salary: How to Make $1,000 a Minute*. 7th ed. Wilmette, IL: Jack Chapman, 2011.

Christakis, Nicholas A., and James H. Fowler. *Connected: The Surprising Power of Our Social Networks and How They Shape Our Lives*. New York: Little, Brown, 2009.

Cialdini, Robert B. *Influence: How and Why People Agree to Things*. New York: Morrow, 1984.

Cohen, Adam. *The Perfect Store: Inside eBay*. Boston: Little, Brown, 2002.

Covey, Stephen R. *The Seven Habits of Highly Effective People: Restoring the Character Ethic*. New York: Simon and Schuster, 1989.

Cringely, Robert X. *Accidental Empires: How the Boys of Silicon Valley Make Their Millions, Battle Foreign Competition, and Still Can't Get a Date*. Reading, MA: Addison-Wesley, 1992.

Deci, Edward L., and Richard Flaste. *Why We Do What We Do: The Dynamics of Personal Autonomy*. New York: G. P. Putnam's Sons, 1995.

DeLong, Thomas J., and Sara DeLong. "Managing Yourself: The Paradox of Excellence." *Harvard Business Review*, June 2011.

Dennis, Felix. *How to Get Rich*. London: Ebury; New York: Random House, 2006.

Dominus, Susan. "Suze Orman Is Having a Moment." *New York Times Magazine*, May 14, 2009.

Donaldson, Michael C. *Fearless Negotiating: The Wish-Want-Walk Method to Reach Solutions That Work*. New York: McGraw-Hill, 2007.

Edmondson, Amy C. *A Fuller Explanation: The Synergetic Geometry of R. Buckminster Fuller*. Pueblo, CO: Emergentworld, 2009.

———. *Teaming: How Organizations Learn, Innovate, and Compete in the Knowledge Economy*. San Francisco: Jossey-Bass, 2012.

Evans, Harold, Gail Buckland, and David Lefer. *They Made America: From the Steam Engine to the Search Engine: Two Centuries of Innovators*. New York: Little, Brown, 2004.

Gates, Bill, Nathan Myhrvold, and Peter Rinearson. *The Road Ahead*. New York: Viking, 1995.

Godin, Seth. *The Dip: A Little Book That Teaches You When to Quit (and When to Stick)*. New York: Portfolio, 2007.

Goleman, Daniel. *Vital Lies, Simple Truths: The Psychology of Self-Deception*. New York: Simon and Schuster, 1985.

Goossen, Richard J. *Entrepreneurial Excellence: Profit from the Best Ideas of the Experts*. Franklin Lakes, NJ: Career Press, 2007.

Green, David L. *IQuote: Brilliance and Banter from the Internet Age*. Guilford, CT: Lyons Press, 2007.

Grunden, Naida. *The Pittsburgh Way to Efficient Healthcare: Improving Patient Care Using Toyota-based Methods*. New York: Healthcare Performance, 2008.

Hagstrom, Robert G. *The Warren Buffett Way: Investment Strategies of the World's Greatest Investor*. New York: John Wiley, 1994.

Halperin, Ian. *Guy Laliberté: The Fabulous Life of the Creator of Cirque du Soleil: A Biography*. 2nd ed. Montreal: Transit, 2009.

Haven, Kendall F. *100 Greatest Science Inventions of All Time*. Westport, CT: Libraries Unlimited, 2006.

Henderson, Harry. *A to Z of Computer Scientists*. New York: Facts on File, 2003.

Hurley, Robert F. *The Decision to Trust: How Leaders Create High-Trust Organizations*. San Francisco: Jossey-Bass, 2012.

Infection Prevention and Control: Current Research and Practice. Oakbrook Terrace, IL: Joint Commission Resources, 2007.

Isaacson, Walter. *Steve Jobs*. New York: Simon and Schuster, 2011.

Jones, Randall. *The Richest Man in Town: The Twelve Commandments of Wealth*. New York: Business Plus, 2009.

Kohn, Alfie. *Punished by Rewards: The Trouble with Gold Stars, Incentive Plans, A's, Praise, and Other Bribes*. Boston: Houghton Mifflin, 1993.

Langer, Ellen J. *The Power of Mindful Learning*. Reading, MA: Addison-Wesley, 1997.

Lemov, Doug. *Teach Like a Champion: 49 Techniques That Put Students on the Path to College*. San Francisco: Jossey-Bass, 2010.

Lewis, Michael. *The New New Thing: A Silicon Valley Story*. New York: W. W. Norton, 2000.

Liberman, Gail, and Alan Lavine. *Rags to Riches: Motivating Stories of How Ordinary People Achieved Extraordinary Wealth*. Chicago: Dearborn, 2000.

Lowenstein, Roger. *Buffett: The Making of an American Capitalist*. New York: Broadway Books, 2001.

Making Health Care Safer: A Critical Analysis of Patient Safety Practices. Rockville, MD: Agency for Healthcare Research and Quality, 2001.

Manes, Stephen, and Paul Andrews. *Gates: How Microsoft's Mogul Reinvented an Industry—and Made Himself the Richest Man in America*. New York: Doubleday, 1993.

Michaelides, Marios, and Peter R. Mueser. "Recent Trends in the Characteristics of Unemployment Insurance Recipients." *Monthly Labor Review*. Washington, DC: Bureau of Labor Statistics, July, 2012.

Misino, Dominick J., and Jim DeFelice. *Negotiate and Win: Proven Strategies from the NYPD's Top Hostage Negotiator*. New York: McGraw-Hill, 2004.

O'Hurley, John. *It's Okay to Miss the Bed on the First Jump: And Other Life Lessons I Learned from Dogs*. New York: Hudson Street, 2006.

Orfalea, Paul, and Ann Marsh. *Copy This!: Lessons from a Hyperactive Dyslexic Who Turned a Bright Idea into One of America's Best Companies*. New York: Workman, 2005.

Orman, Suze. *The Courage to Be Rich: Creating a Life of Material and Spiritual Abundance*. New York: Riverhead, 1999.

_____. *The Money Class: How to Stand in Your Truth and Create the Future You Deserve*. New York: Spiegel and Grau, 2012.

Pinkley, Robin L., and Gregory B. Northcraft. *Get Paid What You're Worth: The Expert Negotiator's Guide to Salary and Compensation*. New York: St. Martin's Griffin, 2000.

Price, David A. *The Pixar Touch: The Making of a Company*. New York: Alfred A. Knopf, 2008.

Prince, Russ Alan, and Lewis Schiff. *The Influence of Affluence: How the New Rich Are Changing America*. New York: Broadway Books, 2009.

Reynolds, Paul D. *Entrepreneurship in the United States: The Future Is Now*. New York: Springer, 2010.

Reynolds, Paul D., and Sammis B. White. *The Entrepreneurial Process: Economic Growth, Men, Women, and Minorities*. Westport, CT: Quorum, 1997.

Schroeder, Alice. *The Snowball: Warren Buffett and the Business of Life*. New York: Bantam, 2008.

Seabrook, John. *Flash of Genius: And Other True Stories of Invention*. New York: St. Martin's Griffin, 2008.

Shane, Scott. *The Illusions of Entrepreneurship: The Costly Myths That Entrepreneurs, Investors, and Policy Makers Live By*. New Haven, CT: Yale University Press, 2008.

Shell, G. Richard. *Bargaining for Advantage: Negotiation Strategies for Reasonable People*. New York: Viking, 1999.

Sinetar, Marsha. *Do What You Love, the Money Will Follow: Discovering Your Right Livelihood*. New York: Dell, 1989. Reprint 1995.

Slott, Ed. *Parlay Your IRA into a Family Fortune: 3 Easy Steps for Creating a Lifetime Supply of Tax-Deferred, Even Tax-Free, Wealth for You and Your Family*. New York: Viking, 2005.

Symonds, Matthew, and Larry Ellison. *Softwar: An Intimate Portrait of Larry Ellison and Oracle*. New York: Simon and Schuster, 2003.

Taylor, Shelley E. *Positive Illusions: Creative Self-Deception and the Healthy Mind*. New York: Basic Books, 1989.

Thompson, Donald N. *The $12 Million Stuffed Shark: The Curious Economics of Contemporary Art*. New York: Palgrave Macmillan, 2008.

Vinjamuri, David. *Accidental Branding: How Ordinary People Build Extraordinary Brands*. Hoboken, NJ: John Wiley and Sons, 2008.

Wallace, James, and Jim Erickson. *Hard Drive: Bill Gates and the Making of the Microsoft Empire*. New York: Wiley, 1992.

Wynbrandt, James. *Flying High: How JetBlue Founder and CEO David Neeleman Beats the Competition—Even in the World's Most Turbulent Industry*. Hoboken, NJ: Wiley, 2004.

Index

About the Author

Lewis Schiff is the executive director of Inc. Business Owners Council, a membership organization for *Inc.* magazine's top entrepreneurs and owners of closely held family businesses, and maintains a blog about behavioral entrepreneurship on Inc.com. Schiff has coauthored two books: *The Influence of Affluence: The Rise of the New Rich and How They Are Changing America*, which charts the rise of America's growing affluent middle class through original research and analysis, and *The Armchair Millionaire*, which describes a wealth-creation system that leverages Nobel Prize–winning methodologies.